Between History
and Romance

Between History and Romance

Travel Writing on Spain in the Early Nineteenth-Century United States

Pere Gifra-Adroher

Madison • Teaneck
Fairleigh Dickinson University Press
London: Associated University Presses

Associated University Presses
440 Forsgate Drive
Cranbury, NJ 08512

Associated University Presses
16 Barter Street
London WC1A 2AH, England

Associated University Presses
P.O. Box 338, Port Credit
Mississauga, Ontario
Canada L5G 4L8

The paper used in this publication meets the requirements of the American National Standard for Permanence of Paper for Printed Library Materials Z39.48-1984.

Library of Congress Cataloging-in-Publication Data

Gifra-Adroher, Pere, 1966–
    Between history and romance : travel writing on Spain in the early nineteenth-century
United States / Pere Gifra-Adroher.
        p. cm.
    Includes bibliographical references and index.
    ISBN 0-8386-3848-1 (alk. paper)
        1. Travelers' writings, American—History and criticism. 2. American prose literature—19th century—History and criticism. 3. Literature and history—United States—History—19th century. 4. Literature and history—Spain—History—19th century. 5. Americans—Travel—Spain—History—19th century. 6. American literature—Spanish influences. 7. Spain—Description and travel. 8. Spain—In literature. I. Title.
PS366.T73 G55   2000
810.9'355—dc21   99-089062

PRINTED IN THE UNITED STATES OF AMERICA

For my parents,
Pere Gifra Pigem and Maria Adroher Bosch,
whose inspiring stories have helped me
travel across time.

Contents

Acknowledgments

I OWE A SPECIAL DEBT TO THE MANY COLLEAGUES, FRIENDS, AND RELAtives who have constantly given me advice, support, and assistance throughout the past years in Illinois, New Jersey, and Catalonia. For her enduring encouragement, I first wish to express my deepest gratitude to Nina Baym, of the University of Illinois at UrbanaChampaign, who provided her invaluable guidance at the genesis of this project and then commented on it at various critical stages. My appreciation also goes to Emily Watts, Bruce Michelson, Leon Chai, and other members of the English Department at the University of Illinois for their insightful suggestions on my work. Furthermore, sincere thanks are due to Mary Suzanne Schriber, of Northern Illinois University, whose knowledgeable criticism helped to sharpen the focus of my book in later writing stages. Several other people have contributed to this book in many other ways. For their editorial assistance, I am grateful to Harry Keyishian, Pat Bazan-Figueras, Christine Retz, Brian Haskell, and Julien Yoseloff. My thanks are also due to my colleagues at Universitat Pompeu Fabra, and to Joan Solà, of the Universitat de Vic, for their support and friendship. I reserve my final thanks for my family and above all for my wife Pilar Prieto, who have patiently waited for this book to appear and have provided unflagging optimism, good humour, and a precious helping hand to disburden me of many distracting matters when I most needed them.

While projecting and writing this book, I have obviously benefited from previous scholarship on this field. Without the colossal research carried out by Stanley T. Williams decades ago, I would not have started this study; I am particularly indebted to him and to such other academics as Iris L. Whitman and Frederick Stimson for having plowed the field of intercultural relations between Spain and the United States. I am also obliged to the scholarship produced by the editors of some of the works I quote throughout the book, and most particularly to those of the Twayne edition of Irving's work and the Harvard edition of Longfellow's letters. I also wish to acknowledge the assistance of several institutions that lent support to my undertaking. The Generalitat de Catalunya and Universitat Pompeu Fabra in Barcelona generously helped me by facilitating research grants and sabbatical time respectively. Likewise, I am sincerely grateful to the Barra Foundation for awarding me with their International Fellowship in American History and Culture to look up relevant materials at the Library Company of Philadelphia. As the subject matter of my study often required the search of rare books and the retrieval of other items difficult to obtain, I would like to thank for their tireless assistance many staff members and librarians at several institutions. In particular, I am indebted to those who helped me at the Main Library of the University of Illinois at Urbana-Champaign, the Fairleigh Dickinson University Library, the New York Public Library, the Library Company of Philadelphia, the University of Pennsylvania's Van Pelt-Dietrich Library, the Library of Congress, and the Biblioteca at Universitat Pompeu Fabra.

My gratitude finally goes to the individuals and institutions that have kindly allowed the reproduction of items in their possession. Full credit is given under each illustration. Quotations from Longfellow's letters are reprinted from *The Letters of Henry Wadsworth Longfellow* in two volumes, edited by Andrew Hilen, by permission of the Belknap Press of Harvard University Press, copyright © 1972 by the President and Fellows of Harvard College. Excerpts from Washington Irving's *Letters: Volume II, 1823–1838*, edited by Ralph Aderman et al. are reprinted by permission of Twayne Publishers. Some of the material on Alexander Slidell Mackenzie and Caroline Cushing appeared respectively in much shorter versions in *Travel Essentials,* edited by Santiago Henríquez, and *Actas del XXI Congreso Internacional de AEDEAN*, edited by Fernando Toda et al. Full citations for these articles are included in the bibliography. I am grateful for permission to reprint.

Abbreviations

RS   Caleb Cushing, *Reminiscences of Spain, the Country, Its People, History and Monuments.* 2 vols. Boston: Carter, Hendee & Company, 1833.

LD   [Caroline Elizabeth (Wilde) Cushing], *Letters, Descriptive of Public Monuments, Scenery, and Manners in France and Spain.* 2 vols. Newburyport, Mass.: E. W. Allen, 1832.

PP   Alexander H. Everett, *Prose Pieces and Correspondence.* Edited by Elizabeth Evans. St. Paul, Minn.: The John Colet Press, 1975.

LL   *The Letters of Henry Wadsworth Longfellow.* Edited by Andrew Hilen. 2 vols. Cambridge, Mass.: The Belknap Press of Harvard University Press, 1966.

LT   *Life, Letters and Journals of George Ticknor.* Eds. George Hillard, Mrs. Anna Ticknor, and Anna Eliot Ticknor. 2 vols. 1876. Boston and New York: Houghton, 1909.

TT   *George Ticknor's Travels in Spain.* Edited by George Tyler Northup. *University of Toronto Studies* 2 (1913).

LII   Washington Irving, *Letters: Volume II, 1823–1838.* Edited by Ralph M. Aderman et al. Boston: Twayne, 1979.

A   Washington Irving, *The Alhambra.* Edited by William T. Lenehan and Andrew B. Myers. Boston: Twayne, 1983.

JIII   Washington Irving. *Journals and Notebooks: Volume III, 1819–1827.* Edited by Walter A. Reichart. Madison: University of Wisconsin Press, 1970.

JIV   Washington Irving. *Journals and Notebooks: Volume IV, 1826–1829.* Edited by Wayne R. Kime and Andrew B. Myers. Boston: Twayne, 1984.

OM [Henry Wadsworth Longfellow], *Outre-Mer; A Pilgrimage Beyond the Sea*. 2 vols. 1833–34. New York: Harper & Brothers, 1835.

YS [Alexander Slidell Mackenzie], *A Year in Spain. By a Young American*. 3rd ed., enlarged. 3 vols. 1829. New York: Harper & Brothers, 1836.

SR [Alexander Slidell Mackenzie], *Spain Revisited. By the Author of "A Year in Spain."* 2 vols. New York: Harper & Brothers, 1836.

TE Mordecai Manuel Noah, *Travels in England, France, Spain, and the Barbary States in the Years 1813–14 and 15*. New York: Kirk & Mercein, 1819.

SS *Scenes in Spain*. New York: Dearborn, 1837.

Between History
and Romance

1

Introduction: Spain, Travel, and Textuality in the Early Nineteenth-Century United States

DURING THE LAST DECADES OF THE EIGHTEENTH CENTURY AND throughout most of the nineteenth century Spain attracted the Western romantic imagination powerfully. Though anchored in economic and cultural stagnation, Spain offered to post-Enlightenment travelers the exoticism of its Oriental, medieval, and imperial past. A journey to Spain not only entailed a literal geographical progression but also a figurative voyage across different historical and cultural periods of that country, such as the Moorish domination and the Christian Reconquest (711–1492), the Golden Age (ca. 1556–1700), and the recent Peninsular War (1808–1814), that appealed strongly to Americans and Europeans alike. No other country in Europe, Théophile Gautier observed, seemed to be as deeply interred in its past as Spain. Many writers, musicians, and painters traveling there in search of experiences did their best to construe the patchwork of old kingdoms, variety of languages, and treasury of folklore manifestly blended before them.[1] They dug enthusiastically about for the historical and artistic ores of Spain, which offered an inexhaustible source of inspiration, and forged them into major themes in the literary, musical, and plastic arts.

Many writers of the United States, even though their young republic had enjoyed few long-established cultural links with Spain, shared the same fascination that European writers and artists felt for Spanish culture in the early nineteenth century. Once and for all, Spain and the Spaniards began to lose their invisibility, becoming more known and, to a certain extent, also commodified by the apparently innocent cultural channels that purported to represent them. This process took place particularly during the late 1820s and the decade of the 1830s with the publication of Washington Irving's historical studies and of several full-length accounts of actual travel. Among the many likely and sometimes obvious reasons for this surge of interest, the following stand out: America had been "discovered" by Columbus through the auspices of Spain; Spain had invaded and dominated the southern part of the hemisphere in which Americans resided; Spain was a Catholic despotism, the very opposite of United States Protestant republicanism; Spain was a very old country whereas the United States was a very new one; and, finally, Spain perhaps was seen as an agent of Western consolidation for having unified its diverse kingdoms and successfully repulsed the Moorish occupants of its territories in 1492. Americans were very significantly turning their eyes toward crucial episodes in the formation of modern Spain at a time when they too were strengthening their own nationhood.[2]

The popular notions of Spain that Americans received, however, became often distorted and fossilized because of their continuous reliance on stereotypes. It is not surprising that by the mid-nineteenth century the representation of Spain and the Spaniards had almost become platitudinous in the United States. Despite complaints against "the present popular impression, that life in the Peninsula is still a mixture of the adventures of Gil Blas and the exploits of Don Quixote,"[3] the fact was that many Americans still equated Spain with exoticism, banditry, poverty, and medievalism. Indeed, the Spanish fad influencing American letters from drama to history and from romance to travel writing drew above all upon these very aspects. Spain was represented as a picturesque, static country that, according to the anonymous author of *Scenes in Spain*, "in the midst of revolutions, remains in so many respects the same" (SS, i). Even Henry David Thoreau, the transcendental traveler who seldom ventured far from his native New England, referred to it in *Walden*, where an excursus criticizing the people's insatiable appetite for information and the type and quality of news they receive concludes with the following remark:

> As for Spain, for instance, if you know how to throw in Don Carlos and the Infanta, and Don Pedro and Seville and Granada, from time to time in the right proportions,—they may have changed the names a little since I saw the papers,—and serve up a bull-fight when other entertainments fail, it will be true to the letter, and give us as good an idea of the exact state or ruin of things in Spain as the most succint and lucid reports under this head in the newspapers.[4]

That Thoreau chose to speak about Spain rather than another country as a hackneyed piece of news is significant; his choice demonstrates that by the 1840s things Spanish had achieved enough diffusion and notoriety in small-town America to make them a sought-after journalistic commodity. In addition, Thoreau's allusions to the Carlist rebellion (1833–40), the southern cities of Granada and Seville, and the gory national sport, show that he was well aware of which particular aspects of Spain interested the average antebellum American reader. His facetious reliance on the usual commonplaces corroborates the popular view of a thrilling, romantic Spain constructed by American and European artists, writers, and travelers.

Proof of the magnetism exerted by things Spanish lies not only in the number of erudite hispanophile works published but also in the success of other sorts of more popular genres. Washington Irving's *History of the Life and Voyages of Christopher Columbus* (1828), *A Chronicle of the Conquest of Granada* (1829), and *The Voyages and Discoveries of the Companions of Columbus* (1831), William Hickling Prescott's *Ferdinand and Isabella* (1837), and George Ticknor's *History of Spanish Literature* (1849) exemplify, on the one hand, the serious approach to Spanish themes that decisively placed United States scholarship in major intellectual debates abroad. Henry Wadsworth Longfellow's drama, *The Spanish Student* (1843), James Fenimore Cooper's *Mercedes of Castile* (1840), and William Gilmore Simms's romances *Pelayo* (1838) and *Count Julian* (1845) manifest, on the other hand, the influence of Spanish elements in popular genres at home. Almost all of a sudden Spain grew into a fashion, a new acquisition for both the cultured and popular audiences of the United States, and travel writing, enjoying an exceptional position halfway between highbrow and lowbrow culture, was there to play an important role constructing, redefining, and circulating notions of what Spain and Spanishness consisted in for antebellum American audiences.

Between History and Romance focuses on the travel writings produced by some Americans who visited Spain in the early nineteenth century, and ascertains the role that these texts played in fostering a romantic representation of that country in the United States. Echoing Lynn Hunt, I address these problems of representation: what these travel writings did, how they did it, and their relation with the world they professed to be faithfully representing.[5] The study, chronologically speaking, attempts to map out chiefly the role of what might be called the "second wave" of travel writings in the early American representation of Spain, as opposed to the "first wave" formed by the travel journals, letters, and memoranda left by the diplomat-travelers of the second half of the eighteenth century. I argue that primarily, though not exclusively, on the period from the mid-1820s to the mid-1830s, the years comprising Irving's Spanish output, we witness a transition from an enlightened to a romantic representation of Spain. That is, a representational shift occurred whereby that foreign nation changed from being conceived as a political allegory of conspicuous political implications for general readerships at home to being portrayed as an hedonistic retreat for individual romantic travelers abroad. It was not, of course, a sudden shift, as for years to come many American travel writers still insisted on political and allegorical readings of Spain, but it definitely was one that aligned American travel writings with the main currents of Continental literature.

The chronological progression of *Between History and Romance* first covers the origins of Spanish travel writing in the United States with a stress on its Enlightenment perspective so that the changing attitudes in the 1820s and 1830s become more evident by contrast. By the time Thoreau wrote about bullfights and the Infanta, a number of Americans had already visited Spain, experienced prima facie some of the events that were taking place there, and written about them. These first American travel writers were not merely journalists anxious to report to audiences back home; they were predominantly politicians and literati who constituted a residue of the eighteenth-century Grand Tour, traveling to further their education, improve their language skills, and more often than not confirm their political views toward the Old World.[6] And even though we can find certain parallelisms between their *Weltanschauung* and that of eighteenth-century traveler-diplomats to Spain like John Adams or John Jay, ultimately their determination to visit a country that many would avoid at all costs sets them aside as a romantic group of travel writers.

During the first decades of the nineteenth century a visit to Spain was still a precarious task about which, out of civic duty, the genteel traveler felt obliged to inform his fellow citizens. Alexander Everett, the American Minister to Spain, and his wife, Lucretia Orne Peabody, for example, encouraged twenty-year-old Henry Wadsworth Longfellow to write about Spain as soon as he returned to the United States.[7] These travelers, aware that they visited a country which, as Alexander Slidell Mackenzie observed, "though inferior to none in interest, has been almost entirely neglected by tourists" (YS, 1:vii), set out to redress this neglect in their travel books. In a period when travel writing, perhaps due to its Enlightenment legacy, still signified an exercise in cross-cultural understanding, it is not strange that suddenly a handful of travel accounts appeared solely devoted to Spain in such a short period of time. Though not too numerous, these travel accounts nevertheless became culturally relevant because they demonstrated that the travel writers from the United States could also contribute noticeably to the overall Western representation of Spain. In writing about Spain on an equal footing with other European travel writers, and choosing a completely American point of view to do it, these writers thus became active participants in the literary coming of age of their nation.

The chapters that *Between History and Romance* devotes to readings of specific works are much more concerned with studying the connections between travel, writing, and textuality as vehicles of representation than with assessing whether these travel accounts are historically accurate or whether they duly reflect the material and social conditions of early nineteenth-century Spain. To do so would mean to step over into the field of material and social history, and even though the boundaries between academic disciplines, as Clifford Geertz has put it, are blurring, my interest rather lies, to borrow Homi Bhaba's expression, in how these travel writers "narrate" the foreign nation, and what conventions and genres they employ to do it.[8] Consequently, throughout the study I demonstrate that for their representation of Spain these writers made use of several major conventions of their genre, but above all resorted to mixing the factual discourse of history and the adventurous discourse of romance. Hence the title of this study, *Between History and Romance*, a phrase adapted from a letter by Washington Irving in which, as I shall explain in chapter 5, he defined the genre status of *Chronicle of the Conquest of Granada*. Like Thoreau, by turning to such conventions these earlier travel writers presented Spain as a symbol: sometimes political chaos, as in Alexander Slidell Mackenzie, sometimes escapism as in Washington Irving, sometimes spiritual fulfillment as in Longfellow. In the case of Caroline Cushing, the only woman writer present in the study, Spain represented the horizon of freedom that her domestic environment denied her. An analysis of what these writings did rhetorically, then, sheds light not only on the writer, but also on the collective anxieties of Americans at home and abroad, and therefore helps place these texts in the broader context of antebellum American culture.

I

The territory of nineteenth-century American travel writing has been charted, but on the whole the role that these writings played in the representation of Spain still remains vastly unexplored. While Lord Byron, Prosper Mérimée, Richard Ford, George Borrow, and many other European travelers who undertook the romantic voyage through Spain have been the object of critical scrutiny, Americans have often been left out from surveys, or, if included, usually represented only by Henry Wadsworth Longfellow and Washington Irving. This neglect of an important body of nineteenth-century American travel writing of over a hundred titles, among them Severn T. Wallis's *Glimpses of Spain* (1849), John Hay's *Castilian Days* (1871), George Parsons Lathrop's *Spanish Vistas* (1883), and Louise Chandler-Moulton's *Lazy Tours in Spain and Elsewhere* (1896), may perhaps come to an end with the recent surge of interest in travel literature and theory. To be sure, some of these narratives of Spanish travel are dull, monotonous, and cumbered by unassimilated factual information, but there is still good reason not to ignore this whole body of writing, or reduce it unjustly to Washington Irving's Spanish cultural production.

Travel writing is becoming less and less a minor area in literary studies today, as cross-disciplinary and new historicist perspectives move away from the previous formalist aesthetics that dictated the preponderance of certain genres over others. Apart from the intrinsic biographical information they contain about their respective authors, travel writings now have come to be scrutinized for the multiple voices and discourses embedded in them and for what these may reveal about American and foreign cultures at a given period. I therefore attempt here to bring together various theoretical concepts from contemporary scholarship on travel and tourism theory in order to overcome the former strictly biographical approaches to the nineteenth-century American representation of Spain. American travel writing on Spain still continues to be only addressed comprehensively in two works written decades ago: Carrie E. Farnham's *American Travellers in Spain* (1921), and Stanley T. Williams's *The Spanish Background of American Literature* (1955). The materialistic approach of the former and the encyclopedic perspective of the latter render them somewhat dated in light of current critical discourses. In contrast, a handful of more recent studies like Dennis Porter's *Haunted Journeys* (1990), Sara Mills's *Discourses of Difference* (1991), Mary Louise Pratt's *Imperial Eyes* (1992), James Buzard's *The Beaten Track* (1993), William Stowe's *Going Abroad* (1994), Terry Caesar's *Forgiving the Boundaries* (1995), Beth L. Lueck's *American Writers and The Picturesque Tour* (1997), or Mary Suzanne Schriber's *Writing Home* (1997) have ingenuously deployed discourses like psychoanalysis, anthropology, tourism, (post)colonialism, semiotics, or feminism to flesh out a new panorama of travel writing that shifts away from content analysis toward rhetorical analysis and questions of representation.

Even though the renewed interest in travel theory has opened up the canon in fostering scholarship on texts other than merely those by canonized American expatriates, it has nevertheless continued leaving the narratives produced by American travelers on Spain mostly in the dark. In his excellent study *The Beaten Track*, for example, James Buzard examines the interaction between travel and tourism in the nineteenth and early twentieth centuries, and the contribution of each one of these cultural practices to the definition of culture in the Anglo-American mind. He also discusses the southern European influence on the British and American unconscious, but in so doing he circumscribes the appeal of southern Europe mostly to Italy, and thus again overlooks the attraction exerted by the Iberian Peninsula despite the long tradition of touristic records about it. The analysis of nineteenth-century American travel writing on Spain therefore begs for a new reexamination of the subject that, continuing to bear in mind biographical data, combines new theoretical standpoints to unravel both the hidden and conspicuous conventions, voices, and discourses these texts employed to represent Spain in the early nineteenth century.

An important aspect of *Between History and Romance* lies not only in its focus on a noncanonical genre, travel writing, but also in its recovery of noncanonical texts and authors. Few of the travel books I examine here are well-known today. Of the various texts discussed at length, the most familiar to general Americanists is without doubt Washington Irving's *Tales of the Alhambra* (1832), the archcanonical American text on Spain for its century, as Hemingway's *The Sun Also Rises* (1926) is for the next century. Not so familiar is Henry Wadsworth Longfellow's *Outre-Mer* (1833–34); though emulating Irving's style, it remains one of his less celebrated books, perhaps because this sentimental travelogue inaugurated his career in creative writing and consequently preceded his canonization as America's household poet. Alexander Slidell Mackenzie's *A Year in Spain. By a Young American* (1829, enlarged in 1836), which enjoyed some popularity in its day, is virtually a forgotten text today, and so is its sequel *Spain Revisited* (1836). The other texts that constitute the core of this study are Mordecai Manuel Noah's *Travels in England, France, Spain, and the Barbary States* (1819), the travel writings of George Ticknor, Caleb Cushing's *Reminiscences of Spain* (1833), and the second volume of Caroline Cushing's *Letters Descriptive of Public Monuments, Sce-*

nery, and Manners in France and Spain (1832), the first full-blown record of Spanish travel published by an American woman writer.

The literary canon regards Irving and Longfellow as the most important antebellum writers to deal with Spain, but others—who will not be analyzed in this study—also contributed to the travel literature on this country. They include Samuel Woodruff's *Journal of a Tour to Malta, Greece, Asia Minor, Carthage, Algiers, Port Mahon and Spain* (1831), Enoch Cobb Wines's *Two Years and a Half in the Navy* (1832), the anonymous *Scenes in Spain* (1837), and Gustavus Horner's *Medical and Topographical Observations upon the Mediterranean* (1839). In the 1840s and 1850s, other travel narratives, some of which reinforced the romantic view of Spain produced by Irving, Longfellow, and the Cushings were these: John A. Clark's *Glimpses of the Old World* (1840), Charles Rockwell's *Sketches of Foreign Travel and Life at Sea* (1842), Francis Schroeder's *Shores of the Mediterranean* (1846), Severn Teackle Wallis's *Glimpses of Spain* (1849) and *Spain* (1853), John Esaias Warren's *Vagamundo; or, the Attaché in Spain* (1851), Bayard Taylor's *The Lands of the Saracen* (1855), John Milton Mackie's *Cosas de España, or Going to Madrid via Barcelona* (1855), and Charles Wainwright March's *Sketches and Adventures in Madeira, Portugal, and the Andalusias of Spain* (1856). At any rate, the importance of Irving and Longfellow has to be stressed because, probably due to their domestic and international reputation, they became the American participants in a contemporary western European textual dialogue about romantic Spain.

As some of their titles vaguely suggest, these works are representative of a variety of literary forms and aims. Harold Smith, in his bibliography of nineteenth-century American travelers, defines travel writing as any publication which "dealt substantially, or significantly, with the author's travels."[9] Here I have deliberately chosen to extend the label "travel writing" to texts not necessarily published but intended toward publication or addressed to a clear audience other than the travel writers themselves. That includes such different types of congeneric texts as letters, diaries, journals, and sketches, some of them published decades after the traveler's death, but nevertheless published writings. I have also observed a certain degree of latitude in including some texts that in principle were not written with lucrative ends in mind nor for broad audiences. George Ticknor's record of his visit to Spain, for example, has arrived to us posthumously and in a fragmentary manner, but it was certainly known to and circulated by his family and circle of friends as well as among his Harvard students by the time it reached the general public in print. Likewise, Caroline Cushing's letters were privately printed in Newburyport in a posthumous, carefully edited two-volume set that made her representation of Spain known beyond the mere family circle for which they were primarily intended.

II

The cumulative power of multiple textual representations became partly responsible for the shift toward a romantic representation of Spain in American travel writing, but equally relevant in that process was the existence of a tight literary network publicizing the country during the 1820s and 1830s. That is, a group of authors who met in Spain, followed similar itineraries there, and shared the common goal of narrating their at that time exclusive experience. Thus, apart from the contingencies of production and reception of their texts, the lives and experiences of these travel writers constitute a relevant facet of travel writing to which *Between History and Romance* pays special attention. In our studies of travel writing, Sara Mills argues, we cannot shut our eyes to the traveler's experience, for "to write on a subject such as travel writing without discussing experience, in however problematised a form, would not be an adequate account since experience, for male and female writers, is the subject-matter of travel journals."[10] Quite often the travelers' own theoretical discussions of their aims and experiences are, unfortunately, vague and confusing, but far from closing their books off from possible readings of experience, this conceptual vagueness opens the door to them. William Stowe, for example, has argued in *Going Abroad* that a paramount function of European travel in antebellum American culture was to enable major and minor travel writers to transgress lines of race, class, gender, and nation in their efforts to construct, improve, or challenge their own literary and social status.[11] Whether it meant to cast oneself as a Byronic revolutionary traveler or as a resolute woman traveler, as Mackenzie and Caroline Cushing respectively did, the Americans who visited Spain made use of this chameleonic convention allotted to and by travel writing, and thus they too shed their old skins to adopt new personas.

There are several points of confluence between the authors that form the object of this study, however, which go beyond their choice to rewrite themselves in their travel writings. These travel writers' backgrounds truly convert them into agents of a cultural gentry capable of carrying out an hermeneutic task of visible public impact. These writers are all from New England or the New York City area. Noah, Irving, and Mackenzie were New Yorkers; Ticknor, Longfellow, and the Cushings were native of Massachusetts. Similarly, they all belonged to a small, influential, and well-connected cultural elite of a certain status and power. Ticknor, for instance, became professor of Spanish at Harvard University from 1819 to 1835, and was followed in this position by Longfellow from 1835 to 1854. Irving and Cushing were appointed American Ministers to Spain several years after their trips there, from 1842 to 1846, and from 1874 to 1877, respectively. Mackenzie, a lieutenant in the navy and brother of Senator John Slidell, achieved historical notoriety as the officer who ordered the execution of some prominent mutineers aboard the ship *Somers*. Finally, although they did not write any major travel text about Spain, Obadiah Rich and Alexander H. Everett figure behind some of the former writers as sponsors of their literary ventures. Rich, the Massachusetts bibliophile and ex-consul at Valencia, possessed one the greatest collection of original materials on Hispanic America, of which Irving made ample use to write his Columbian works. Everett, the Minister Plenipotentiary to Spain who had attracted Irving to Madrid to write about Columbus, also played an important role by encouraging these writers to publicize their accounts of Spain through his connections with the *North American Review*, of which he was editor from 1830 until 1835.[12] This journal duly noticed and evaluated some of these travel books and thus carried out a significant cultural work disseminating Spanish themes.

In creating a dominant reading of Spain and the Hispanic world in antebellum America, the hermeneutic role that these travelers, scholars, and institutions played paralleled the formation of Western discourses on the Orient that also took place in nineteenth-century Europe. Edward Said's explanation in *Orientalism* (1978) of how the West has conceived the Orient illuminates, to a certain extent, many aspects of the early American representation of Spain discussed in this study. Said defines Orientalism, among other things, as the ideology fostered by the emergence of an academic discipline about the East and the continuous reminding of the binary opposition East-West.[13] However, the idea I especially want to stress from his work is that travel literature can contribute to discourse formation and the construction of the Other. Just as the Vicomte François de Chateaubriand, Gérard de Nerval, Gustave Flaubert, and many others invented, according to Said, a literary version of the Orient, Irving and other Americans likewise created an idealized version of Spain for their readerships in the United States. Through this version, Spain, like the Orient, became a stable and homogeneous system of representation, an idea that helped more or less define American culture by comparison, transatlantically for travel writers comparing with Spain, continentally for those looking south of the border and to the Caribbean. This idea—and here the connections with Said's work are more visible—had to be ratified, sanctioned, and typified by academia. It is no coincidence, then, that the origins of Hispanism as an academic discipline in America had as founders Ticknor, Longfellow, and Irving, nor is it surprising that some of the travel writers who visited Spain eventually participated in political and military activies connected to Spain and South America.[14] Caleb Cushing, for example, traveled in Spain in 1829, took part in the Mexican-American War, went to Colombia on a diplomatic mission in 1868, and served as Minister to Spain from 1874 until 1877. Travel writing and discourse formation are then totally conjoined in the early American representation of Spain.

Washington Irving, though not the self-proclaimed leader of a literal school of travel writers, always seems to be the group's galvanizing figure. This is especially noticeable at the textual level. The overall design of his *Sketch-Book* had a great influence on Longfellow and Cushing, but his *Life and Voyages of Christopher Columbus* was even more widely popular. In *A Year in Spain*, Mackenzie shows familiarity with *Life and Voyages of Christopher Columbus* and the *Chronicle of the Conquest of Granada*, and also speaks of Irving as one of the leading writers of the English language (YS, 2:176; 3:65, 264). Caroline Cushing, who also cites Irving's book on Granada, mentions that while visiting the archives of Indies in Seville her guide referred to the research Irving carried out there for his Columbian work (LD, 2:159, 217). Likewise, the author of *Scenes in Spain*, visiting the same archives, mentions Irving's investigations there to prepare that biography. He also cites Mackenzie, and when it comes to describing the Alhambra concludes that, after Irving's description of the palace, any attempt to delineate it again would fall short of it (SS, 7, 99, 152). Finally, Caleb Cushing also cites Irving's *Columbus* (RS, 2:258, 288). The travelers' acknowledged indebtedness to Irving's authority thus became an almost inexorable convention in their writings.

In addition to the intertextuality launched by his Spanish books, Irving's own presence in Spain may be said to have stimulated early nineteenth-century American travel writing on Spain. Commissioned by Everett to translate Navarrete's papers on Columbus, he moved to Spain in 1826 and began to use Obadiah Rich's library and live with the bibliophile's family. Already a literary lion, he was regularly visited by Americans in Madrid. Visits by Mackenzie and Longfellow to learn Spanish coincided with Irving during 1827. The former, who had entered Spain in October 1826, departed in April 1827—though he was to return in 1834—whereas the latter arrived in March 1827 and remained until November of the same year. During their sojourn in the capital each met several times with Irving, as his journals attest.[15] Longfellow had read and admired Irving's *Sketch Book* while an undergraduate at Bowdoin College in the early 1820s, and now was eager to make its author's acquaintance. Mackenzie (at that time he still maintained his last name of Slidell) was a young lieutenant wandering in Spain with a leave of absence from the navy. Caleb Cushing, on the other hand, did not meet Irving in Madrid, but in Paris in 1829 when Irving was on his way to a diplomatic position in London where he would complete the manuscript of *Tales of the Alhambra*. Cushing, by then already planning to write a sort of Spanish sketchbook à la Irving, conversed with him and took the opportunity to request literary advice.[16]

Mackenzie became the traveler who held a more enduring literary association with Irving. In 1827, when Longfellow and Mackenzie met Irving in Madrid, the latter was constantly busy with the composition of *Life and Voyages of Christopher Columbus*. But before leaving Madrid, Mackenzie read parts of Irving's manuscript in progress, and offered suggestions on the route taken by the Spanish admiral as well as on other topics of nautical information.[17] Years later Irving reciprocated by correcting and reviewing the English edition of Mackenzie's *A Year in Spain* (London, 1831),[18] a work which, as his nephew Pierre subsequently recalled, in his last years became "one of his favorite books, during his long illness." He added, "He read it again and again. Its graphic pictures seemed to carry him back to pleasant scenes, and out of himself. When reading to him, as we did constantly, to produce sleep, we always avoided it, as we found it excited his imagination, and roused rather than soothed him."[19] After his return to the United States, Irving supported Mackenzie's literary career: he tried, unsuccessfully, to convince his publisher to print *Spain Revisited* (1836), which he considered "the work to go beside the Year in Spain and to complete the picturing of the Country" (LII, 860).[20]

In contrast to Mackenzie, Longfellow's literary relation with Irving in Madrid and afterward seems less intense. The young Bowdoin graduate was welcomed by the Everetts and Richs, but when it was his turn to visit Irving a mixture of admiration and disappointment overcame him. Irving, by then absorbed with the composition of *Life and Voyages of Christopher Columbus*, did little more than accept Longfellow's letter of introduction from George Ticknor and pick up other letters addressed to him by the Storrows (later, in the polite exchange characteristic of genteel travel, Irving wrote him letters of recommendation—for Scott and other eminent authors—to facilitate his access into other circles). Subsequently Longfellow had more opportunities to socialize with him, and years later he would write about his literary mentor with sentimental veneration:

> One summer morning, passing his house at the early hour of six, I saw his study window already wide open. On my mentioning it to him afterwards, he said: "Yes, I am always at my work as early as six." Since then I have often remembered that sunny morning and that open window so suggestive of his sunny temperament and open heart, and equally so of his patient and persistent toil.[21]

Longfellow's more enduring literary association of those days was with Mackenzie. Both lived in the same boardinghouse and made an excursion to the environs of Madrid, particularly to Segovia and the monastery of El Escorial. Mackenzie wrote about that trip, and also included a description of his companion in *A Year in Spain*:

> A young countryman who had come to Spain in search of instruction. He was just from college, full of all the ardent feeling excited by classical pursuit, with health unbroken, hope that was a stranger to disappointments, curiosity which had never yet been fed to satiety. Then he had sunny locks, a fresh complexion, and a clear eye, all indications of a joyous temperament. (YS, 2:7–8)

A few years later, on 15 October 1829, when he was a professor of Spanish at Bowdoin, Longfellow wrote his friend about this book, admiring its force, and admitting the sentimentality of his own work:

> Your book on Spain is very much admired here. It makes me, however, very melancholy when I read it, for open where I will, I find something unknown to me before. I was as long in Spain as you were—enjoyed the same advantages whilst there—and now having before my eye as a record of what you did, and the information you collected there, I feel rather sad, that I should have effected so little, when you have effected so much: for instead of a treasure of useful and valuable information, such as you have brought away from Spain, I have only dreamy sensa-

tions, and vague recollections of a sunny land. I quarrel with myself everyday for not having seen more Bullfights . . . and sometimes fret myself into a fever for not having been hard-hearted enough to see the tragedies of the Plaza de Cebada. (LL, 1:323)

Finally when Longfellow was beginning to enjoy a comfortable literary career, he gave Mackenzie literary advice, and when the latter was under pressure for the *Somers* incident, Longfellow sent him a letter of support.[22]

III

If an important reason for concentrating on the writers of the 1820s and 1830s is the cultural work they did in creating a culturally sanctioned academic reading of Spain through travel writing, another reason is their relation with the sociopolitical circumstances from which they arose and to which they responded. The travelers' journeys and the publication dates of their travel books coincided in the United States with the Jackson administration (1828–36) and a general rise of nationalism, whereas in Spain those years witnessed a great deal of political turmoil. Spain was immersed in political chaos. It had recently lost its American colonies, its inhabitants were still recovering from the ravages of Napoleon's invasion, and the government continued moving back and forth between constitutionalism and despotism.[23] Ferdinand VII, restored to the throne by his subjects in 1814 after recognizing the Constitution of 1812, found his attempts to suppress the same document quelled by a popular revolution six years later. His dominions were falling apart: in 1821 Spain ceded Florida to the United States, and by 1825 most South American colonies were independent. Pressed by necessity, in 1823 he summoned the Holy Alliance to intervene and restore him to power. The ten years that ensued, known as the "ominous decade," during which Irving and others were in Spain, saw a great deal of political repression and the presence of occupation forces.[24] In his travel book Enoch Cobb Wines, who visited the Balearic Islands and Barcelona, states that "the slaves of sultan Mahmoud are in a condition far preferable to that of the subjects of Ferdinand the Seventh."[25] The civil war of succession from 1833 to 1840, on which Thoreau commented, made Spanish politics still more international, with foreigners supporting both the liberal cause of Isabella and the reactionary claims of Don Carlos. Whether by ommission or by implication, American travel writing inscribed these foreign sociopolitical events and thus directly or indirectly commented on their significance for the domestic reader.

The romantic representation of Spain, however, hinged less on contemporary historical issues than on textualized versions of the past or pastoral representations of the present. Pivoting on the reaction to industrialization and change, this representation was given impetus by Lord Byron, Wilhelm von Humboldt, Prosper de Mérimée, and the Vicomte de Chateaubriand, among many others, and reached its peak of popularity especially near the middle of the century through the travel narratives of Théophile Gautier, Richard Ford, and George Borrow, as well as the bizarrely contorted engravings of Gustave Doré.[26] It was an arcadian and nostalgic view of Spain as a simple, rural, and motionless country that offered a contrast to the bustling society of the United States. George Ticknor and Alexander Slidell Mackenzie are the first travel writers to develop the alluring and primitive underside of Spain for American audiences. Their representation, however, was still significantly permeated with didactic and political concerns characteristic of the eighteenth century mindset. Irving, Longfellow, and to a certain extent the Cushings, as we shall see later, became then the travel writers who opened the unbounded escapist possibilities of the voyage to edenic Spain to the imagination of many readers in the United States.

The idea of a scenic, romantic Spain, however, did go back to the late eighteenth century when many British travelers in search of the picturesque began to look for untrodden touristic routes. They found in Spain—one of the least known European countries, according to Dr. Johnson—a constant source of sketches, compositions, and landscapes.[27] Their accounts, however, did not constitute mere applications of the aesthetic principles of the picturesque school advocated by William Gilpin, Richard Payne Knight, and Uvedale Price. On the contrary, more often than not travel books became specialized analyses of the economy, religion, and politics of the country, a characteristic that carried over into the travel writings of early romantic travelers in the nineteenth century like the German Wilhelm von Humboldt and the French Alexandre de Laborde. With the Horatian conventions in mind, these writers not only sought to teach but to delight, and therefore highlighted both the factual and the adventurous discourses of their narratives by combining history and romance into a single genre.

The romantic travel book on Spain, though making use of these informative artistic, sociohistorical, and political conventions, nonetheless leaned more toward the subjective and projected before its readers the profile of a masculine traveler who delighted in the perils of trekking across Spain. The first decades of the nineteenth century, for example, produced several travel writings by foreigners who had fought with or against Napoleonic armies in the peninsula. From the same period dates the representation of Spain left by Lord Byron, who was there in the summer of 1809. It would not be an exaggeration to say that the first canto of *Childe Harold's Pilgrimage* did more to publicize romantic Spain in Europe and the United States than many of its contemporary travel books put together. The first sketch in Cushing's *Reminiscences of Spain*, for example, appears preceded by "Oh, lovely Spain! renowned, romantic Land!," the frequently quoted line xxxv from Byron's poem (RS, 1:2). Similarly, Octavia Walton LeVert begins the Spanish chapters of her *Souvenirs of Travel* (1857) with the same Byronic quote.[28] James Buzard has claimed that by creating "an aristocracy of inner feeling" Byron challenged the exclusiveness of the Grand Tour and in a sense reconfigured Continental travel, but perhaps even more important is Byron's role in gendering European travel. His influence remained so strong that being a Byronic traveler "amounted to figuring oneself as a lone male wanderer, unfettered by the familial and female influences of home."[29] Early American travel writing on Spain took advantage of this conventional Byronic posing in the travel text and thus accentuated the travelers' subjective and sentimental side. It also favored the representation of intrepid male travelers rambling in feminized scenarios linguistically and ideologically naturalized to be traveled on. Only Caroline Cushing, the woman travel writer in the group of authors I discuss, challenged this gendered view of the peninsular tour and demonstrated to American audiences that women could also travel in perilous Spain.

Leaving Byronic gestures aside, the impulse to travel abroad is nevertheless always difficult to characterize. Dennis Porter, for example, in a psychoanalytical study of some nonfictional travel accounts from the Enlightenment to the postcolonial era, calls attention to the essentially ambivalent nature of travel. It is an activity almost beyond the traveler's control, "fueled by desire" and at the same time manifesting "powerful transgressive impulses."[30] Desire, particularly its unconscious type, becomes the ineluctable force which drives travelers to pursue the satisfaction of their yearnings in lands other than their own. But, very frequently, when they leave the patriarchal country and ignore their filial duties toward *pater* and *patria*, they are beset with guilt, which, along with desire, ends up inscribed in the texts they produce. This is, for example, what Jeffrey Rubin-Dorsky argues in his study of Irving's career in Europe from 1815 to 1832. Far from being the blissful period they have often symbolized, those years reveal Irving torn between his wish to stay abroad and his will to return to his homeland.[31]

Another rhetorical convention of travel writing that betrays the impulse to travel is what Porter terms the traveler's "sense of belatedness," the notion of belonging or returning to the foreign places he or she visits.[32] In similar terms, Christopher Mulvey has referred to "the time-and-space journey," which he defines as "a mythological and psychic one in which the traveler might reconstruct his childhood of tales, books, pictures, legends, and dreams."[33] This imaginary exodus, which manifests to what degree the textualization of Spain was built into the traveler's complicated psyche, is inscribed in several travel narratives of the period I discuss. Consider, for instance, Harriet Trowbridge Allen's exultant exclamation upon entering Spain: "I can hardly realize, as yet that we are in Spain. . . . I feel at home amid these familiar names recalling as they do many a story and legend of romance, of knight and cavalier and Moorish warrior."[34] These outpourings, a somewhat common rhetorical convention in travel writing, illustrate that for many travelers the motive of their voyage to Spain also was to realize an idealized past of textual romantic associations that, rather than inspiring awe or instilling a sense of cultural disadvantage, furnished the traveler with pleasure. In other instances, paradoxical as it may seem, the pleasurable impulse to travel came from the very insecurity found abroad. Such is the case, for example, of Sarah Rogers Haight, who affirmed that notwithstanding the danger, "there [was] also excitement and novelty in travelling through a country under martial law, and where one may at any moment be in the midst of an insurrection or an 'émeute'."[35] Or take this passage by Alexander Slidell Mackenzie, who, upon leaving war-torn Spain in 1836, affirmed that life was not the same any more in safe France: "I began to miss the excitement which had kept me alive in Spain by the precariousness of my existence, the daily probability of being robbed, the daily possibility of seeing others murdered, or being murdered myself; and even this sprightly land [France] became to me one of unmeaning monotony, until I sank into an ennui bordering on melancholy." (SR, 2:379). The romantic death-wish implicit in Mackenzie's words no doubt conveys the bitterness and dissatisfaction of the romantic agony, but also communicates the message of pleasure and gratification encoded in touristic discourse.[36]

Today travel brochures, advertisements, and photographs have accustomed us to this discourse of pleasure, but early nineteenth-century travel writing had to transmit it with subtlety and decorum. Pleasure, however, was not the only discourse disseminated by the travel writings examined here. The discourses of American nationalism and exceptionalism are equally manifest. Nonfictional travel writings, considered a powerful medium of education, had to follow certain conventions. To the inevitable compendium of geographical and historical facts, writers added cross-cultural comparisons, usually to the advantage of their own civilization. It is not strange, then, that the travel book was capable of influencing a great number of readers morally and politically. Mary Louise Pratt has noted, for example, that in eighteenth- and nineteenth-century Europe travel books "engaged metropolitan reading publics with (or to) expansionist enterprises whose material benefits accrued mainly to the very few."[37] For Pratt, the European political and economic expansion that took place since 1750 found in the nonfictional travel book and in the figure of the explorer who wrote it two of its best allies. The scientific traveler, with his ever-scrutinizing eye, catalogued, surveyed, and objectified the Other. Thus, while the European economic and military powers were securing their hegemony over indigenous peoples, travel writers were carrying out what Pratt calls an "anti-conquest," the creation and implementation of several representational strategies that ultimately exonerated the colonizers from their guilt.[38] Not all travel writers, however, do thoroughly accept the colonial discourse that impregnates the ideological foundations of their genre. Sara Mills has demonstrated that British women travelers of the late colonial period contested the imperialist discourse that, along with those of patriarchy and femininity, conflicted with their representations of themselves and otherness.[39] Like these British women travelers, the Americans who wrote on Spain also found their own personal discourses interlocked with public ones. Sometimes they became indirect agents of these public discourses, and when they articulated them they did so with certain misgivings.

The cultural work of the travel book partially explains the installation of nationalist and exceptionalist discursive orders in mid-nineteenth-century America. However, when it comes to the particular case of Spain, this view needs to be taken with reservations. It can be argued, for example, that Bayard Taylor's *Eldorado; or, Adventures in the Path of Empire* (1850) and Herman Melville's

Moby-Dick (1851) subconsciously engaged American audiences in the commercial expansionist enterprises of prospecting gold in California and whaling in the Pacific, respectively. The American expansionism promulgated by Manifest Destiny is tangible in both texts, where exploitation of other peoples' natural resources is sanctioned. But whereas it is not difficult to establish a connection between the rise of American travel writing and American global imperialism during the second half of the nineteenth century, the same cannot be so simply said of the decades I study here, decades during which the United States was still striving to define itself as a nation and still suffered from cultural and geographical insularity.[40]

To begin with, some of the earliest American foreign policies, such as the 1823 Monroe Doctrine, had not yet been clearly articulated. Likewise, the number of Americans abroad producing travel literature was not very large. It was a period, as Nina Baym reminds us, when "American tourists were not the colonizers but the colonized; they were traveling from the outback to the cultural center."[41] For those of British stock, which they almost all were, England was the cultural center, and a voyage there confronted American travelers with their ancestry.[42] Hawthorne, appointed United States consul in Liverpool, titled his British travel sketches *Our Old Home* (1863). Irving, in *Bracebridge Hall* (1822), affirmed that "England is as classic ground to an American as Italy is to an Englishman. . . . He for the first time sees a world about which he has been reading and thinking in every stage of his existence."[43] Yet if Italy was regarded as both the shrine of Western art and the locus of hedonism, and England was classic ground to Americans, then what was Spain to them? It was a textualized paradise, a land of noble peasantry and civilized values gone awry, where, unaware of it, the agents of a rising empire were romanticizing the subjects of a battered one. Even though it may be rather difficult to elucidate, American exceptionalism thus had an impact on early American travel writing on Spain, and vice versa, for the representation these travel writers produced prefigures a discourse on Spain and the Hispanic world—of political corruption, tame populations, and unused natural resources—that many a proponent of Manifest Destiny surely used to valorize imperialist enterprises south of the border.

IV

Apart from the political background in which these travel writings appeared, which included this subtext of American exceptionalism, the discourses that surface in the American romantic representation of Spain are permeated with many descriptive, thematic, and narrative conventions of travel writing that shed light on the private and public concerns imposed on the travel writers. Important among these rhetorical conventions is the travelers' disclosure of their motives for visiting Spain, which may range from improving one's health to studying the language, literature, and history, or even the choice of Spain as a novelty in travel writing.[44] However, in describing the shift from an enlightened to a romantic representation of that country, the most productive convention from a literary point of view is the fusion of *history* and *romance* within the arena of travel writing. Instead of struggling with their own medium of expression, which sometimes proved unsatisfactory owing to the elusive heterogeneity of the travel book itself, travel writers took advantage of its shapelessness to inform it with variegated narrative discourses like history and romance.[45] These two genres, in particular, could easily mingle within the travel book to make the object of representation more palatable to readers, and they could also help to articulate the discourse of adventure and the discourse of facts necessary to represent a politicized or an escapist narration of Spain whenever it was convenient.

The dark aspects of early nineteenth-century Spanish history constitute a significant part of the politics of representation in these travel writings, yet also a matter of romance. Irving explained that in his *Chronicle of the Conquest of Granada* he had tried to avoid pure scholarly history, which audiences would find too dry, and therefore came up with a genre "between a history and a romance." Like Irving, other American travel writers on Spain narrated Spain as a text that oscillated between two major poles of inscription: the factuality of its historical actualities and the fictionality of its romantic expectations. Many of these travel books consequently became a hybrid genre fusing travel account with romance to achieve two purposes. One is to romanticize history to avoid a direct confrontation with the realities of the present; the other is to use this same romance to make the object of representation, Spain, more marketable to American audiences.[46] History, and more particularly romanticized history, is then both a tool used to represent and, in some cases, to escape the anxiety of what Irving in *The Sketch Book* called "the commonplace realities of the present."

The fact that history became a major underlying convention in these travel narratives to form a sound idea of Spain and the Spaniards is supported by the number of Spanish historical works published in the United States during that period, beginning with the results of Irving's archival research and continuing with Prescott's scholarship. The romantic travelers' notion of history, however, often wavered between the mere recollection of past events fit for moral reflection and its perception as a convention that turned Spain and the Spaniards into a sort of thematic fun park where leisurely middle-class travelers could live through experiences of romance. These travelers regarded history as an unfolding process where the poverty, political strife, and absolutism of the present were seen as a direct consequence of past and recent historical episodes, but seldom did they outspokenly challenge the causes nor the effects of that process. For them the historical and literary associations of Spain were so palpable everywhere that they gradually came to interpret the country as a kind of living history.

The literary climate in which these travel writings occurred still held nonfictional prose in high esteem, even though public tastes were shifting to an ever-increasing market more and more dominated by prose fiction. History was one of the chief genres in antebellum America, and so was the travel book, which William Charvat defines as "a kind of contemporary history." The same literary historian argues that the former genre—and, implicitly, the latter—had social prestige "because it was useful and educational, and because its methods were in accord with the reigning Scottish Common-Sense philosophy, which celebrated actuality and denigrated possibility."[47] Notwithstanding their reputation, travel and history books had to compete during the 1820s and the 1830s with the romance and the novel. James Fenimore Cooper, who had popularized the Waverley type of historical fiction with *The Spy* (1821), continued his successes with the publication of the first titles of his Leatherstocking saga. Historical romances like Lydia Maria Child's *Hobomok* (1824) and Catharine Maria Sedgwick's *Hope Leslie* (1827) were becoming the mark of literary nationalism.

The competition among genres in antebellum America, to be sure, was not solely a matter of social prestige, but became rather a question of sales, copyrights, and editions. That is why Irving, to make his *Columbus* more lucrative, changed Navarrete's papers to create a work that, as Charvat estimates, earned him $25,000.[48] More astonishing, perhaps, is the fact that in 1838, in the middle of a recession, the two luxurious volumes of Prescott's *History of the Reign of Ferdinand and Isabella* sold out at $7.50 each set.[49] The same profit was reaped by its cousin genre. "Travels sell about the best of anything we get hold of," said editor George Putnam to John Lloyd Stephens, author of *Incidents of Travel in Egypt, Ara-*

bia Petraea, and the Holy Land (1837). "They don't always go off with a rush, like a novel by a celebrated author, but they sell longer, and in the end, pay better. By the way, you've been to Europe; why not write us a book of travels?"[50] Putnam's mercenary remark importantly reminds us that the travel book, unlike other genres, could endure periods of weak publication. In the case of the early travelers in Spain, however, in addition to the market opened by Irving's venture into Spanish culture, they published in a period of relative economic stability at home between the financial depressions 1819–1823 and 1837–1844. Longfellow's *Outre-Mer*, his first literary venture, was published with moderate success, but before he could make any profit on his next book, *Hyperion*, its New York publisher, Colman, failed.[51]

Travel and history books nevertheless managed to maintain their quotas in the literary market through periods of crisis. However, faced with the competition of new literary genres, it is not strange that travel writers and historians chose to experiment and often turned self-consciously to the romance and the novel to enliven their texts, at least in a suggested if not overt manner. The borderline between these genres was extremely hard to draw, and as William Gilmore Simms pointed out in a review of Prescott's *History of the Conquest of Mexico* (1843), writers cultivating them did so with some apprehension:

> Never was history, in itself, more thoroughly like romance; never was the narrow boundary between the possible and the certain, more vague, shadowy and subtle. Truth seems to hang forever over the abyss of doubt;—the probable loses itself in a wide empire of uncertainties, in which the historian, trembling always lest he should lose his guide, grasps unscrupulously, at last, upon the nearest forms which promise a refuge for his thought; and is delighted, finally, to lose himself in any faith which will put at rest his incredulity.[52]

Admittedly, Simms's anxieties echo the romantic suspension of disbelief advocated by Coleridge, but instead of succumbing to methodological scepticism or pure solipsism, the historian—like the romancer and the travel writer—delights in experimenting lost "in any faith," that is, in any new genre. The travel books I concentrate on also chose this way out, and their generic elasticity gave them carte blanche to mix history, romance, and other conventions to produce, invigorate, and commodify a lasting romantic representation of Spain in the United States.

However experimental or destabilized their vehicle of representation might be, romantic travel writers, mixing their historical facts and contemporary observations with romance, must have experienced the same methodological anxieties that Hawthorne was to voice in his prefaces years later. The era of meticulous travel description was waning, and now the travel writer, like Hawthorne's romancer, had "a right to present that truth under circumstances, to a great extent, of the writer's own choosing or creation."[53] What was increasingly necessary was that the nonfictional travel book be imbued with romance, something that, according to many, could not be convincingly situated in the United States. On the one hand we find those who, like Sarah Josepha Hale, acknowledged the American landscape could not offer the poetical associations travelers found in Europe, but, following the nationalistic fervor of the time, urged for the beginning of a collective effort to charge it with New World ones.[54] For others, on the other hand, to write "about a country where there is no shadow, no antiquity, no mystery, no picturesque and gloomy wrong, nor anything but a common-place prosperity, in broad and simple daylight," was as difficult as it later was to Hawthorne's romancer in *The Marble Faun* (1860).[55] Or, according to Cooper in *Notions of the Americans* (1828), the United States was a country whose culture lacks, among other things, "annals for the historian," "manners for the dramatist," and "obscure fictions for the writer of romance."[56] Hawthorne had also observed in his preface to *The Marble Faun* that "Romance and poetry, like ivy, lichens, and wall flowers, need Ruin to make them grow," a remark which, though referring to another country (Italy) and genre (romance), nevertheless calls attention to the same elements the romantic travel writer in Spain had to make use of—namely ruins, history, and imagination.

The theme of ruins surely is one of a number of gothic conventions of romance that make themselves most manifest in these travel accounts. While Irving explored the multiple influences that ruinous settings like the Alhambra could have on those who inhabited them, including himself, other travel writers like Mordecai M. Noah and Caroline Cushing used the contemplation of dilapidated buildings to trigger moral ruminations with strong didactic messages. The battered castles, poor inns, and once-magnificent churches of Spain often stood for them as icons of a fallen glorious past. However, this was not the only convention of gothic romance that these travel writers deployed to represent Spain. Sometimes they resort to narratorial personas whose perceptions can be called into question. This is true, for example, of Caleb Cushing, Longfellow, and Irving, who portray themselves as experiencing romantic dream visions. On other occasions they use the metaliterary convention of a found manuscript, as Irving does with Fray Antonio de Agapida's parchments to chronicle the events of the siege and fall of the kingdom of Granada. Finally, they also represent the ghastly side of Spain with the conventions of gothic romance, as is the case in Mackenzie's gory accounts of highway robberies and capital punishments, or in Caleb Cushing's fictionalized account of the Inquisition, "Garci Pérez, a Tale of the Holy Office." In each of these and other conventions, Spain was nearly turned into a setting of gothic fiction where travelers and readers alike could experience the chills of romance.

The traveler's rewriting of the Spaniard as an exotic Other constitutes another convention of the literature of travel on Spain that also displays powerful connections with romance. The Spaniards presented a crux to American travelers because cultural identification was not always easy to consummate. These travelers were both fascinated by the splendorous past of Spain and repulsed by its decayed present.[57] They also held the country in high esteem because of its Columbian and literary associations, especially whatever was connected to Cervantes and the Golden Age. And yet, apart from its Western bonds, Spain could not offer to Anglo-Saxon Americans the ancestral heritage of other European places. Granted, the voyage to Spain permitted an introduction into the European past, but it also offered an encounter with the somewhat different background of the Orient. By a rhetorical exercise not too difficult to effect, the Spaniards, through their medieval and Oriental affiliation, could be rewritten as picturesque emblems of non-European otherness and thus afforded the American traveler a cross-cultural experience between East and West on European soil. The binary opposition East-West that, according to Said, fosters the discourses of Orientalism, is noticeable in these representations. Irving's *Chronicle of the Conquest of Granada* (1829) and *The Alhambra* (1832), Bayard Taylor's *The Lands of the Saracen* (1858), and the anonymous *Traces of the Roman and the Moor* (1853), all works that explicitly capitalize on the Arab connotations of their titles, are obvious orientalist works on Spain. The exoticism of the Spaniards, however, is not only present in the titles of books but elsewhere. The illustrated travel accounts published in the second half of the century also include many drawings of Moorish Spain. The orientalist narration of Spanish otherness demonstrates not only the fondness for exoticism in antebellum literature but also the homogeneity of the overall American discourse on Spain arising in that period.

To a significant extent, however, the inscription of picturesque and orientalized Spaniards betrays more than a conventional fad for the exoticism of romance, as these early travel books on Spain often reveal a true ethnographic curiosity.[58] George Borrow, the famous Englishman who in the 1840s traveled and peddled Bibles in Spain, once expressed, "My favourite, I might say my only study, is man."[59] He lived for a long period of time among the gypsies, and came to be considered an authority in that community. Irving also fashioned himself as a romantic, amateur ethnographer living among Spanish noble savages during his sojourn in the community of Alhambrans. The past century's notion of the traveler-cum-anthropologist, however, has recently been contested. As Valerie Wheeler puts it,

> Literate, but not literary, anthropological, but not anthropologists, exploring, but not explorers, travel writers produce something like ethnography but not ethnography. . . . Though the traveler had an honored place in nineteenth-century anthropology as one who provided data for the armchair anthropologist to analyze, travel books today are considered a minor form of ethnographic writing.[60]

Still, the early Americans in Spain participated in the same ethnographic curiosity that enticed travelers to more exotic cultures, a curiosity that lasted until the turn of the century and beyond. Consider, for example, James M. Buckley's account in 1895 of the Spaniards' ethnic affiliations: "In the streets of the cities every variety that could result from the admixture of the original population with the Goths, Moors, Romans, Greeks, and Phoenicians appears." And he adds, "While two thirds of the people have the Spanish type, one in three looks as much like an Englishman or an American as the majority of the natives of those countries, having the lighter complexion and even the same general expression of countenance."[61]

If the travel book was considered in the past a serious ethnographic document depicting the Other as faithfully as possible, its artificial nature, its subtle power relations, and above all its unreliable quality as linguistic construct have now been brought to the forefront by new historicist inquiries. Vincent Crapanzano, making a clear linguistic analogy, defines the ethnographer's threefold task: he has to translate, decode, and interpret the foreign culture for his readers. Reading culture is like translating, but since what is being translated is a society, not a text, and societies are temporally determined, the representation of the Other becomes therefore slippery, if not almost unattainable.[62] The traveler, then, like the ethnographer, had to face this unsurmountable obstacle and devise ways to represent the Other to his or her audiences at home with a certain degree of verisimilitude. Irving and Caroline Cushing, for example, strove to achieve this with the interpolation of foreign words and expressions. Longfellow and Caleb Cushing, in their sketchbooks, to capture the essence of Castilian character included their own translations of Spanish poetry, a reminder that perhaps the first step in attempting the translation of the Other begins with their language.

V

The emphasis that anthropologists have recently laid upon inscription, representation, and textuality nevertheless calls attention to a series of conventions, mechanisms, or strategies of cultural interpretation that, as James Buzard has remarked, gained momentum especially after the Napoleonic Wars. One especially important convention is the notion of the travel book as a cultural product, as an image-making commodity that customizes continental Europe to the Anglo-American visitors and helps them define the notion of "Culture" versus "culture" at home and abroad. The other, returning to the connection between anthropology and travel, is the notion of textuality. Most travelers making the Continental tour, explains Buzard, found themselves enmeshed in a textual maze, so that they had to adopt one of two attitudes: either give in to a near tyranny of accounts of the places visited, or try to transcend this textual maze by writing something original improving what had already been said about a place. Very often it was the latter they chose to do, yet quite unsuccessfully, since when the travel writers, by claiming that they had reached a real foreign experience off the beaten track, positioned themselves outside mainstream culture, the latter immediately devised mechanisms that turned their antitouristic statements into orthodox culture. It was because of this yearning for originality that the Continental tour ultimately became "an affair of 'writing' more than of 'reality'."[63] *Between History and Romance*, as it was previously mentioned, will not then be a conscientious critique of the lack of historical accuracy in travel books about Spain. On the contrary, bearing in mind these travel books' "writing" more than their "reality," it shall argue for the fictionality embedded in their textual representation of that country.

The next six chapters will thus examine how the textual knowledge of Spain took place in the early nineteenth-century United States and how the literary network that brought about that knowledge cast off its original didactic conventions of Enlightenment travel writing to embrace a fertile combination of the factual and the nonfactual, that is, of history and romance. The touristic discourses present in these travel writings became diluted in their component of suggested romance. Still, by paying attention to history and romance, among some of the other rhetorical conventions deployed by these texts, one may identify some new insights into antebellum American culture which these generic conventions provided to contemporary readers through their textual exploration of foreign lands and, more especifically, of Spain. As a starting point, chapter 2 follows several objectives. First, it gives an overview of Spain as a topic in American letters prior to the 1830s, focusing briefly on some of the most influential Spanish themes. Second, it discusses some works by Philip Freneau, Joel Barlow, and other writers of the colonial and early national periods, especially some diplomats who traveled to Spain and whose letters and official papers provided the first genuinely American representation of that country. And finally, it provides details about the actual infrastructure of travel to Europe, and to and within Spain proper, explaining why until the 1830s there had been so little access to the country.

Having examined the Enlightenment view of the first travel accounts on and literary representations of Spain, the following two chapters focus on the late enlightened or pre-romantic views circulated by the first nineteenth-century travel writings. Chapter 3 discusses Mordecai Manuel Noah's censorious *Travels in England, France, Spain, and the Barbary States* and George Ticknor's posthumous letters and journals. These early nineteenth-century representations of Spain serve to illustrate the still common ideology of the rational Enlightenment from which subsequent travelers try to deviate, but which in some other cases they follow rather closely to examine the situation of Spain after the Napoleonic invasion. In a sense, both Noah and Ticknor, together with Mackenzie, bridge the first generation of Enlightenment travelers in Spain like John Adams, John Jay, and James Monroe, and romantics like Irving, Longfellow, and the Cushings. Chapter 4 focuses on Mackenzie's *A Year in Spain*, alluding briefly to his subsequent *Spain Revisited*. Although today Mackenzie is perhaps remembered only as one of the officers involved in the court-martial later fictionalized in Melville's *Billy Budd*, his first travel book remains one of the most powerful accounts of Spain in the nineteenth century. Read and edited by Irving, translated, widely reviewed, and banned in Spain, this account is undoubtedly the most subversive in the decade. While manifesting Byronic conventions of romantic travel, Mackenzie's transgressive representation of Spain also reveals a solid preoccupation with political events in that country, and exemplifies what might be called a Painesque view of Spain akin to the ideas of the political or revolutionary Enlightenment. This travel book manifests that history is not a romantic tool to escape the present but, on the contrary, a process in the making.

In contrast to the apparent political commitment of the late Enlightenment or pre-romantic travel writers, the remaining chapters in the study converge on romantic travel accounts that promoted a less involved and rather escapist representation of Spain. Using the definitive edition of Irving's letters and journals, chapter 5 discusses the politics of his representation of Spain focusing, above all, on *The Alhambra*, but also paying attention to other Spanish writings such as *Life and Voyages of Christopher Columbus* and *Chronicle of the Conquest of Granada*. I argue that *The Alhambra* reads almost like an ethnographic text where Irving, aided by his informant Mateo Ximenez, attempts to attain a "thick description" of Spain by doing intense fieldwork in the palace and its environs. His dialogic account of the inhabitants of Granada, however, is finally marred by his continuous reliance on the "storied and poetic associations" of their history. By mingling a sort of primitive perennial present and the Oriental past in one single setting, Irving tries to keep at bay the threatening forces of contemporary Spain, and his few allusions to the sociopolitical turbulence beyond the walls of the palace are sometimes more telling than his romantic raptures. Related to Irving's *The Alhambra* by its generic affiliation, chapter 6 provides a reading of Longfellow's *Outre-Mer* that concentrates upon his rejection of enlightened rationalism and political involvement for religious sentimentalism. With its strong emphasis on subjectivism and his negation of otherness and historical information, Longfellow's sketchbook, like Irving's, becomes a good example of the reactionary romantic travel account. Its representation of Spain, unlike that circulated by the politically charged accounts of Noah, Ticknor, and Mackenzie, inscribes the country and its citizens as if they were suspended in a blissful historical void beyond the influence of progress and change. The very representation of Spain that relies on romantic conventions, moral lessons, sentimental musings, and literary associations also makes itself manifest in chapter 7, which examines Caleb Cushing's Irvingesque sketchbook *Reminiscences of Spain*, a travel narrative still charged with the culturally inflected apparatus of the learned travel book. In contrast to that cultured rhetoric, the same chapter also offers a counterimage in analyzing the second volume of Caroline Cushing's *Letters Descriptive of Public Monuments, Scenery, and Manners in France and Spain*, a work that adds a gender dimension to the whole study by problematizing such issues as the transgression of the female's domestic sphere or the notion of Spain as an exclusive romantic getaway for the male traveler.

Having placed these texts and writers within the broader perspective of antebellum American culture in the late 1820s and the 1830s, and having connected them with other issues in the study of travel literature, this study looks further afield by way of conclusion. It argues that, despite efforts to represent Spain with fidelity to American audiences, during the remaining decades of the antebellum period and even later the country continued to be envisioned as a site of medievalism, orientalism, and the exotic due to the influence of the earlier romantic representations, especially those by Irving. No doubt this unchanged view has something to do with the lasting influence of the conventions of history and romance in American travel writing. No doubt, too, it is the result of the inexhaustible capacity of travel writing as a genre to renew and reinvent itself with the adoption of new rhetorical conventions, viewpoints, and discourses. "The dialogue of American travel writers with each other and with their audiences," Terry Caesar has observed apropos of nineteenth-century American travel writing, "ultimately evolved into an epistemological experience of seeing America itself through the mediation of abroad."[64] The authors and works discussed in this study, as I hope to demonstrate, also engaged themselves in this epistemological experience and therefore played a minor though patent role in America's understanding and commodification of what was commonly known as the country of olives and oranges, the land of history and romance.

2

First Impressions: Writing from and about Spain in the Colonial and Early National Periods

In the late eighteenth century, once the United States had achieved political independence and began to vindicate its own national identity abroad, Spain still appeared as a species of terra incognita to average Americans, and continued to be so during the first decades of the following century. In a survey on the state of the peninsula, Alexander H. Everett noted that there was "no country, whose domestic condition or its internal affairs are more misinterpreted than those of Spain."[1] Everett probably did not know then of the number of early records on Spain available to us today, nor could he anticipate, of course, that, within a few years after his remark, a host of American travelers including his friend Irving would produce full American representations of Spain. Even then, the perception that it was difficult to acquire a true understanding of Spain ran so deep that not long after the publication of the travel books discussed in this study, an anonymous essayist complained that "after all that has been said and written about the country, and after the numerous visits that have been made to it, Spain still seems to be a region unexplored."[2] However, as this chapter shall demonstrate, before the Irving generation brought out its travel books on Spain, that country had made itself certainly visible in early American letters, and that visibility helped to propagate enduring first impressions of Spain in the United States.

Colonial Americans certainly had their share of information about peninsular affairs, but it was especially the epistemological project of the Enlightenment that spread its intellectual light over all areas of knowledge, including Spain. The surge in romantic literary works of Spanish inspiration, including travel books, that took place in the 1820s and 1830s in the United States did not arise ex nihilo. Rather it manifested both an already strong influence of

44

Spanish themes on American letters, and what Stanley Williams has termed a "widening consciousness of Spanish culture" in the earlier decades of the century. Indeed, as Stimson, Williams, and other scholars have shown, British-Americans drew a great deal of material from Spain and South America for their emerging literature. The most important Spanish themes in early American letters, according to Frederick Stimson, are the "black legend" disseminated by the British, the emancipation of South America, Columbus, the noble savage, Spanish poetry, the civilization of the Caribbean, and certain episodes in peninsular history.[3] These plots, characters, and landscape descriptions, however, were usually extracted from prior texts, a circumstance which manifests that the textualization of Spain began quite early in the colonial United States.

Most American notions about Spain in the colonial and early national periods derived, however, from foreign accounts, or from stereotypes of Spanish indolence, religious bigotry, and pride. Because of the difficult transatlantic voyage and the precariousness of internal travel in the Iberian Peninsula, few citizens of the young United States had direct contact with the Spaniards. Transatlantic relations were few and far between; consequently the American traveler in Spain embodied otherness to the Spaniards as much as they did to the American. Stereotypes in fact became current signifiers for cross-cultural exchanges, and their pidgeonholing of national characters prefigured, as Percy Adams observes, a later American literary tradition that encompassed "the international novel, Grand Tour literature, and the *Bildungsroman*."[4] Stereotypes were and are used because, as Homi Bhabha points out, they constitute a very important factor in the "ideological construction of otherness." Their paradoxical manner of representation, depending both on fixedness and constant repetition, provides a sensation of truth.[5]

The travel accounts of the late colonial and early national periods provide sufficient evidence of the extent and use of such stereotyping. John Jay, for instance, wrote to Congress explaining that many Spaniards believed Americans to be savages. In Barcelona, George Crowninshield did all he could to convince the Catalans around him that he was neither an American Indian nor an Englishman. Stereotypes, however, were deeply ingrained in both parts, for, as Severn T. Wallis would lament almost by mid-nineteenth century, "we have a sort of indefinite idea of the Spaniard, which places him about half-way between a bloody-minded grand-inquisitor and an 'illustrious hidalgo' of Major Monsoon's Portuguese regiment."[6] Far from being a ludicrous figment of Wallis's imagination, the type of representation of Spain that he brings up is precisely that which colonial Americans had held for a long time. Given the ignorance and misinformation of things Spanish, it is not surprising that history and romance—the very two elements with which one could forge an idea of Spain without actually traveling there—eventually came to be powerful rhetorical conventions for the textual construction of Hispanic otherness in antebellum America.

I

During the early colonial period, the American image of Spain was rather different, and perhaps less mediated by the visual impact of stereotyped iconicity, than it later was in the antebellum period. Judith Adler has noted that before Lockeian thought—based on the apprehension of reality through images—began to influence European sightseeing and precepts on how to represent otherness, cross-cultural representations were above all based on discourses and ideas.[7] Notions about Spain were as widely circulated in Europe as stereotypes, especially among its political competitors, and thus Edith F. Helman's affirmation that "New England shared the views and prejudices of Old England about Spain" should not come as a surprise.[8] American representations of Spain were profoundly political, in effect a replication of British biases arising from economic, political, and religious rivalries. Thus, it is not strange, for example, that the poems where Anne Bradstreet cites Spain ("The Four Elements," "A Dialogue Between Old England and New; Concerning Their Present Troubles, Anno 1642," and "In Honour of Queen Elizabeth") allude to such Anglo-Spanish commonplaces as the defeat of the Spanish Armada, the sack of Cádiz by the Earl of Essex, Sir Francis Drake's piracy, and King Philip II's Catholic fanaticism.[9] Yet, as Americans developed their own social and political idiosyncrasies, they also began to transform their views of Spain.

It was particularly in the final decades of the eighteenth century that these views slightly began to derive from somewhat different political and cultural standpoints. Benjamin Franklin, for example, depicted Spain as a power to be taken into account during the revolution in "Dialogue between Britain, France, Spain, Holland, Saxony, and America" (1776).[10] Similarly, as Zardoya has noted, while loyalist poets like Joseph Stanbury and Jonathan Odell attacked Spain because it was an enemy of England, patriots like Joel Barlow, John Trumbull, and Philip Freneau praised it because it was supporting the rebels' cause.[11] Before the Revolution, however, Freneau had attacked Spain's depredation of South America in "The Rising Glory of America," characterizing Cortés and Pizarro as the "pride of Spain / whom blood and murder only satisfied" and asserting that "Gold, fatal gold, was the alluring bait / to Spain's rapacious tribes."[12] No doubt readers of Freneau's poem, influenced by textual stereotypes, stored in their subconscious images of armor-clad *conquistadores* looting the New World, but no doubt, too, these readers received and assimilated the current discourses on Spain which these early American works were feeding them.

The representation of Spain and its American possessions were in fact part of the overall discourse of self-affirmation that was being articulated in the emergent British colonies. Private and public libraries played a very important role in the development of the national idiosyncrasy of these territories by circulating and textualizing things Spanish among colonial Americans. Some colonists carried all or part of their book collections with them to the New World, and when they were firmly settled continued to acquire books on very different subjects. In Philadelphia, for instance, one of the first private libraries was that of James Logan, the bibliophile friend of William Penn, who bequeathed more than two thousand volumes to the city upon his death in 1751.[13] Some private libraries included French or English translations of Spanish literature as well as originals, and their owners used whatever resources they had at hand in order to obtain them. Samuel Sewall, for example, requested the purchase of some Spanish books in London, and William Bentley, not satisfied with his English translation of *Don Quixote*, ordered the original directly from Madrid.[14] In that period the acquisition of such bibliographical rarities was entrusted to travelers or to book dealers in Europe. Some of these bibliophiles, like John Miller or Obadiah Rich, acted as a sort of self-appointed cultural agents, playing an influential role in the development of American scholarship and the early representation of Spain.

Travel books on Spain were also well-known in the American colonies, especially after the rediscovery of Spain by British travel writers during the second half of the eighteenth century. Short excerpts from European travel books on Spain became a stock presence in many periodicals during the late colonial and early national periods. Moreover, some of the first libraries, such as the Harvard Library, the Library Company of Philadelphia, and the Burlington Library Company in New Jersey, owned copies of the best travel books on Spanish-speaking areas.[15] In consonance with the call for an increasingly patriotic literature, however, Americans soon began to demand their own representations of foreign countries. Mordecai Manuel Noah, for example, rallied for that in the preface to his *Travels in England, France, Spain, and the Barbary States* (1819), arguing that in order to be truly independent Americans must assert their own views of foreign lands too. In short, to develop a representation of Spain independent of foreign influence was part of the development of an independent national identity.

Many American travel writings of the Enlightenment nurtured this national identity strongly, and in so doing they constituted an interlude between the bizarre notions of Spain held by the seventeenth-century colonists and the imaginative fancies of nineteenth-century romantics. The Enlightenment travelers' analytic approach to every facet of life precluded a representation of the country tinted with rhetorical conventions like history and romance. The agriculture, population, wealth, and industry of the peninsula, among other topics, were duly compared to and contrasted with those of the new American republic. The style that these eighteenth-century travel writers used, Percy Adams remarks, was plain and focused on concrete facts rather than on general information. The rise of middle-class and female readerships as well as the influence of learned and scientific societies demanded a new style capable of reaching a larger number of readers.[16] Ironically, though, the first American travel writings on Spain, dating from the years of the Revolutionary War, only reached a small number of readers and thus had practically no influence on their successors. The letters, diplomatic correspondence, diaries, and journals of John Adams, John Jay, James Monroe, and other travelers were initially accessible to very few, and when some of these writings appeared in the nineteenth century, publishers were responding to scholarly interest about the writers' careers and to filiopietistic attitudes toward their memory rather than sound interest in Spain. Written decades before Hispanism emerged as an academic discipline in the United States, these Enlightenment travel writings nevertheless stand as the earliest testimony of how the first American travelers saw and chose to represent Spain.

Given the poor circulation of these Enlightenment accounts, American audiences discovered influential thematic conventions to represent Spain elsewhere. Topics like Roman Catholicism, Cervantes, and Columbus, for example, which later appeared also in the romantic travel books, were to be found not in the earlier American travel writings on Spain but rather in genres like history and the popular romance. Charles Brockden Brown's epistolary romance *Wieland; or, The Transformation* (1798) is one of such a number of popular works that built this notion of Spain as an exotic, remote place. When Clara Wieland, the narrator of this romance, inquires into the origin of Henry Pleyel's friendship with the enigmatic Carwin, she is answered by way of a traveler's tale. Pleyel reveals he met Carwin in the Roman theater of old Saguntum, in Spain, and from those ruins they returned to Valencia together. During the month he spent in that city he befriended Carwin but never was able to determine his past because "his garb, aspect, and deportment were wholly Spanish." He proceeds, "A residence of three years in the country, indefatigable attention to the language, and a studious conformity with the customs of the people, had made him indistinguishable from a native, when he chose to assume that character." Nor was that all; the duplicitous Carwin also "had embraced the catholic [sic] religion, and adopted a Spanish name instead of his own."[17] Pleyel no doubt admires Carwin's chameleonic disposition. His friend clearly succeeded at achieving a degree of cultural flexibility that opinionated travelers, perhaps like Pleyel himself, failed to attain abroad. But for Clara Carwin's conduct appears to be much more reproachable. To have contacts with another culture and even at times fashion oneself as an Other could somehow be tolerated, but to dispense with one's identity and, even worse, one's religion was degrading enough to merit ostracizing.

Brown's *Wieland* points, briefly but significantly, to more than the fears of cultural contamination awakened in characters like Clara Wieland during a period in which the Alien and Sedition Acts made people distrust any sign of foreignness. Pleyel's anecdote also calls attention to some of the textual and generic conventions with which Spain was most prevalently identified during the early national period. The meeting in the ruinous theater, the fear of contagion of the Romish faith, and the supposedly unbounded freedom enjoyed by travelers like Carwin all show the type of ingredients necessary for what audiences considered to be a likely representation of Spain. Brown's use of these conventions to enhance the gothicism and exoticism of his epistolary novel is not coincidental. On the contrary, it proves, as Frederick Stimson has noted, that not only Brown but many early romancers chose Mexico, the Caribbean, and Spain as settings for their stories—often framed by renowned historical periods or events—of cruelty, love, and piracy. Moreover, it shows he was writing within cultural codes of what Spanishness already constituted in the British American colonies during the late eighteenth century.[18] In short, Spain was being deployed as a text whose major narrative everybody knew yet upon which writers could play only its own minor variations.

II

The process of self-affirmation that the United States was carrying out at that time entailed a systematic rejection and adoption of European literary themes and genres. In this process, the "Anglo" dimension of the national identity still continued to play its role in the definition of Spanish otherness so that representative themes like religion, Cervantes, and Columbus sometimes were seen from diverse standpoints. What many early nineteenth-century American travel books did share, however, was their deployment of such thematic conventions to enhance the romance of travel writing. This is true, for example, of their staunch anti-Catholic discourse, obviously deriving from a strongly held Protestantism. Paradoxical as it may seem, as we saw in Charles Brockden Brown's *Wieland*, the Catholic religion attracted and at the same time repelled Americans. For Cotton Mather and Samuel Sewall, for example, the presence of growing communities of Catholics in Spanish America was both a threat and a challenge. As Williams observes, these two men were attracted by the goal of converting their southern neighbors to Protestantism, beginning with Mexico, and they learned Spanish with that goal in mind. Mather, with fairly good composition skills, wrote the first book in Spanish in British North America, *La Fe del Christiano* (Boston, 1699), consisting of "certain Articles, back'd with irresistible sentences of Scripture."[19] Despite their religious biases, the travel writers' hostility was nevertheless not directed against the ordinary Spaniards, for whose devotion and piety they expressed sympathy, but against the friars and clergy they target as evil exploiters of the people's poverty, ignorance, and superstition. The entries in George Crowninshield's log diary of a voyage to the Mediterranean in 1815 reflect quite well the view many antebellum Protestant Americans held of the Spaniards' religion. In Málaga, while visiting the cathedral, Crowninshield calls some of its frescoes, "a sample of the mummery by which the story of Christianity has been transmitted to us," and adds that "England was under this influence, and the whole paraphernalia of priests and friars, till happily freed by the spirit of enquiry. Spain is now three centuries in the rear of England, but a new order of things must take place."[20] Even twelve-year-old John Quincy Adams, who accompanied his father in his trip across northern

Spain, noted the power of the church in his diary: "Poor creatures they are eat up [sic] by their preists [sic]. Near three quarters of what they earn goes to the Preists [sic] and with the other Quarter they must live as they can. Thus is the whole of this Kingdom deceived and deluded by their Religion."[21]

Clearly a convention closely connected to the travel writers' anti-Catholic discourse was the Inquisition with its images of secret tortures, book burnings, and autos-da-fé. For the early travelers, their interest in this institution was more than historical curiosity; they were concerned that it continued to exist in Spanish contemporary life. John Adams recalls that when the attorney general of Galicia was showing him some of the local institutions at La Coruña, he could not avoid asking a few questions about the Inquisition which his host tactfully dodged. Crowninshield relates that during his visit to Barcelona, the consul Mr. Thorndike gave him "an iron instrument 'contrived to silence the mouths of heretics' . . . taken from the Inquisition, when its recesses were opened by order of the French general commanding Barcelona."[22] Finally, in 1818 Ticknor demystified the legends surrounding the persistence of the Inquisition, observing that since Ferdinand VII had restored it in 1814, its role was merely that of censuring books. For years to come, however, the American traveler continued to make a point of visiting the remains of the furnaces and dungeons used by the Holy Office in cities like Toledo, Granada, or Saragossa. Once more, the historical associations these ruins conveyed could be transformed into a marketable textual convention of gothic romance that travel writing could easily incorporate into its narrative discourse.

Another Spanish influence on early American literature and the subsequent nineteenth-century representations of Spain was Cervantes, especially his masterpiece *Don Quixote* (1605–15). Mentioning characters, episodes, and settings from that classic was so common that soon it became a major textual convention of travel writing on Spain. Travelers were also keen on alluding to *Gil Blas de Santillana* (1715–35), Alain René Lesage's picaresque novel set in Spain, but neither as often nor as much as they did with *Don Quixote*. The Spanish novelist was already known in seventeenth-century New England. Zardoya notes, for example, that Shelton's translation of *Don Quixote* was read by Anne Bradstreet, and a copy of the same translation was owned by one Richard Alcock, a Harvard medical student who died in 1676.[23] During the following century, American taste for Cervantes's works increased considerably, so that they could be found in many bookstores of the Eastern seaboard in English or in French translation.[24] Libraries, too, owned copies of the Spanish master, as the collection of Don Quixotes at the Library Company of Philadelphia demonstrates. The Cervantesque holdings of that institution, apart from a British translation dating from 1675, boast several copies of Tobias Smollett's translation printed in London, Dublin, and Philadelphia, as well as editions in Spanish from Madrid and Antwerp. Moreover, the library also had versions in French and Dutch, and a translation into "Hudibrastick verse" made by Edward Ward in London in 1711. In a period averse to fiction, *Don Quixote* played a dual role. On the one hand, it afforded the best antifictional tool for detractors of novels, and perhaps that is the reason why Jefferson, not precisely an auspicious champion of fiction, chose *Don Quixote* as the only novel for the library of the University of Virginia. He is said to have read it twice because it satirized feudalism. But Cervantes, on the other hand, provided a model for early American works like Hugh Henry Brackenridge's *Modern Chivalry* (1792–97, 1804–5), Tabitha Tenney's *Female Quixotism* (1801), Washington Irving's *Knickerbocker's History of New York* (1809), and Royall Tyler's unpublished farce, "The Island of Barataria."[25]

For American travelers in Spain, however, *Don Quixote* was more than a formal model. In the first place, it was a metafictional work whose main protagonist's aimlessness invited reflection upon the very essence of travel literature itself. Even though Cervantes had written this novel precisely to ridicule chivalric romances, travelers could not find a literary piece more suitable to both the romance of travel as a physical act and travel as a literary venture. Consequently, they liked to compare themselves to the Castilian knight, carrying their few belongings, wandering in unpredictable roads, and sojourning in inhospitable inns. In 1818 Ticknor whiled away the days of his dreadful journey from Barcelona to Madrid reading *Don Quixote* to his fellow travelers. "This I read aloud to them," he wrote his parents, "and I assure you it was a pleasure to me . . . to witness the extraordinary effect this extraordinary book produces on the people from whose very blood and character it is drawn" (LT, 1:186). In the second place, Cervantes's masterpiece became a sort of travel guide to Spain; notwithstanding its obsoleteness many travelers read it before departing. In those pre-Baedeker times, any book providing an introduction to Spain was no doubt useful enough. The anonymous author of *Scenes in Spain* (1837), apparently not a very widely read author, had nevertheless learned his Cervantes well, as a profusion of allusions testified. To him and to many other travelers *Don Quixote* was a constant resource for

Engraving from a French edition of *El ingenioso hidalgo Don Quijote de la Mancha* (Paris: Bossange y Masson, 1814) showing Cervantes's knight on the road with his squire Sancho. Don Quixote became not only a pretext for travelers to read the Spanish landscape with many literary associations in mind but also constituted an apt romantic symbol for those who roamed aimlessly. From the author's collection.

interpreting what they saw; one of the most usual rhetorical exercises in nineteenth-century travel books is attempting to see the inns and the people literally as they are described in that novel. In short, literature could come alive, and its characters could be inscribed in a story where, instead of Cervantes, the narrator was the traveler himself.

The knight of La Mancha incarnated the quintessential Spanish hidalgo and at the same time provided a universal symbol of idealism, but it was never as fully Americanized as other historical or fictional characters. In speaking about the incorporation of history and romance in the early representation of Spain, it is inevitable to think of the figure of Christopher Columbus, for many Americans not only the most vital link between their country and Spain but their very forefather. Columbus is one of the New World myths that Americans reworked and reinterpreted to help them develop a genuinely national literature after the revolutionary period. At first the most widely available English source on the Genoese admiral was William Robertson's *History of America* (1777). Once Barlow and Freneau published their Columbian poems, and Washington Irving adapted his *Life and Voyages of Christopher Columbus* (1828) from Martín Fernández de Navarrete's *Colección de los viajes y descubrimientos que hicieron por mar los españoles desde fines del siglo XV* (1825), the Columbian myth was totally engrafted in American letters. Its influence lasted well beyond the romantic period.[26] Despite being the originators of the Columbian vogue, Freneau and Barlow would become invisible in travel writings as Irving's *Columbus* became the reference source on the mariner. As we saw in the previous chapter, travel writers who were contemporaries of Irving duly describing the sights connected with Columbus's life often also called attention to the places where Irving conducted research for his romantic biography. To a certain extent, then, it was Irving who canonized Columbus as a conventional textual presence in American travel writing.

In general, the ideological project of the Columbian theme was not to represent Spain, but Columbus himself and the pan-Americanist ideal he embodied. In fact, Spain often functions as his adversary. The personality and career of the Genoese admiral were used to symbolize several issues in which the new republic was interested, ranging from Columbus as an agent of civilization to Columbus as a symbol of freedom due to the opposition and difficulties he had to surmount.[27] In Freneau's embryonic poem "Columbus to Ferdinand" (1770), the navigator is warmly presented as a romantic outcast who has invested his life in a project everybody rejects and now pleads to the monarch "Supply the bar-que, and bid Columbus sail." Freneau, in "The Pictures of Colum-bus, the Genoese" (1774), continues his sympathetic portrait of Columbus, but adds some glimpses of the sociopolitical circum-stances surrounding his enterprise. In successive pictures, the Spain of Columbus's times is revealed as a bleak, narrow-minded, xenophobic nation: the king's minister distrusts Columbus because he is a foreigner, the Church refuses to consider his theories, and the royal treasury has no funds to support his enterprise. As the Queen's page tells Columbus, "Long wars have wasted us; the pride of Spain / Was never before so high, nor purse so mean."[28] Queen Isabella, who had strong reservations about the success of the trip, is now portrayed as a vain sovereign who boasts it was she who sent Columbus to America. The connection between Freneau's Colum-bian poems and those of Barlow lies, however, more in their pan-Americanist message than in the story of Columbus's ordeals. In Picture XVIII of his second poem, Freneau presents Columbus en-chained, sad, and dying, but reassured because the continent he encountered will become the land of freedom. Barlow's goals for *The Vision of Columbus* (1787), revised and expanded as *The Co-lumbiad* (1807), were the same as those in Freneau's last scene. He wrote that the single poetical design of *The Vision of Columbus* was "to gratify and sooth the desponding mind of the hero . . . to convince him that his labours had not been bestowed in vain, and that he was the author of such extensive happiness to the human race."[29] The Angel accompanying the admiral in Book IX of *The Vi-sion of Columbus* assures him that he will not have to complain any more about "courts insidious, envy's poison'd stings, / The loss of empire and the frown of kings" for the vision of the new continent and its new society would repay his pains.[30] In essence, Columbus provided Americans with a patriotic icon that, apart from giving them brief glimpses of Spanish life, also called attention to the vir-tues of New World democracy and republicanism to the detriment of Spanish monarchy and despotism.

III

The relevance of Spain to British-American politics and Ameri-can origins meant that the few early travelers to Spain arrived with preconceived notions of the country. However, their ability to cor-rect these notions and to transmit more "accurate" views to their countrymen was limited not only by their small numbers, as we saw before, but also by mixed ideas about the use of foreign travel itself for an American. At the very least, in a culture rooted in pragmatic, commonsensical principles, travel must have seemed to many a symptom of pernicious leisure. Enlightenment elites in Europe had considered the Grand Tour a unique formative experience reserved exclusively for future statesmen and scholars, but in the United States some leaders of the new country had their doubts. To be sure, a trip to the cultural shrines of Europe offered the American traveler many rewards. It meant an encounter with one's Western past, a close look at the often oppressive political systems of the Old World, and the possibility of establishing literary, scientific, and diplomatic ties with eminent people. The sustained effort that this cultural practice demanded was extremely worthwhile because, by experiencing the fullness of European reality, the Enlightenment traveler could reinforce not only the experimental quality but also the nationalistic discourse of his account. Still, this view was not universally accepted, for as Thomas Jefferson intimated from Paris to his friend Peter Carr in 1787, traveling also took a heavy toll on each individual:

> This makes men wiser, but less happy. When men of sober age travel, they gather knolege [sic] which they may apply usefully for their country but they are subject ever after to recollections mixed with regret, their affections are weakened by being extended over more objects, & they learn new habits which cannot be gratified when they return home. Young men . . . do not acquire that wisdom for which a previous foundation is requisite by repeated & just observations at home. The glare of pomp & pleasure is analogous to the motion of their blood, it absorbs all their affection & attention, they are torn from it as from the only good in this world, and return to their home as to a place of exile & condemnation. Their eyes are for ever turned back to the object they have lost, & it's [sic] recollection poisons the residue of their lives.[31]

Anticipating the "sadder and wiser man" in Samuel Taylor Coleridge's *Rime of the Ancient Mariner*, Jefferson's mature traveler is capable of balancing the domestic and the foreign intelligently, whereas his young traveler is exiled, condemned, and poisoned, as the carefully chosen words indicate. Jefferson's letter implies, moreover, that the exclusivity of European travel, traditionally a male ritual, belongs to the sage fathers of the nation, and thus apparently discards potential travelers on the grounds of gender, race, class, and, of course, age.

Jefferson believed that the future of the nation depended much more on the yeoman farmer strongly attached to his American plot of land than on the traveler gathering the latest scientific and technologic developments in other countries. There was something beneficial in isolationism, for a long residence abroad, apart from causing the personal psychological harm Jefferson described, could also contaminate the nation's moral fiber with vicious foreign habits. That is precisely what pressed Royall Tyler, in the preface to *The Contrast* (1787), to ask "Why should our thoughts to distant countries roam, / When each refinement may be found at home?" and warn that the Dimples of the new republic were likely to reject the "homespun" values of their mother country, replacing them by those ready-made in Europe.[32] Fortunately for those sharing Tyler's views, each corrupted Dimple returning from Europe would be neutralized by several virtuous republicans like Colonel Manly, the play's hero, who boasted of never having left his native shores and insisted that he had no desire to visit Europe.

With these ideas in the national atmosphere, it is not strange that during the second half of the eighteenth century and the first quarter of the nineteenth century the majority of Americans traveling in Europe went there for some practical purpose, mainly diplomacy or business. Some also pursued an artistic or academic training they could not obtain at home. Few traveled for travel's sake until after the end of the Napoleonic Wars, and tourism as such barely existed. The two largest colonies of Americans gathered in London and Paris. In the former resided artists like John Singleton Copley, Gilbert Stuart, Benjamin West, Samuel F. B. Morse, and Rembrandt Peale, drawn primarily by the cultural models they could find there. Politicians and diplomats, more visible in London when Anglo-American tensions subsided, at first tended to converge in the French capital. Some, like Franklin, Jefferson, Adams, or Silas Deane, were there to obtain recognition and aid for the American rebels; others, like Paine and Barlow, to experience firsthand the revolutionary experiments of the French.[33] Italy was also visited by artists like Allston and Irving in 1804, and soon followed future scholars such as Prescott, Ticknor, Everett, and George Bancroft.[34] Spain, though, remained geographically and ideologically isolated from the Continent's main political and intellectual centers, and thus, despite the increasing number of Americans in Europe during this period, only a few travelers with very specific goals in mind risked the arduous journey there.

Most of the few Americans who went to Spain during the colonial and early national period—diplomats, merchants, and traders—did not go with a view to writing a travel book on the country. Except for Ticknor, artists and scholars would not appear until the late

1820s. They did textualize the country, though, and their representations of Spain have come to us in the letters, journals, and diaries they wrote. In 1779 the Continental Congress appointed John Jay Minister to Spain, entrusting to him the signing of a treaty whereby Spain would recognize the independence of the United States. Jay left the United States in September 1779 and reached Madrid in April 1780. After numerous negotiations, the Spanish government did not recognize the independence of the United States, but agreed to make a loan and supply ammunitions to the rebels. Moreover, in addition to negotiations pertinent to the ongoing Revolutionary War, Jay sought the Spanish government's permission for Americans to navigate the lower Mississippi river and have access to the Gulf of Mexico.[35] The same year John Adams was sent by Congress to establish peace negotiations with the British government in France, but a leaky ship forced a docking at the Spanish port of El Ferrol. Consequently, Adams, his two sons, and his secretary Francis Dana had to proceed to France across northern Spain.[36]

David Humphreys, one of the Connecticut Wits, was sent to Madrid in 1791 by Secretary of State Jefferson to keep watch on mounting Anglo-Spanish tensions, and returned there in 1796 as Minister Plenipotentiary until 1800. In a long letter addressed to President Washington from Lisbon on 16 February 1791 Humphreys reported on the wretched state of Spain:

> I should but repeat a common observation in mentioning that since the expulsion of the Moor & the establishment of Spanish colonies in America, Agriculture, Manufactures, Commerce, & every species of Industry have languished throughout Spain in an extraordinary degree. . . . During the late reign a number of Natives more enlightened and zealous for the national prosperity than the rest, under the title of friends of their Country, established oeconomical Societies for the purpose of reanimating the national spirit and directing their fellow Citizens to useful pursuits. . . . From everything that has fallen within my notice I cannot doubt that the Spaniards naturally possess wit, sprightliness, genius & capacity for improvement. But they have almost insuperable bars to surmount. The rigours of unlimited Monarchy & the clogs of long established superstition must be gradually removed. Genius is depressed; merit unrewarded. No original Performances which breath a spirit of liberality in politics or religion would be permitted to be published.[37]

Humphrey's position was subsequently occupied by Charles Pinckney (1801–5), James Bowdoin (1805), George Erving (1814–19),

Hugh Nelson (1823–25), and Alexander Hill Everett (1825–29), among others. Everett facilitated Irving's incorporation to the American legation in Madrid to translate Navarrete's papers on Columbus, and likewise his cultural work fomenting the early representation of Spain in the United States cannot be left out of consideration.

The commissions held by these traveling diplomats sometimes consisted not only in representing the new republic, but also in negotiating treaties and solving arbitrations with the Spanish authorities. When the latter could not be readily attained, the United States government appointed special mediators. James Monroe, for example, was sent to Madrid in 1805 as Envoy Extraordinary to negotiate Spanish claims to Florida, settle boundaries of Louisiana, and receive payments for injuries by Spanish spoliation of American commerce in the Mississippi.[38] On other occasions, however, some politicians traveled to Spain with nondiplomatic goals. This is true, for example, of William Jarvis, merchant and consul, who smuggled 3,500 heads of fine Merino sheep out of the peninsula while Spain was occupied by the Napoleonic Army in 1808. David Humphreys had attempted something similar in the 1790s, but did not succeed due to Spanish protectionism of that breed.[39] Whether it was owing to political or geographical isolation, the Spanish borders remained tightly shut, and paradoxically it was this image of the country as a remote cultural preserve full of thrilling contrasts that decades later was to attract flocks of romantic tourists in search of the last glimpses of pastoralism in Europe.

IV

The geopolitical situation of Spain had indeed kept the country isolated from the northern European centers. Spain was cut off from France by the impressive barrier of the Pyrenees. Likewise, its interior, dominated by the barren plateau of the central *Meseta* where the Castiles are located, was bisected by the Cordillera Central. To go from Castile to Andalusia travelers had to trek across the Sierra Morena, another important physical obstacle. Only the basins of the Duero, Tagus, and Ebro rivers offered a smoother geography. The coastline was equally rugged, with few inlets and natural ports. Given the rough physical features of the country and the poor condition of its roads, who would want to go to Spain to suffer a rigorous tour unnecessarily? As the narrator in Thomas Atwood Digges's *Adventures of Alonzo* (1775) put it, "The badness of the roads—the uneasiness of the calashes—the tiresome ding-dong pace of the mules, with the continued tinkling of their bells, and above all, the forlorn accommodation of their inns, render travelling in Spain fit only for Lovers or Philosophers."[40] By land, travelers often crossed the natural barrier of the Pyrenees at the border posts of Hendaie and La Jonquera. Still, if in their case the approach to the Spanish border from Paris or another capital was swift overall, their traveling within Spain was slower than for those who came by sea. Arthur Lee, for example, left Paris in early February 1777, reached Bordeaux on the eighteenth, and finally arrived at Vitoria on the twenty-sixth. However, he then wrote Franklin in Paris that he expected to arrive in Madrid around 6 April.[41] The physical toll of a trip across Spain must have been high, if we judge from an entry in John Adams's diary, written in Burgos on 1 January 1780: "It is five and Twenty Years that I have been, almost constantly, journeying and voyaging, and I have often undergone severe Tryals, great Hardships, cold, wet, heat, fatigue, bad rest, want of sleep, bad nourishment, &c. &c. &c. But I never experienced any Thing like this Journey."[42] On many occasions the traveler had to wait for a safe means of transportation and thus each segment of the trip had to be delayed for several days. Peninsular travel became thus so bothersome that a few decades later Mordecai M. Noah categorized Spain as "the last country, which should be visited for pleasure; health and business are the only rational inducements, for a journey through Spain" (TE, 193). Like him, posterior travel writers also complained about their Spanish journey, but in the long run their jeremiads paradoxically became no more than just another literary convention whereby domestic audiences could reap enjoyment from their author's textual sufferings.

Even though travel writers forged their own personal view of foreign travel in their texts, the length and difficulty of the voyage to Spain in the early years cannot be overstressed. To begin with, there was no regular transatlantic packet service between North America and any place in Europe, let alone Spain, until after the War of 1812. The first regular line of sailing packets between New York and Liverpool, established in 1818, took three weeks for the eastward passage, and five weeks for the westward one. The duration was shortened in 1838, when a race from Bristol to New York between the steamships *Great Western* and *Sirius* was won by the latter in only ten days.[43] For those whose destination was Spain the voyage took much longer. If traveling with the newly inaugurated regular lines, they had to go to England first and there take a boat from Portsmouth, London, or Liverpool to Bilbao, La Coruña,

Cádiz, Valencia, or Barcelona. It took Mordecai M. Noah, for example, twelve days to sail from Falmouth to Cádiz on a British packet in 1813. The alternative, employed by those on the Grand Tour circuit of Europe, was to cross the Channel to France, and then take the overland route to Spain.

Before and after the inauguration of these regular transatlantic lines, many American travelers wishing to proceed directly to Spain found passage in merchant ships sailing between Newburyport, Salem, and such Spanish ports as Málaga, Barcelona, Cádiz, and Bilbao. These vessels with spartan accommodations were a frequent sight in Spanish ports. When George Coggeshall moored at Cádiz, for example, after his first voyage from New York in 1800 on the schooner *Charlotte*, he discovered that "there were, at this time, ten or twelve American vessels lying in this port, and among them a large letter-of-marque ship belonging to Salem, Mass."[44] Although Cádiz no longer held the monopoly of commerce with America, it continued to be, due to its situation, one of the ports receiving many vessels from South America and the Caribbean. An American traveler thus might voyage south to New Orleans, Havana, or Veracruz, and there connect with European ships. John Jay, having left Pennsylvania on 26 October 1779 with his wife and secretary, encountered a very bad storm off the coast of Martinique that dismasted their ship. They had to stop there and then sail to Spain with a French vessel, finally arriving in Cádiz on 22 January 1780. Likewise, the French frigate *Sensible*, on which John Adams was traveling to France, suffered a leak and had to put to in northwestern Spain. The vicissitudes of a voyage did not end here, for the traveler had to count on fog, adverse winds, and extremely calm seas.

To the hazards of physical phenomena the traveler also had to add the instability created by political conflicts and the threat of privateers. During the Revolutionary War and the War of 1812, for example, American ships in the Atlantic were often harassed by British naval units. Likewise, Algerine pirates made travels in the Mediterranean too insecure until in 1815 the expedition led by Stephen Decatur put an end to their intimidations. Mordecai M. Noah's account of his trip to Europe and North Africa in 1813 combines both perils. The schooner *Joel Barlow*, on which he was sailing to Tunis to ransom the enslaved American crew of the brig *Edwin*, was impressed by the British frigate *Briton* in the Bay of Biscay and forced to continue to London. Travelers also had to take into consideration the menace of privateering before embarking on a trip, not only because their ship might be assaulted by a privateer, but because it could engage in that activity itself. In his memoirs, George Coggeshall relates that in 1814 the British apprehended his privateer and conveyed it to Gibraltar. He narrates that he dodged the military security there and managed to escape to the Spanish town of Algeciras and seek refuge there.[45]

Only after 1815, with the conclusion of the Napoleonic Wars, came a general peace that facilitated safe access to Europe. There was, at least, no major conflagration engaging most of the Continental nations, and consequently the travelers of the 1820s and 1830s had much less to worry about than their predecessors. Travelers in the first decades of the nineteenth century found that communication from Madrid to France through the Basque provinces had definitely improved. Victor Marie Dupont, one of the French emigrés to Delaware, left Paris on 26 April 1801 and arrived in Bourdeaux four days later. From Bayonne he departed on 5 May and finally reached Madrid after only six days of travel along post roads.[46] By Irving's time two decades later one could travel from Bordeaux to Madrid in five days. From Catalonia, however, the trip continued to be tiresome, taking Ticknor thirteen days to travel the four hundred miles between Barcelona and Madrid in 1818. Spain, which for centuries had been a cluster of more or less autonomous and sovereign regions, had become much more unified during the eighteenth century as the Bourbon monarchs imposed a centralized French model with everything converging in the capital. Travelers on diplomatic or cultural business had to report inevitably to the capital. The main roads, as anything else in Spain, were highly centralized by the time the first Americans visited the peninsula. The journey to Madrid, however, often included a trip to Toledo and to the centers of royal power at the monastery of El Escorial and the palace of La Granja. Seville, Granada, Valencia, Barcelona, and other cities might also be visited, but the notion of the pilgrimage to Andalusia and, especially, Granada, still had to be developed into a convention of romantic travel writing.

Safe access to Spain, however, did not mean the end of the traveler's problems, for turbulent internal political conditions created lawlessness and insecurity. Noah and Ticknor, traveling in Spain in 1813 and 1818, respectively, could still witness the destruction wrought by the Spanish guerrillas and the French and British armies. In many areas of the peninsula, moreover, smugglers, bandits, and insurrectionists made travel difficult, and, for some travelers, fascinating. Mackenzie, for example, was robbed twice: the first robbery, near the border between Catalonia and Valencia ended with the murder of the postillion; the second took place outside Madrilejos, en route from Madrid to Seville. Longfellow, anxious for adventure, lamented that he had traveled from Madrid to Seville very safely, yet acknowledged that "almost every village we passed through had its tale to tell of atrocities committed in the neighbourhood" (OM, 2:117). Apart from travelers' tales and gazette news, there were also mementos on the road; entering the old Kingdom of Valencia, Mackenzie observed that "the whole road was skirted with stone crosses, that had been raised opposite to as many scenes of robbery and assassination" (YS, 1:83). Likewise, in the northern province of Alava Caroline Cushing's attention was attracted "by the view of little wooden or stone crosses, elevated by the side of the road, to show that on that spot some person had been cut off from life" (LD, 2:16). Little by little Spain was being textualized as a harsh and dangerous locale where, apart from the occasional woman traveler, only male travelers dared to ramble.

If internal peninsular travel was regarded as a difficult, back-breaking activity only fit for the male traveler it was partly because the technical achievements and mechanical inventions that increasingly networked European countries were scarcely seen in Spain. Robert Spiller remarks that in Britain "Macadam had perfected his process [of paving] by 1811, and by 1820 most of the main highways . . . were in excellent condition, hard and smooth, so that the stagecoaches on post roads seldom stuck in the ruts or were delayed by other similar inconveniences."[47] In Spain, on the contrary, the roads were too often tortuous, muddy, or steep, so that until 1866, when the basic railway network was completed, travel continued to be very slow.[48] In a stoical letter to his father from Madrid, dated 23 June 1780, John Jay wrote he would give him an account of his journey from Cádiz to Madrid that he would definitely find amusing. The amusement he is describing, however, is far from pleasant:

> The distance is between three and four hundred English miles. We were told at Cadiz that it would be necessary to take with us beds, hams, tea, sugar, chocolate, and other articles of provision, as well as kitchen utensils for dressing them, for that we should seldom find either on the road. We were further informed that these journeys were usually performed in carriages resembling a coach and drawn by six mules. . . . We travelled at the rate of between twenty and thirty miles a day, and the same mules brought us to Madrid that we set out with from Cadiz, at which they had arrived from Madrid only a day before we left it. We stopped but once in the course of the day. At the end of the journey they appeared to be in as much flesh and spirits as when we set out.

The manner of driving them is in my opinion greatly to their disadvantage, very fast up and down hill and slow on plain ground.[49]

So much for a northbound trip from Andalusia to the capital in the 1770s. Several decades later, when Ticknor traveled westward from Barcelona to Madrid, the situation had not changed considerably. In a letter to his parents he described the ordeal of travel:

In the first place, imagine roads so abominable that the utmost diligence, from four o'clock in the morning until seven at night, would not bring us forward more than twenty-one or twenty-two miles! Imagine a country so deserted and desolate, and with so little travelling and communication, as to have no taverns; for I do not call the miserable hovels where we stopped by that name, because it is not even expected of them to furnish anything but a place to cover you from the weather. And, in the last place, imagine a country so destitute of the means of subsistence, that, even by seeking every opportunity to purchase provisions, you cannot keep so provided that you will not sometimes want a meal. (LT, 2:185)

Writing out of desperation, Jay and Ticknor point to some of the most uncomfortable aspects of traveling in Spain. Yet in so doing they also make use of two motifs that Percy Adams lists among the most significant commonplaces of travel writing: the coach (or coach journey) and the inn.[50] These two extremely productive conventions of travel writing, repeated ad nauseam in posterior accounts, attest the powerful economy of the genre and once again reveal the generic codes writers used to render a representation of Spain as the land of romance.

These travel texts deal with the Spanish inns not only as potential settings of adventure but as notorious places for their almost uninhabitable condition, which no doubt was a deterrent for travelers.[51] Smoke, dirt, fleas, meals cooked with rancid oil, and meager food supplies were only a few of the things plaguing travelers. Ticknor described to his parents the three existing types of lodging travelers could find: *fondas*, maintained by the government and always supplied with food and beds; *posadas*, private inns with beds but normally without food; and *ventas*, houses with a room and a fire, where you have to provide the rest. He attributed this scarcity of lodgings to the fact that nobody traveled in Spain, noting that in a journey of thirteen days they encountered only a few muleteers and carts, and just one coach like their own (LT, 2:17–18). John Jay, however, affirmed that the *posadas* were "more tolerable than had been represented to us," having "very good rooms, but swarming

The diverse and often uncomfortable modes of transportation endured by the American traveler generated abundant descriptions and complaints that proved a productive rhetorical convention for the romance of travel. Many of the conveyances used are visible in this plate from volume 2 of the folio edition of Alexandre de Laborde's *Voyage pittoresque et historique de l'Espagne* (Paris: Didot, 1806–20). Courtesy of Arxiu Històric de la Ciutat de Barcelona.

with fleas and bugs. The mules were generally lodged under the same roof, and my bedroom has frequently been divided from them by only a common partition."[52] John Quincy Adams also wrote that they "did not once lodge with the mules," but slept in "chambers in which any body would think a half a dozen hogs had lived there six months."[53] Accommodation in some areas was so scarce that travelers had to carry all of their belongings with them. That was true, for example, of John Adams and his companions as they traveled across northern Spain: "We are obliged, in this Journey to carry our own Beds, Blanketts, Sheets, Pillows &c., our own Provisions of Chocolat [sic], Tea, Sugar, Meat, Wine, Spirits, and every Thing that We want. We get nothing at the Taverns, but Fire, Water, and Salt. We carry our own Butter, Cheese, and indeed Salt and Pepper too."[54] The best solution for travelers in that period, and especially for people of the same social class, was probably to use letters of recommendation that would facilitate lodgings in the homes of local authorities at any major city. This was the case for some of the Enlightenment travelers named in this chapter, and also of Mordecai Manuel Noah and George Ticknor, who will be treated in the following.

In the early American travel writings on Spain, as, in fact, in all travel books, the process of traveling as much as the representation of one's destination both occupies a significant amount of space and becomes part of a definition of the nation and its people. For many of these American travelers, then, the dilapidated buildings they encountered no doubt seemed to symbolize a nation gone to wrack and ruin, and the poorly maintained roads along which they were plowing represented lack of communication at all levels of Spanish life. Moreover, it was not difficult for them to equate the filthy inns they slept at and the sunburned, garlic-smelling people they saw there with a dirty nation. Still, although the dreary panorama of bad roads, poor inns, and bad food was far from an invitation to traveling in Spain, and occupied much space in travel narrations, it also held, as more than one writer would put it, all the charms of romance.

3

Toward Romantic Spain:
Mordecai M. Noah, George Ticknor,
and the Allure of a Fallen Empire

MORDECAI MANUEL NOAH (1793–1851) AND GEORGE TICKNOR (1791–
1871), if perhaps not the actual initiators of an American tradition
of travel writings about Spain, are at least the figures who bridge
the first wave of Enlightenment diplomat-travelers described in the
previous chapter with the posterior wave inspired by Washington
Irving. Ironically, though, as is the case with most of the writers in
this study, they have not been remembered as travel writers. First,
because the intricate circumstances of composition and publication of their representations of Spain virtually concealed their
genre identity as travel writings. Second, because the status of
travel writing in literary scholarship has been neglected until recently. And third, because the authors' shift toward different literary and nonliterary activities after their European sojourn has
directed what attention they have received to their civic accom-
plishments. Still, before Irving's voluminous output of Spanish
themes literally monopolized the commodification of romantic
Spain in America, the early nineteenth-century Spanish travel
writings of Noah and Ticknor came forth with a new perception of
the country. Not because these writings represented Spain at a very
crucial period when, immediately after the Peninsular War, it was
trying to leave behind the clash of arms, maintain its fragile constitutionalism, and decide the future of its American colonies, but because they marked a progressive shift from the objective spirit of
inquiry of the Enlightenment travel account to a more subjective
involvement with the object of representation. For all that, even
though in form they were still intellectual offspring of the Enlightenment, in essence Noah and Ticknor prefigure the American romantic narration of Spain.

Their relative obscurity today belies the prominence these two men enjoyed in their respective geocultural niches. Noah, a Knick-erbocker, was a politician and Jewish activist as well as editor of several New York newspapers and amateur playwright. During his political career, which often faced anti-Semitic opposition, he was consul in Tunis and also held the posts of sheriff, surveyor of the port, and associate judge in New York. As a Jewish activist he pro-moted the creation of an international Jewish settlement ("Ara-rat") on an island in the Niagara river.[1] His first theatrical ventures, *The Fortress of Sorrento* (1808) and *Paul and Alexis* (1812), were not well received, but after his journey to Europe and North Africa he became, as he told William Dunlap, "domiciliated in the green-room," producing successful plays like *She Would Be a Soldier* (1819), *The Siege of Tripoli* (1820), *Marion* (1821), and *The Gre-cian Captive* (1822).[2] As for Ticknor, one of the leading Boston Brahmins, his "niche in history rests," according to David Tyack, "upon his attempted educational reforms at Harvard, his liberal and commanding role in founding the Boston Public Library, and his erudite *History of Spanish Literature.*"[3] Moreover, one should add to these achievements, as it is very relevant to the present study, Ticknor's mentoring of future academics-cum-travelers and his dynamic capacity in the formation of Hispanism as both a dis-course and discipline in the United States.

This chapter examines Noah and Ticknor as early romantic in-terpreters of Spain, yet somehow as transitional figures between the Enlightenment and the romantic representation of that coun-try. To dub them exclusively late Enlightenment travel writers might seem somewhat limiting, particularly bearing in mind that subsequent representations of Spain by Irving and Longfellow, de-spite their romantic tone, also occasionally exhibit formal traces of eighteenth-century travel literature. Noah and Ticknor were heirs to the Age of Reason at least chronologically, since they were both born in the last decade of the eighteenth century, and stylistically, for they had been educated under Neoclassical precepts favoring a polished prose with urbane diction. Noah's style, for example, was defined as "facile, fluent, of a humorous turn, pleasing in expres-sion, though sometimes ungrammatical, with a cheerful vein of moralizing, and a knowledge of the world,"[4] and the style of Tick-nor's manuscripts, as well as that of his *History of Spanish Litera-ture*, is nearly impeccable. Moreover, intellectually both authors also shared the ideological and aesthetic convictions upheld by most writers and critics of early nineteenth-century America, namely, a belief in the moral decorum of their profession, a nation-alistic bias, a politically conservative discourse, and a clear didactic aim. To that we have to add the influence of Scottish Common-Sense philosophy with its empiricist methods of analysis and its skeptical view of fictitious representation that restrained the kind of poetical reverie typical of Irving.[5] With this intellectual baggage, then, it is not surprising that these travelers' representations of Spain equally concentrated upon the twofold role of edifying their audiences and narrating their personal travel experiences.

The paradigms of nonfictional travel writing inherited from the late decades of the previous century are present in the representations of Spain left by Noah and Ticknor. The emphasis on teaching and delighting, which is paramount in the literature of travel of the eighteenth century, appears manifestly at work, but other narrative and descriptive conventions of the genre, as we shall see later in this chapter, are also discernible.[6] Important among these are the combination of natural, historical, and artistic observations with philosophical reflections; the blend of formal and colloquial linguistic registers; the incorporation of the discourses of history and adventure; the interpolation of digressive biographical elements; and, finally, the presence of a strong narrative voice foregrounded throughout the text. It is through these and other textual strategies that both authors converted their textualizations of Spain not only into a repository of information about the foreign nation they visited but also about the gender and class privileges they embodied.

I

Travelers like Noah and Ticknor often inscribed in their texts the ideological hegemony of their own culture. This was accomplished, as Mary Louise Pratt has shown, mainly through the manipulation of descriptive conventions and narrative voices. Travel accounts deployed two important types of narrators that, notwithstanding their apparently dissimilar representations of the foreign nation, shared similar ideological traits. The first type of narrator corresponds to what Pratt calls "the seeing man," a traveler who scans the land and depopulates it of its native inhabitants, a male who, deploying a rhetoric of scientific exploration, eliminates his own presence in the text and thus creates an essentialist discourse on the paradisiacal nature of the Other and his habitat. The second type of narrator is "the experiential unhero," a sentimental traveler more interested in making himself present throughout the text than in describing the landscape and producing information. In other words, a traveler who, using the language of emotions, narrates his personal experiences and his interaction with the Other. Formally speaking, then, the first type of narrator, with emphasis on presumed objectivity, falls within the descriptive modes of Enlightenment travel writing, while the second, drawing on the traveler's subjectivity, places the text in the realm of the romantic travel book. Pratt observes, however, that ideologically speaking these two narrators constitute complementary facets of the same bourgeois consciousness, for one represents the official language of the public sphere and the other the introspective language of the private sphere.[7] As transitional figures between the Enlightenment and Romanticism, Noah and Ticknor waver between these two types of narrative point of view. Sometimes they record their sojourn in Spain as if they were merely contemplating its geography, economy, and art, and sometimes they prefer to relate their interaction with the Spaniards, yet always assuming their superior condition as citizens of the United States of America.

The presumed cultural superiority of the traveler by no means deterred the presence of other voices in travel texts. However, what originally might read like a dialogic travel account, to put it in Bakhtinian terms, sometimes ends up becoming a monologic text where the voice of otherness appears muted through the traveler's own voice. Neither Ticknor nor, particularly, Noah, sought a high degree of cross-cultural rapport with the Other they were representing, and if they did it was with certain misgivings. They did not pursue, like Alexander Slidell Mackenzie, a crude, almost seditious representation of Spain mildly tinged with revolutionary rhetoric. They sought, instead, a rational involvement with Spain manifested in a reflective attitude more akin to that of the Enlightenment philosophers and historians. Yet it was a representation of Spain that had its moments of dialogic cultural exploration, a representation where the country was observed almost microscopically albeit through the lenses of history and the filters of romance. Noah's case is paradigmatic of the traveler's cultural solipsism, for, as Stanley Williams points out, he traveled "able to keep inviolate all his prejudices concerning Spain's tyranny, her hatred of South American independence, and her feeble arts."[8] His reluctance to attempt a strong cross-cultural communication may in fact be imputed to his forced sojourn in Spain, for travel incidents obliged him to stop there even though, as we shall see later, he had never intended to visit the country. In spite of this, he purposely incorporated his textualized Spain into the nationalistic discourse of the period by turning his journey into a philosophical exploration of a decadent imperial power and the causes of its decline. In short, for

Noah Spain became a good example of civilization gone wrong, an idea that years later Ticknor also exploited when discussing the rise and decline of Spanish literature. But Ticknor, more open to otherness than Noah, embraced both the positive and negative aspects of Spain, thereby confronting what David Tyack calls "the riddle of Spain." For a New Englander like him it was certainly problematic to harmonize progress with the romantic appeal of a backward country that one often associated with the exploits of Don Quixote and Gil Blas.[9]

The Spanish travel accounts of Noah and Ticknor did not leave a profound impression in America when they were written in the second decade of the nineteenth century. Noah related his journey to Spain in the second chapter of *Travels in England, France, Spain, and the Barbary States in the Years 1813–14 and 15* (1819), which, despite being his only nonfictional travel book, enjoyed a fair publication history.[10] One may guess that one reason for whatever success the book had was its political appeal, for Noah wrote it in part to exonerate himself from political accusations made against him after he resigned as American consul in Tunis.[11] Ticknor's travel journals from his 1815–19 European *Wanderjahre* had much less diffusion than Noah's book, mainly because they were not written with a view for publication, but for circulation among family and friends.[12] Apart from an 1825 essay on Spanish amusements, his travel writings were published posthumously, along with parts of his correspondence, as *Life, Letters, and Journals of George Ticknor* (1876), deferring, as it were, his representation of Spain.[13] It is still plausible, however, to suppose that the ideological and literary repercussions of Ticknor's travel writings were equally felt in his lifetime, albeit through other channels. His representation of Spain was not only known in the influential circle that had access to his journals and letters, but also to the male elite at Harvard attending the lectures on Spanish literature initiated soon after his return from Europe. These lectures, not always strictly dealing with belles lettres, publicized Ticknor's discourse on Spain and the Spaniards, and no doubt influenced the representation of Spain by the upcoming New England intelligentsia. Ultimately, with the publication of his *History of Spanish Literature* (1849) Ticknor's views on Spain reached their broadest circulation, far beyond the Harvard walls.[14] His three-volume magnum opus was widely acclaimed by scholars everywhere, and soon was translated into Spanish and German. It did not transcribe any portion of his travel journals directly, but manifested his reliance on his travel notes and Harvard lectures.[15] In brief, it signified the end of a continuum begun with his journals.

More important, however, in explaining why Ticknor never made the logical leap from travel journal to travel book is the fact that he had his own reservations about the literariness of travel books, at least as manifested in a letter from his friend Alexander H. Everett. "I do not quite agree with you in a remark," wrote Everett from Madrid in July 1828, "which I recollect, you once made when I was talking with you upon this subject and urging you to publish your own travels that works of this kind belong to a low order of writing." And although he urged Ticknor, for his own advantage and the public good, to write "two or three separate works—as for example, one on Germany—another on Spain—a third on France, Italy, or England" (PP, 221), Ticknor never did it. Had he written it, he would have probably become the dean of nineteenth-century American travel writers in Spain. At any rate, despite his never having published his travel writings in full narrative form, Ticknor's manuscripts can be considered almost finished products. Their prose is polished and, in a preface-like annotation he made in his journals in 1868, he explained, among other things, that they had constituted for him a valuable means of gathering information on foreign countries that could be sent home and read by his family.[16] This demonstrates that Ticknor was well aware of the rhetorical potential that journals, like any other forms of travel writing available to him, really had.

Apart from their slim diffusion, the Spanish travel writings of Noah and Ticknor share also a fortuitous genesis, for neither author contemplated making a journey into Spain, let alone writing about it, when they departed for the Old World. Their writings betray no period of mental preparation before crossing the Pyrenees similar to Irving's wait at Bordeaux years later. Noah had never considered a visit to Spain, a country he disliked for having expelled its Jewish population in 1492. He had accepted to undertake a diplomatic mission in the Mediterranean because, as Isaac Goldberg observes, it would afford him with two plans he had long cherished: to see the ruins of the ancient civilizations of North Africa, principally Carthage, and to obtain information about the Jews in the Barbary States, who centuries before had sought refuge there.[17] Likewise, Ticknor had focused on Germany, France, Britain, and Italy as part of his educational tour, but not on Spain. Still, unlike his compatriot, for whom Spain in the end meant little more than despotism and bigotry, for Ticknor Spain signified more than that. True, he found it economically degraded and politically corrupt, but he also approached it as a locus of desire, the realm of romance, literally a slice of the agrarian past that he felt the United States and other countries were losing. The outcome of his Spanish trip would be more significant than Noah's, too, for his association with things Spanish never ceased thereafter.

It was through several travel contingencies, then, that both authors ultimately reached the peninsula. Noah was on his way to a consular position in Tunis when his odyssey began. He left the United States toward the end of May 1813, but before he could reach France a British man-of-war impressed his ship in the Bay of Biscay forcing him and the other passengers to continue to London. After this unplanned stop in England Noah was given permission to embark in Falmouth on a British packet bound for La Coruña and Cádiz, where, unwillingly, he began his Spanish journey. Ticknor's journey to Spain, like Noah's, was also the result of chance. In 1816 Ticknor had left the United States to make the grand tour of Europe and pursue studies at the University of Göttingen. He would probably have lingered there and continued with his *Wanderjahre*, but for a letter that he received from President Kirkland of Harvard toward the end of July 1816 offering him the recently endowed Abiel Smith Professorship of Romance Literatures. This offer made him reconsider his plans. "Here is at once a new subject of study proposed to me, to which I have paid no attention since I have been here, and which I have not taken into the plan of my studies in Europe," he wrote to his father on 9 November 1816. And with a quasi-puritanical sense of calling, he added, "If I am to be a professor in this literature [Spanish], I must go to Spain" (LT, 1:117). However, he continued with his course of studies until, almost a year later, he replied to the Harvard offer from Rome on 6 November 1817.[18]

II

The digressive and biographical conventions of travel writing are two clear textual strategies present above all in Noah's narrative. These conventions are connected with a secret diplomatic task commissioned to Noah by Secretary of State Monroe, that of negotiating the release of the crew of a Salem brig recently enslaved by Algerine pirates. Noah employed an American naturalized Spaniard, Richard Keene, to act as neutral envoy to the Barbary States. But when Keene finally ransomed some of the sailors at a higher price than authorized, Noah, aware that his negotiator had had to employ personal funds, decided to reimburse him partially. This action, along with charges of espionage against Keene, produced Noah's later problems. In 1815, not long after he had taken up his consulship in Tunis, Monroe forced him to resign on the grounds of his Jewish religion and accusations of embezzelment. A legal battle ensued between Noah and his detractors, ending in 1817 when he was finally vindicated and cleared of all charges.[19] Since Noah wrote his travel book to exonerate himself from these allegations, it is not surprising that he fastidiously detailed the particulars of his voyage. This emphasis on one's affairs would not have surprised readers, who during the Enlightenment and later had begun to consider personal information as an essential part of travel writings. Audiences were particularly eager to read about the foreign adventures of travel writers who were public figures at home. Personal information also was a kind of guarantee for the authenticity of the more general observations on the foreign place, and, more importantly, it contributed to the existence of a narrative organization, a primordial element for the literariness of nonfiction travel writings.[20] Besides, in the case of Noah's eventful voyage, this personal information contributed to the romantic nature of the travel account, placing the traveler amid a tumultuous world of intrigues typical of popular fiction.

The narrative structure of Noah's travels in the peninsula can be divided into two main parts. First, the short excursions he made around Cádiz while he was expecting news from his intermediary, and, second, his slow and eventful approach to France along the Mediterranean coast. During his residence in Cádiz, Noah, following a method of inquiry typical of the Enlightenment, surveys the living conditions of the city and what constitutes its civilization. Accordingly, he begins with a close look at its markets, edifices, and trade, and continues—after interpolating the circumstances of his personal mission—with a historical survey emphasizing the ancient history of Cádiz and the modern sieges conducted by the British and the Dutch. On the whole, he notes that "the lively appearance of the city, with its small turrets, white houses, spacious buildings, passage boats, and ships of war, gave tokens of opulence, importance, and comfort" (TE, 64). Behind that façade, however, Noah soon discovers the Spanish socioeconomic crisis and tries to account for it. Nothing has been more conducive to the city's economic decline, he affirms, than the reliance of the Spanish government on its colonies. He asserts, in typically enlightened rhetoric, that because of that Spaniards "lost sight of that great maxim, which nations never should forget, that industry, science, and the arts, are the only true sources of wealth and national character" (TE, 67). His personal background is no doubt foregrounded here, for during his boyhood in Philadelphia he had been an indentured gilder and carver, a job he combined with the emulation of Benjamin Franklin's rigid studious and moderate life.[21] Consequently, Noah employs a mercantilistic and utilitarian discourse that pays tribute to manual work, education, and enterprise.

The caustic anti–Roman Catholic discourse so prevalent in nineteenth-century Anglo-American writing also informs Noah's textual construction of Spain. Noah believed that Roman Catholicism was one of the most important causes of national backwardness in Spain, and even though he admired the people's pious daily vespers, he saw in the numerous religious ceremonies a mind-shackling power, epitomized by the Inquisition. For him spiritual despotism lay at the root of the decay and poverty of Cádiz and, by extension, of the whole country. Besides, he considered the friars and priests as "the principal cause of that decay of moral and national character, of that want of energy and education, which constitute the safety, and, sometimes, the glory of a nation" (TE, 141). In his view, the enlightened French invaders could have provided a way for the Spanish people out of their moral degradation. In his analysis of the Peninsular War Noah laments that the Spaniards rejected Joseph Bonaparte so vociferously, for his reign would have been positive for the Spaniards. He also debunks the vaunted Spanish patriotism, reminding readers that the famous victories of the Spaniards would not have been possible without their British allies, and that the local people fought against the French not out of national pride but personal convenience.

The narrative structure of Noah's Spanish travels is forwarded through the descriptions of several successive short trips he made in the outskirts of Cádiz but, above all, through the episodic nature of his progression along the Mediterranean coast. While he was in Cádiz Noah visited Algeciras, the plains of Tarifa, Puerto de Santa María, and finally Jerez de la Frontera, near the battleground "wherein Roderic, the last king of the Goths, was defeated" (TE, 138). Yet once the American captives in Algiers were released, he became impatient to proceed to his Tunisian consulship. Noah made no secret of his distaste for Cádiz: even though "an attachment in time might be formed to the city, and to the mode of living," he observes, in fact "the prejudices of the people, their zeal and bigotry in religious affairs, the want of spirit and enterprise, the absence of literary institutions, seminaries of learning, and works of science and the arts, cannot fail to render a long residence, exceedingly irksome to the inquiring mind" (TE, 162). In short, he was leaving the southern city with the conviction that to an enlightened mind like his it was an unbearable place. No sooner had he departed from Cádiz than he realized his coasting vessel was followed by Algerine pirates. From that moment on his trip became a constant change of means of transportation to speed up the journey and shun the alleged corsairs. Noah clearly exploits the rhetorical possibilities of what Mary Suzanne Schriber calls the "vehicle convention" of travel literature, which consists in talking about travel conveyances as if they were actors in the book, not just means of transportations.[22] On horseback he traversed San Roque, Estepona, and Málaga. Then he sailed in a *felucca* to Almería, Cartagena, and Palos, "the port from which Columbus had first sailed," which he considered "an interesting place for Americans" (TE, 170). Finally he managed to reach Alicante by hiring an antiquated coach, and from there he continued toward Barcelona, first on a farmer's cart, then a brig, and finally a small wagon with two mules.

The Enlightenment interests displayed in Noah's representation of Cádiz are also evinced in his description of Barcelona. That is, his utilitarian discourse celebrates industriousness, manual labor, and education. His discussion of Barcelona, however, begins with historical information. He tells his readers that the city was briefly occupied by the Moors but then returned to Christian hands, and also adds that the Jews played an important role in establishing its commercial status. After this, Noah begins his economic assessment of the Catalonian capital, where "every body appears at work" despite the visible postwar economic recession. He remarks the presence of "calico printers, gun-smiths in great numbers, and manufacturing the best quality of fowling pieces; locksmiths, needle and nail makers, lace manufacturers, silk weavers, and almost every species of mechanical art" (TE, 184). He also praises the existence of an educational infrastructure consisting of good libraries and professional "schools of art where drawing, architecture, and other branches of the arts are taught" (TE, 186). But neither the industriousness of the local people nor the existence of economic facilities have prevented the inevitable: "The commerce has dwindled to insignificance and very few merchants of great capital now carry on business. Formerly a thousand vessels annually arrived and sailed from Barcelona; the number at present does not exceed two hundred" (TE, 186).

No other episode in Noah's travels, however, transcends the symbolic importance of his final departure from Spain. Travel writings often charge with strong liminal significance the act of border-

Portrait of thirty-four-year-old Mordecai Manuel Noah posing as a dignified man
of letters, by J. F. Smith. From the frontispiece to his *Travels in England, France,
Spain, and the Barbary States in the Years 1813–14 and 15* (1819). Courtesy of
The Library Company of Philadelphia.

crossing, which may come to signify not only the entrance to new geographical and political states but also the accession to new territories of the mind. Noah's text endows his crossing of the Spanish border into France with the symbolism of a passage from the past to the present. The Spanish marble slab at the border, full of inscriptions honoring the Spanish monarch, makes a strong contrast with the French one bearing only the name of the country. To Noah, that marks "the difference of national character; the [Spanish] one, weak, flimsy, and impotent, the other powerful, collected, and undaunted" (TE, 189). The crossing of the Pyrenees also invites Noah to reflect on the country he has left, which he gravely does in a set of concluding general remarks typical of eighteenth-century travel books. He lists religious, educational, military, and social concerns and analyzes them in a rather distant yet moderate style. He also adds observations on the future of South America, repeating that the independence of the Spanish colonies will be beneficial for both the metropolis and the colonists, yet adding that to be completely free South America must reject "Spanish laws and customs" and adopt "a perfect system of religious freedom, of education, science, and the arts," for "without these indispensable attributes of liberty, they will only be released from foreign chains, to put domestic shackles on themselves" (TE, 194). In these last utterances, the voice of the enlightened pan-American discourse is clearly heard.

III

The deployment of digressions and biographical elements to forward the traveler's narrative, so important in Noah's travel book, is equally important in Ticknor's account of his journey to Spain. Yet for Ticknor the personal experiences related in travel writing are neither a vindication of done deeds nor a justification of a particular mission. Rather, they constitute a means to obtain cultural authority and concomitantly fashion for himself a public persona as well-traveled man of letters. European travel, as William Stowe has observed, operated like a gender and class ritual full of conventions whereby nineteenth-century Americans attained abroad the cultural polish they needed to maintain or further a certain sociocultural status at home. Those who followed the "liturgy of travel" very specifically detailed by scores of guidebooks could finally aspire to become members of a "new clerisy" of worldly wise Americans. More importantly, however, is the fact that upon their return those who wrote about their travel experiences could improve their gender and class position even more powerfully. As Stowe notes, travel writers

> had the opportunity to rewrite and in a sense to relive their travel experiences, and to recast themselves as the kind of narrators, protagonists, and travelers they most wanted to be. Like spiritual autobiographies and saints' lives, travel chronicles attest to certain nonordinary events, reformulate them to match approved cultural patterns, and depict their protagonists as ideal incarnations of respectable models from the objective, superior scientific observer to the sensitive, sympathetic reformer, the social critic, the intrepid explorer, the professional writer, and the responsible, respectable American.[23]

Ticknor's journals and letters, in a certain sense, meaningfully bracket off certain years of his life in Europe to prepare for himself the role of Harvard scholar and Boston intellectual he was to hold until his death.

Ticknor is in fact the American author who inaugurates the conventional itinerary of visiting Spain that will be more or less present ever after in nineteenth-century American travel writing. That is, a journey that could be said to be complete only if it entailed a stay in the capital and a visit to Andalusia. When Ticknor entered Spain on 30 April 1818, he was aware, like Noah, that he was there more for business than for pleasure, and organized his life accordingly. As he would write many years later, "My object was to increase a very imperfect knowledge of the language and literature of the country, and to purchase Spanish books, always so rare in the great book-marts of the rest of Europe."[24] However, his departure from Spain five months later would be more regretful than that of his compatriot, a clear indication that his relation with the country he was representing had been deeper and more lasting notwithstanding the cold, inquisitorial surface of his letters and journals. Once he crossed the border Ticknor moved on to Madrid without delay, carrying letters of introduction that would present him to the diplomatic and cultural circles of the capital. Thomas Jefferson, for example, had given Ticknor a letter of introduction to the American Minister George W. Erving, where, among other things, he described the young scholar as "a young gentleman of high repectability and . . . among the first in our country in point of erudition. . . . You will find in him the most perfect correctness of conduct, and virtue which will make him a valuable addition to your friendships."[25] During his first days of cultural acclimatization, Ticknor already perceived in the people traits he was to term quintessentially Spanish: a staunch national pride and an unflagging religious faith. In Girona, "a genuine field of Spanish heroism" (TT, 10), Ticknor saw palpable evidence of the bloody French siege of 1808. In the same town he also lamented what he regarded as the people's slavery to the Roman Catholic religion, expressed in their submission to the numerous ecclesiastics to whom they bowed down much more often than the Italians did. A few days later, when Ticknor arrived in Barcelona, where he remained from May 3 to May 10, he continued to be surprised by "the people's fanaticism in religion" but was equally captivated by their "fanaticism in pleasure," considering the large crowds attending public balls, theaters, and other popular entertainments (TT, 16).

This dialectics of repulsion and attraction pervades Ticknor's travel journals and his *History of Spanish Literature*, and brings to the foreground the contest between his Enlightenment formation and his romantic situation. In his introduction to *George Ticknor's Travels in Spain*, George T. Northup conjugates Ticknor's two cultural allegiances by saying that he "represents the scientific, rather than the literary, side of the romantic movement," for "in a land where nearly every traveller turns dreamer, Ticknor saw things as they were" (TT, 5). In this respect, Ticknor's analysis of the Spaniards' religious ethos is a good example of the cultural dilemma he faced. As a romantic, on the one hand, he admired the unifying Christian zeal that brought about the reconquest of Moslem Spain, but, on the other hand, as an enlightened New England Protestant and like many of the Boston Unitarian intellectuals, he could not help detesting the economic and spiritual rule of Roman Catholicism over the Spaniards. The major New England historians, like their fellow American travelers writing on Spain, decried the alliance between crown and altar, and scorned many characteristics of the Roman Catholic church. David Levin cogently demonstrates, for instance, that "ultramontanism, the Inquisition, the privileges and claims of priests, the intercession of saints, the Immaculate Conception, transubstantiation, faith in the value of relics, the confessional, ritual, the need to baptize dying infants . . . are the Catholic ideas that receive the most attention" during that period.[26] Similarly, to Ticknor the early religious fervor that had united the Spanish people during the Reconquest became a corrupted and degrading influence as it grew into fanaticism and bigotry after the fall of Granada, and especially with the introduction of the Inquisition in Spain.

Ticknor's writings follow the convention of juxtaposing the hardships of traveling abroad with the pleasures of being there. For thirteen days, from May 11 until May 23, Ticknor was constantly en route between Barcelona and Madrid, enduring the hardships of bad roads and poor inns, enjoying the company of his three fellow travelers, including José de Madrazo, the royal painter, and witnessing the devastation wrought on the country by years of warfare against the Napoleonic troops. The destruction was still so conspicuous that the city of Lérida, he noted, had "nothing to verify the beautiful description Lucan gives of it but its fine situation," while ruinous Saragossa made "Leipzig, Lützen, and Waterloo" look, by comparison, "ordinary fields of battle" (TT, 19–20). Ticknor found solace during this trip, as we saw in the previous chapter, in reading *Don Quixote*, and no doubt a highlight before reaching Madrid was his stop at Alcalá de Henares, seat of the renowned university but also "birthplace of Cervantes, the unimitated, the inimitable Cervantes" (TT, 25). In his life in Madrid, like Irving several years later, Ticknor tried to strike a balance between a rigid course of studies and regular social calls to fellow Americans, foreign diplomats, and local aristocrats.[27] He usually started the day early, at half past five, studied until eleven, and then worked until one with a Spanish tutor. After a short lunch, at half past one he received his second instructor, José Antonio Conde, a specialist in medieval literature who read poetry with him for about three hours. That concluded his daily academic program, so that after dining normally at five, Ticknor was left with ample opportunities to walk, ride, or observe Madrid society of 1818. If he frequented the diplomatic soirées more often than the local ones it was because he found the Spanish aristocracy and, especially, the middle class, dull, narrow-minded, ignorant, and bad mannered. For example, he regarded Ferdinand VII, to whom he was introduced, as a "vulgar blackguard" (LT, 1:191). He preferred to spend his social time with George Erving, Sir Henry Wellesley, and the Duke de Laval, the American, British and French ambassadors respectively, and also with Caesare Balbo, the Sardinian representative's son.

The social criticism inherent to Enlightenment travel writing does not escape Ticknor's observation. In addition to reports on his academic and social occupations, Ticknor also sent to his family miscellaneous information on the capital filtered through his critical eyes. He found Madrid, for example, to have few remarkable monuments, although he admitted the existing ones were full of historical associations. Yet, if these monuments meant something for Ticknor, it definitely was not Spanishness, but royal power and centralization. Instead of displaying the Spaniards' own view of themselves, they stood as memento of the former paternalistic enlightened despotism of Charles III. Ticknor, too, regarded the city, though not filthy, as neither healthy nor clean enough, an example being the dirty and badly kept General Hospital. On the public institutions in Madrid his opinions varied. While he found the Library "abominably administered," he considered the Museum of Natural History and the royal sites great places for the art lover. Similarly, he commended the free public education run jointly by the municipality and a religious order, and praised the two academies of language and history (LT, 1:197). Ticknor also took note of the various popular summer amusements. For him the Prado, the promenade where everybody walked and met every afternoon, was "something that no European city can boast within its walls" (LT, 1:190). Officers, monks, civilians, and all sorts of people mingled there daily; even the royal family took rides in their carriage among the multitude along the Prado. He thought that of the two theaters in town, the Teatro del Príncipe and Teatro de la Cruz, the latter was more interesting because it staged more Golden Age drama and less French drama in translation, at that time the fashion in Madrid. Finally, he held the bullfight as the paragon of Spanish recreation; he saw it as the most popular entertainment because it allowed Spaniards to vent their anxieties and express, in a nearly democratic arena, thoughts otherwise seditious.[28]

No matter how comfortable he was in Madrid, Ticknor had to put an end to his cultural immersion before he might feel the harmful effects that, according to Thomas Jefferson, foreign travel caused on young Americans abroad. In early September Ticknor visited El Escorial—"a monument of the magnificence, the splendor, the superstition, and perhaps the personal fears of Philip II" (LT, 1:214)—San Ildefonso, and Segovia,[29] and then left Madrid a week later to make the romantic journey across the Sierra Morena into Andalusia, "the Italy of Spain" (LT, 1:223). He departed from the capital regretfully: "I had come there with sad and dark thoughts; but, instead of the solitary, melancholy life I had imagined I was to lead, I found myself, on the whole, more pleasantly situated there, and passed my time . . . more profitably, than I have done anywhere in Europe" (LT, 1:220). Ticknor reached Cordova on September 17, and during his three days there he met the Duke of Rivas, with whom he visited some mountain hermits. Interestingly, on the way to that religious establishment Ticknor describes a bucolic scene that resembles some of Goya's early paintings. It is the type of pastoral situation that Ticknor enjoyed and which reoccurs in later passages of his Andalusian journey:

There, by the side of a little fountain that gushed from the rocks, we found a cloth spread on the ground and covered with a breakfast of cold meats, fruits, and wine, which the Duke had sent up to beforehand. In this romantic spot, under the shade of some pomegranate-trees, and with a magnificent view of Cordova, the rich plain that spreads for fifty miles above and below it, and the Guadalquivir winding through the whole of it, we stretched ourselves on the grass, and I made a breakfast such as is so often described in works of fiction, but which I never realized before, and which I can never forget. (LT, 1:225)

Looking at the scenery with romantic emotion, almost unnoticedly Ticknor effaces the boundary between fiction and reality, between the historicity in which he was steeped and the romance he unconsciously wished to reproduce. In Andalusia Spain was becoming for him a country of romance, a realm of the imagination. In essence, a reality liable to be turned into a text.

The insecurity of the Spanish roads, the beauty of the Alhambra, and the paintings of Murillo are some other powerful commonplaces mentioned by Ticknor that subsequent nineteenth-century American travel writing capitalized on. Following the post road for safety, Ticknor arrived in Granada on September 24 to visit the Alhambra,[30] about which he said in a letter to a friend: "The Alhambra, a name which will make my blood thrill if I live to the frosts of a century. . . . It was a riotous, tumultuous pleasure, which will remain in my memory, like a kind of sensual enjoyment" (LT, 1:232). He then proceeded to Gibraltar through Málaga, the first part of the trip escorted by *cosarios* transporting goods, since "the roads are so infested with robbers that no other mode of travelling is safe" (LT, 1:232). Ticknor left Gibraltar on October 3 and traveled to Cádiz. There he met the literary scholar Nicolaus Böhl von Faber, who was to receive Irving in 1828. Five days later he took the steamboat up the Guadalquivir river to Seville, "the capital seat of the genuine Spanish school in painting," to look at the pictures by Murillo (LT, 1:239). Again he was asserting his condition of young scholar not only well-versed in Spanish language and literature but in Spanish architecture and painting.

Ticknor's Spanish travel writings also conclude with the conventional redemptive nature of his border-crossing. After a week in Seville Ticknor decided to go to Lisbon, but hearing that the direct route through Badajoz was infested with robbers he prudently joined a party of *contrabandistas* for protection. The days he spent with these men who made a living smuggling dollars from Seville to Lisbon and carrying back British goods were some of the most

Portrait of George Ticknor by Thomas Sully, 1828. Courtesy of the Trustees of Dartmouth College.

exhilarating in his life because of the freedom he felt and also because of the mundane attitude his fellow travelers manifested. He took pleasure in

> sleeping out every night but one, and then in the house of the chief of our band; dining under trees at noon; living on a footing of perfect equality and good-fellowship with people who are liable every day to be shot or hanged by the laws of their country; indeed, leading for a week

as much of a vagabond life as if I were an Arab or a Mameluke,—I came soon to have some of the same sort of gay recklessness that marked the character of my companions. In short, I had fine spirits the whole way, and did not find myself to have been long in coming to the borders of Portugal. There I bade farewell to the only country in the world where I could have led such a life; the only one, indeed, where it would have been safer to be under the protection of contrabandistas and outlaws, than under that of regular government, against which they array themselves. (LT, 1:242)

Comparing this border crossing with Noah's, one has little difficulty concluding that Ticknor experienced the lure of desire, well embedded in this excerpt, much more powerfully than his compatriot. But the feelings expressed in this passage could have unsettling implications for a law-abiding patrician from New England like Ticknor. William Charvat has shown that in the first decades of the nineteenth-century New England critics decried literary representations of antisocial figures.[31] Worse than to represent them, to travel with outlaws and be pleased with their company was against the decorum of letters in his time. Thus, it was safer to restrict the record of these somewhat subversive camaraderie with smugglers to the privacy of a journal than to jeopardize one's public image by publishing it.

IV

Having focused this discussion of Noah and Ticknor above all on the circumstances of composition and their itineraries, and having at the beginning described their travel accounts as late Enlightenment works that nevertheless prefigure the romantic representation of Spain, I will now return to their relationship with the ideology and literary conventions that shape the form and content of the nonfictional travel book. Although, formally speaking, Noah and Ticknor did deploy many conventions of nonfictional travel writing inherited from the previous century they did not follow to the letter some other paradigms of the genre. They avoided, for example, a merely picturesque representation of Spain. They also disregarded the type of formal arrangement that focused solely on one specialized discourse (for example, economic, archeological, agricultural, or artistic) and placed the others at the periphery of the traveler's experience. Since the travel book had to reflect the variety and complexity of the country it was meant to narrate, they aimed, instead, at an eclectic type of cultural cartography that created a multilayered travel text in which the economic, architectural, social, and military discourses, to name a few, shared equally in the representation of otherness. In such a representation the traveler was conceived both as an anonymous objective narrator and as a subject relating his self-exploration as well as his encounter with otherness.

In departing from certain formal conventions of eighteenth-century travel literature both authors were on their way to situate their writings in the romantic period; yet, ideologically speaking, their accounts still belonged to the neoclassical didactic tradition. According to Charles Batten, Enlightenment travel accounts ordinarily show these major traits: the just implementation of the Horatian maxim *prodesse et delectare*, the interpolation of encyclopedic observations and abstract musings with autobiographical elements, and the adoption of a wide range of voices ranging from those of the philosophical and sentimental traveler to those of the picturesque and splenetic traveler. Travel writers enlightened readers with facts about foreign countries and also delighted them with the autobiographical parts of their narratives. Too much encyclopedic information, on the one hand, would make a travelogue rather dull, while a narrative solely focused on biographical information, on the other, would be frowned upon by critics who termed it too egotistical.[32] On the contrary, the romantic travel book capitalized much more powerfully upon the subjective. As Percy Adams notes, by and large "travel books have varied in the amount of subjectivity they include. That is, the less they have, the more they seem like a guidebook; the more they have, the more they approach the novel and seem to be lying."[33] By stressing above all the conjunction between the "spontaneous overflow of powerful feeling" and the traveler's "emotions recollected in tranquility" after the journey, the romantic travel book thus remained closer to the fictional discourse of the novel than to the scientific, exploratory discourse of the travel accounts of the Age of Reason. Moreover, the rhetorical conventions displayed by the discourse of picturesque aesthetics for nature description and for the representation of otherness soon became more popular than the former long encyclopedic accounts of foreign geographies, economies, and peoples. For Ticknor and Noah, however, the key to a balanced nonfictional travel account still was an equal amount of objective and subjective material. The idea of balance itself was a legacy from the Enlightenment they could not altogether escape.

Alexander H. Everett voiced this balanced and didactic view of nonfictional travel literature in the above-mentioned letter to Ticknor where, interestingly enough, he linked the former tradition of travel writing represented by Johnson and Clarke with the romantics Chateaubriand and Humboldt. Apart from referring to his friend's dislike of travel books, Everett also observed:

> It is unfortunate in general that our intelligent travellers so seldom publish any thing upon their return from Europe. Few books are so instructive and certainly none so entertaining to a mature mind as good travels. . . . A book of travels admits the display of every kind of merit whether of style or substance that can belong to any composition, excepting those that are proper to the highest strains of impassioned eloquence & poetry; and these are also excluded from philosophy, history, and other sorts of writing that are generally esteemed as of the first class. (PP, 221)

His encomium of the didacticism implicit in travel writing was, of course, limited and reflects the idea, no doubt shared by Noah and Ticknor, that notwithstanding the praise given to the teach-and-delight method in nonfictional travel writing, the genre was nevertheless low on the literary hierarchy.

More often than not travel writers chose a historical discourse to convey their instructive message within the framework of their travel narratives. In the twofold task of enlightening and recreating, however, the first goal always had primacy. Emphasizing facts instead of adventure is, as William Spengemann points out, a "peculiarly American" choice, whereas according to Terry Caesar it clearly differentiates American writers from their British counterparts.[34] The travel writings of Noah and Ticknor exemplify quite well this conviction that history was a subject matter that could morally edify their readership. In the preface to *Travels in England, France, Spain, and the Barbary States*, for example, Noah voices the difficulties travel writers experience in trying to please the diverse preferences of their readers. Some are fond of travel narratives focusing on scientific and educational themes, while others prefer agricultural, social, or artistic subjects. In his view, however, the most important subject in a travel book is history, "a study which is deemed of essential importance to the progress of learning and civilization, and the successful advancement of governments" (TE, v). These two authors understood that the cultural work offered by history—within and without the framework of nonfictional travel writing—was chiefly the moral instruction of the literate masses. Thus, it is not surprising that Ticknor—always certain of his role as moral and cultural arbiter reaching out to the masses—in a letter to Sir Charles Lyell explained he had written his *History of Spanish Literature* "as much for *general* readers as for scholars" (LT, 2:253).

The use of contemporary history in the Spanish travel writings of Noah and Ticknor also underlines their embedded nationalistic bias. Terry Caesar, in his analysis of American travel writing, argues that the early American travel book "had to be, inescapably, American."[35] Noah, for example, constantly expresses his pan-American call for the independence of Spain's American colonies. Moreover, by comparing the concurrent socioeconomic and political situation of Spain with that of the United States, both authors not only informed American readers about ongoing peninsular problems, but also implicitly reminded them that such problems could hardly ever arise in their virtuous republic. The circulation of British and French travel books on Spain, as we saw in the previous chapter, had been keeping American readers informed of what was occurring in the peninsula. But to people like Noah that constituted a form of cultural subordination to Europe that had to be redressed because it made Americans "too apt to receive erroneous impressions through foreign sources" (TE, vi). If an enlightened republic was to disseminate its worldview, then it had to necessarily produce its own representations of otherness. Ticknor did this cultural work silently in his journals and openly in his Harvard lectures and his *History of Spanish Literature*, both of them an extension, as I argued before, of his travel writings. With that in mind, one may contend that Ticknor was trying to offer to the public a genuinely American literary history of Spain that would supersede the standard European works of Bouterwek and Sismondi by going a little further and also becoming a cultural exploration of the peninsular ethos.

Noah's sense of the importance of history is clear throughout *Travels in England, France, Spain, and the Barbary States*, but he put forward his views on the relationship between historical consciousness, nationalistic discourse, and travel writing most systematically in a speech delivered on 25 November 1821, two years after the publication of his travel account, to a group of mechanics in New York:

> Nothing betrays a loose course of reading than to be familiar with the history of every other part of the world better than that of your native land. Commence, then, at *home*, and in addition to the discoveries in America, familiarize yourself with the history of the United States, its early struggle for freedom, its laws, governments, soil, climate, produc-

tions and manufactures; the names and populations of states, their mountains and rivers. Once thoroughly informed on these subjects, the mind may pursue its inclination. The history of Rome, of England, France, and Spain, and every work containing useful information of foreign countries, or ancient or modern events together with voyages and travels, which blend novelty with instruction, and amusement will always be sought after with avidity.[36]

Striking a nationalistic key, Noah advises American citizens to become more patriotic by acquiring an eighteenth-century type of encyclopedic knowledge of their country, and also of foreign countries. His indebtedness to Enlightenment thinking is likewise present when he lists the literary models for the educated worker of the Republic: rhetoricians like Kaimes, Blair, and Burke; statesmen like Jefferson, Madison, and Hamilton; and historians like David Hume, William Robertson, and Edward Gibbon.

Along with the nationalistic agenda embedded in the Spanish travel writings of Noah and Ticknor, another instructive message in their historical discourse is the premonitory illustration of the fate of great empires.[37] The concern with the rise and fall of empires, well illustrated in Noah's above-mentioned allusion to three of the major eighteenth-century historians, was shared by many historians and intellectuals in nineteenth-century New England who were evaluating the goals of a nation that not long before had promulgated the Monroe Doctrine and now was living through the Age of Jackson. The negative representation of the Barbary States in Noah's book, for example, with history going backward in that area and degenerating from the former high culture of Carthage to the ruthlessness of the present, probably caused apprehension to readers. Even those certain of a providential plan for the progress of the American nation must have felt some degree of alarm.[38] The representation of historical Spain was an especially apt subject for instruction because it could be used for the purposes of political allegory. It was not, however, a political allegory fraught with the revolutionary overtones of Mackenzie's later Spanish travel narratives. By showing the twofold example of Spain in the demise of the Hispano-Arabic civilization and the disintegration of the Spanish-American empire, Noah and Ticknor taught a powerful historical lesson to the American readership using an enlightened method of inquiry. Instead of responding aesthetically or emotionally to the ruins of the past, as romantic travelers like Irving and Longfellow would do in the following decade, they fashion themselves as philosophical travelers rationally inspecting the causes of economic decay and political degradation in Spain.

Noah, as we saw before, regarded Spain on the whole as a country that had ignored the mercantilistic maxims of the Enlightenment and consequently let itself be burdened by its colonial ballast. An anonymous review of Noah's book also focused on this point, noting that it was the "inordinate inherited wealth" of several centuries that had destroyed the country's capacity to work.[39] Noah's most extended historical reflection, which he situates on the outskirts of Algeciras during one of his trips outside Cádiz, seeks answers to the Spanish crisis. Strolling along the road to San Roque, he discovers several half-interred human bones from the Peninsular Wars; these initiate a reverie on the fortunes of time, and more particularly on the history of Spain up to the fall of Granada. He outlines the different barbarian invasions, then details the degradation of the Goth monarchy and the plot prepared to precipitate the Arab invasion of the peninsula, and finally chronicles the Arab domination, interpolating such episodes as the exploits of El Cid and the Christian victory at Navas de Tolosa. The last pages of his historical digression try to account for the decline of the Muslim power in Spain culminating with the fall of Granada. Noah interrupts this long historical reverie with a strong plea to the Spaniards to compare the prosperity they enjoyed during the medieval period with their current "misfortunes brought on by ignorance and fanaticism, by indolence and tyranny." Since historical events, he implies, do not take place by accident but by human causality, he admonishes Spain to redress its state with the following enlightened course of action:

> Arouse yourself! shake off your indolence! and give your prejudices to the winds! Raze your inquisitions to the ground; turn your monasteries into seminaries of learning; place your priests between the handles of a plough; tolerate all religions; call back the Moors and the Jews, who gave you character and wealth; declare your provinces in South America, Sovereign and Independent. (TE, 125)

In the end, he returns to the early scene on the road to San Roque, and concludes: "Every thing around me gave tokens of decaying power; of a retrograde of national strength, and national character; the fields looked green; nature had remained true to her general course—man only had changed" (TE, 134). The classical *ubi sunt* theme and the philosophical sense of passing time akin to the meditative poems of his contemporaries, such as William Cullen Bryant's "Thanatopsis," cannot be ignored here, nor can we fail to notice some trace also of philosophical skepticism. He constructs a similar reverie as he crosses the Ebro river at Tortosa. After imagining Hannibal passing over it and leading his Carthagenian forces against his enemies during the Iberian campaigns, Noah returns to the transitoriness of his position and calmly observes that "the river still gushed with vehemence . . . but the chieftains of antiquity, who had given celebrity to these plains, existed only in history" (TE, 178).

Ticknor's travel journals contain a similar moment of historical speculation triggered by his view of the dilapidated city of Saragossa. "As we approached the city," he wrote, "the sides of the road were marked everywhere by lines of ruin which appeal equally to the heart and to the imagination." Touched by this Dantesque panorama, Ticknor alights from his carriage and approaches the debris of a large convent used by the locals as a defense against the French troops. Here he contemplates a ghostly sight: "The peasants were ploughing round it, and, as I passed over the fresh mould, I trod at every step on pieces of leather, fragments of arms and helmets, and sometimes saw human bones which still remained undecayed and unhidden after the cultivation of nine summers, so terrible was the carnage and so little the respect for the dead!" (TT, 20). Like Noah's, Ticknor's agitated reaction immediately gives way to a calmer consideration of what he sees. Trying to find an explanation for the heroic resistance at Saragossa, Ticknor remembers the Spanish spirit in the sieges of Numancia and Saguntum, and also in the wars with the Goths and the Moors, "the moral spirit of the people, who, however humble and abject they may be to their domestick rulers, never submit to foreign usurpation, whatever form it may assume" (TT, 21). In other journal passages as well as in his *History of Spanish Literature* Ticknor reiterated this concept of Spanish pride as a source of both moral force and physical destruction. Unchecked pride turned into bigotry had been, according to Ticknor, a chief cause of decline in all things Spanish. The other cause of Spanish degeneration—and in this point he held the same opinion as Noah—was the strict control Roman Catholicism had exerted on the people, which turned their natural piety into religious fanaticism.

The thrills of travel no doubt constituted another arena of fusion between history and romance, for the romance of the traveler's yarn could be set against the historical backdrop of contemporary Spain. Travel writing is generically different from history writing even though it incorporates some history. A travel narrative investigating only the historical causes of current Spanish problems, however, would have inevitably been too dry for a readership that sought a little more than factual information. Moreover, it would have obscured the genre identity of the travel narrative. Consequently, to enliven the otherwise dry objectivity of the historical discourse in their travel writings Noah and Ticknor introduced quasi-imaginative conventions of the genre like the picturesqueness of landscape and character, the thrill of the traveler's adventures, and the interest of some fictional digressions. Blended with historical facts, these somewhat romantic elements animated the serious surface of the travel book.

The romantic emotional response to nature or to ruins is an important convention of travel writing that Noah and Ticknor employ in their accounts. Yet, they never appear to be narrowly subject to a structured framework of picturesque aesthetics. Picturesque tourism, which had begun to make itself noticeable in Britain in the second half of the eighteenth century, employed the aesthetic category of the Picturesque to represent nature as a feminized entity that the trained gaze of the male traveler could improve. Picturesque travelers had close links to landscape studies, from which they obtained ideal pictorial models to improve the vistas they originally contemplated, and consequently made ample use of the jargon of painting when they had to textually reorganize these vistas. However, as the aesthetic category of the Picturesque became popularized in the early nineteenth-century, the application of the term expanded not only to rural but also to human and urban compositions. The Picturesque then, as James Buzard points out, came to be synonymous with the authentic, with whatever it was that retained traces of authenticity, and thus established a bridge between classical ideas of artistic oneness and romantic theories of organic wholeness.[40] Admittedly, the Spanish travel writings of Noah and Ticknor refer to Spain as a feminine entity, yet never with the intention of reorganizing its external features. Rather than acting like picturesque travelers eager to leave their traces on a feminized landscape, their use of the feminine pronoun in reference to Spain corresponds to the male traveler's conventional illusion that he is exploring virgin territory. Moreover, Noah and Ticknor never display the pictorial vocabulary inherent to picturesque tourism nor try to arrange like harmonic compositions the landscapes, towns, cities, and persons they see throughout their Spanish travels.

The picturesque then provides Ticknor and Noah with a frame of reference to represent Spain as a country that still maintains itself immersed in old customs and beliefs. Ticknor, for example, begins his *History of Spanish Literature* with a brief description of the rough peninsular landscape; yet his purpose is not to paint an imaginative picture but to strengthen the correlation between the land and the character of the Spaniards, that is, the genius loci. He had already provisionally formulated this connection in a letter to a friend from Madrid in July. Talking about the ordinary people of Spain, he confessed:

> Spain and the Spanish people amuse me more than anything I have met in Europe. There is more national character here, more originality and poetry in the popular manners and feelings, more force without barbarism, and civilization without corruption, than I have found anywhere else. Would you believe it?—I speak not at all of the highest class,—what seems mere fiction and romance in other countries is matter of observation here, and, in all that relates to manners, Cervantes and Le Sage are historians. For, when you have crossed the Pyrenees, you have not only passed from one country and climate to another, but you have gone back a couple of centuries in your chronology, and find the people still in that kind of poetical existence which we have not only long since lost, but which we have long since ceased to credit on the reports of our ancestors. (LT, 1:188)

The charged arcadian tone of the previous passage is reiterated in this excerpt by phrases like "poetry in the popular manners," "civilization without corruption," and "poetical existence." Spain was becoming in the eyes of Ticknor a sort of living history, an idea that later romantic travelers would greatly strengthen. The picturesqueness of their accounts is then more thematic than structural, and, in addition to allusions to the Spanish scenery, is particularly evinced in local color topics like bullfighting and dancing.

The picturesqueness of character sketches becomes another source of amusement whenever the travel writer's conventions of the genre run dry. Noah and Ticknor provided more entertainment with representations of the common people and descriptions of particular characters than with landscape descriptions. Ticknor, for example, in characterizing some of the diplomats attending the social calls in Madrid, manages to convey their chief psychological traits in sketchlike sentences. He describes Sir Henry Wellesley, the British ambassador, as "a man of not more than common talents, but of sound judgement, and altogether a respectable English gentleman," and George Erving, the American Minister, as a man "with a talent, a clear head, and considerable knowledge, though very little literature" (LT, 1:209, 212). But in contrast to Ticknor's stereotyped genteel characters almost extracted from a novel of manners, Noah's more melodramatic descriptions offered the flavor of darker types of fiction or even drama. His representations of clergymen and anything related to Roman Catholicism, for example, often seem drawn from an Elizabethan revenge tragedy. Witnessing several friars doing contraband in La Coruña, he observes: "The long cloaks and hoods of the friars are admirable adapted for the purpose of smuggling; their sacred character, or the terrors of the Inquisition, prevents them from being searched, though ever objects of suspicion" (TE, 62). Even more prone to inspire terror is his account of how Roman Catholic clergymen literally subdue their parishioners: "A multitude of priests and ecclesiastics, of various grades, who fill the houses, churches, and convents," cautions Noah, "are ever ready to enforce their precepts, and enjoy their rights, by terrors wholly temporal, and ever hostile to the interest, and spirit of true religion" (TE, 87). Portraits like this no doubt entertained and rendered a picturesque image of Spain, but sometimes they paradoxically must have made some readers wonder whether the travel writer's adventures were taking place in a dystopian or in an utopian milieu.

The discourse of adventure constitutes another entertaining convention of these travel writings. On the surface, for example, *Travels in England, France, Spain and the Barbary States* reads like a normative piece of nonfictional travel writing with diverse descriptions and observations of the country. However, the complicated diplomatic mission at its core and the developments arising thereafter convert it into an entertaining political thriller or a sort of picaresque travel book where Spain is the backdrop for the protagonist's adventures. The constant urgency of Noah's progress to France after the release of the American captives at Algiers, the continuous change of means of transportation, and his paranoia of feeling himself persecuted by Algerine pirates, all give narrative impetus to his movements. Noah also occasionally enlivens his narrative with some humor like, for example, his nocturnal bath in Almeria to cool down a temperature too hot to sleep. Noah explains—in an episode that perhaps more than one male reader found a little spicy—that he bathed naked in the Mediterranean, only to discover that he had accidentally slipped in among a group of women whom local soldiers were guarding from intruders (TE, 168–69). In another episode Noah relates that during a boat ride several foreign travelers played at guessing the age of a Spanish marchioness, and his American friend was the one who flattered her most with his comments (TE, 62–63). There is no way, of course, of ascertaining the veracity of these and other episodes in Noah's and Ticknor's travel writings. What is true, though, is that they add a nearly fictional dimension that neither author wanted to push too far. Romance as pure imagination, then, is almost absent. Talking about mythical characters of romance linked to Cádiz, Noah mentions the ancient hero Hercules and the Carthagenian generals Hannibal and Asdrubal (TE, 77–79). In his *History of Spanish Literature* Ticknor also was to refer to the medieval Spanish romances. In essence, the romance of their Spanish travel writings depends as much on the traveler's trajectory as on his representation of the Spanish people.

V

The narrative voices of Noah and Ticknor, as we saw earlier in this chapter, tend to situate themselves within the category of the experiential traveler who sympathizes with the Other he is representing. Ticknor's interest in the Spaniards as protagonists of historical events—and also, as we saw before, as living instances of romance—demonstrates a type of anthropological interest not present in Noah's representation of Spain. For Noah, that country is conceived almost as an abstract entity whose economic and social structure he aims to describe with the zeal and prejudices of the Age of Reason. Ticknor, doing the same to some degree, goes a step further by trying to find the nexus between history and its actors in a sort of romantic spirit of the place. Noah's representation of Spain constituted a sort of hiatus in his literary career, for eventually he would return to journalism and playwriting, areas that would bear virtually no trace of his Spanish experiences. Ticknor, on the other hand, never lost his interest in Spain. He could have visited again, as Franco Meregalli observes, in his second and third European trips yet he refused to do so.[41] His Harvard lectures on romance languages and literatures and his formidable *History of Spanish Literature* proved, however, that he still remained attached to Spain. Through his writings and through his indirect advice, he promoted the interest of subsequent writers in the peninsula, a place where many of them would yield to the hedonism he had embraced and rejected. Some of them would also continue his historical and anthropological exploration of Spain, his interest in the local people and their traditions, thereby bringing the cultural work of textualizing Spain in antebellum American culture a further step ahead.

4

The Young American Abroad: Alexander Slidell Mackenzie and the Call of Revolutionary Traveling

EVEN THOUGH GEORGE TICKNOR'S LECTURES, DISSEMINATED BY THE future educated elites attending his courses at Harvard University, became an initial attempt to articulate for the American public a more or less comprehensive American representation of Spain, Alexander Slidell Mackenzie should be credited as being the first American writer known to have actually published a full-length travel account of Spain in the United States. It is not implausible to suppose that in Madrid Alexander Everett might have urged Mackenzie—as he had previously done with Ticknor and was to do with Longfellow—to produce a travel book on Spain. At any rate Mackenzie's *A Year in Spain. By a Young American* (1829) was duly dedicated to the American diplomat and mentor. This compelling book not only launched Mackenzie's literary career firmly but also revealed, adopting the personality of the Byronic hero and using a Painesque type of subversive Enlightenment rhetoric, that behind the Cervantesque and antiquarian anecdotes of Spain circulated by other travelers lurked a nation whose history was profoundly violent. This chapter argues that in order to create a text that could generate serious attention to the despotism Spain was suffering, Mackenzie above all highlighted the bodily representation of Spaniards in pain. His text could thus appeal to American audiences, which were already being stirred by the lachrimosity of sentimental fiction and poetry, the first impulses of reformist literature, and the ideological upheavals of some of the revolutions taking place in the Old World. The sharp contrast between the state of affairs in Spain and the United States instilled, in essence, a self-gratifying jingoistic message for which the travel writer became a keen yet subtle agent.

Today Alexander Slidell Mackenzie appears as no more than a

footnote in many literature and history books. With no full biographical study yet written about him, information regarding his life and works is fragmentary and in most cases concerns his thirty-three-year career in the Navy.[1] He entered the service as a midshipman in 1815 at the age of twelve and remained there until his death in 1848, taking part in martial operations in Brazil, Argentina, and Mexico, a fact that denotes his textual as well as military involvement with the Hispanic world. Historians, in particular, have paid much attention to his participation in the scandalous *Somers* case. In the fall of 1842, when the training brig *Somers*, commanded by Mackenzie, was returning from a mission in the West African coast, an attempted mutiny by naval apprentices was aborted and the three alleged plot leaders expeditiously hanged from the yardmast. Because one of them was Philip Spencer, the son of Secretary of War John Spencer, Mackenzie and the other officers responsible for the sentence were tried for their hasty decision. A military court, however, affirmed their innocence as well as their scrupulous enforcement of military discipline.[2] This incident gained Mackenzie both adversaries and supporters at once and also cast a dark cloud over the rest of his life and career.

In the world of letters Mackenzie always remained an amateur writing nonfiction. For one thing, he had to relegate his literary career solely to whatever moments of leisure his naval profession allowed him. For another, he never reached a sufficient level of popularity to enter the literary world full time, even though he could name James Fenimore Cooper, Henry Wadsworth Longfellow, and Washington Irving, his neighbor in Tarrytown, as his literary friends. Mackenzie nevertheless combined his self-taught literary knowledge with the perceptive sense of realism he acquired in the Navy to write several detailed and entertaining travel books. *A Year in Spain* was followed by *The American in England* (1835) and *Spain Revisited* (1836), and at his death he left a long unfinished manuscript entitled "A Journal of a Tour in Ireland." If one excludes the articles collected in *Popular Essays on Naval Subjects* (1833), Mackenzie's writings are ideologically charged with a clear nationalistic bias. This is especially true of the biographies of American war heroes that he wrote during the 1840s: *The Life of Commodore Oliver H. Perry* (1840), *Life of John Paul Jones* (1841), and *Life of Commodore Stephen Decatur* (1846). Summing up, then, in both his literary and naval careers Mackenzie can be considered an epitome of the emerging American expansionist mentality of Manifest Destiny at a time when this concept had not yet been explicitly formulated.

I

Mackenzie's representation of Spain, as is the case with other travel books discussed in *Between History and Romance*, arises from a long process of cultural textualization and personal travels rather than from a chance acquaintance with the country. His first contacts with Spain probably date from his early years in the Navy, for during routine voyages in the Mediterranean his ship almost certainly called at Port Mahon in the Balearic Islands. During those years, however, he also constructed his own romantic idea of Spain by reading on shipboard more or less the same type of books—*Don Quixote, Gil Blas, Gonsalve de Cordove, Civil Wars of Granada*— that Irving had read as a boy on the banks of the Hudson. Moreover, to recuperate from an attack of yellow fever he had suffered the year before in the Caribbean, in 1825 Mackenzie requested a leave of absence and sailed for Europe. He spent a year in France and afterward made the tour of Spain, which he related in *A Year in Spain*. Several years later, having been granted another leave of absence on account of an ocular affliction, he departed for England, and from there traveled to Spain in early 1834. He spent two months in Spain, where he found Ferdinand VII already dead and the country torn by a bloody civil war between the apostolical followers of Don Carlos and the constitutionalist supporters of the Queen regent, Maria Cristina. The impressions of that second Spanish sojourn—during which he visited, above all, Castile and the northern provinces—later became *Spain Revisited*. Mackenzie closed his representation of Spain with this travelogue where, like modern war correspondents, he capitalized on his eyewitness stance to textualize abroad before the domestic hearth. That is, he added new authorial value to the role of "young American in dangerous Europe" that he had chosen for himself as a travel writer.

The transgressive and gratifying nature of travel, inscribed in the text through the young traveling narrator's voice, achieves prominence in *A Year in Spain*. There Mackenzie affirms that his motivations to visit the country were leisure and the improvement of his command of Spanish. However, one also discerns a strong sense of adventurousness in his decision, for even though some people warned him that the country was full of robbers, he felt that "the little danger that might be incurred would heighten the pleasure of every scene and incident, reached with some risk, and enjoyed with a sense of insecurity" (YS, I: 16). Given the sociopolitical circumstances of Spain in those days, Mackenzie's words seem to be hiding a slight feeling of blissful death-wish behind their rhetoric of pleasure. In the fall of 1826 the twenty-three-year-old Mackenzie entered Spain through Catalonia, where the Spanish functionaries at the border rummaged his trunks lest he was trying to smuggle books banned in the kingdom, as indeed he was. A piece of silver secretly slipped into the officer's hand, however, avoided the hassle and permitted him to enter Spain with some works by Voltaire. Just at the very moment he was physically crossing two national borders, he presents himself as the metaphorical transgressor of the boundaries of what is and is not legal.

Mackenzie's itinerary follows the conventional route of many a traveler. He spent the first weeks of his sojourn in the principality of Catalonia. As he traveled to Barcelona, and also during his successive days in that city, Mackenzie was surprised by the military and religious control over the country. The presence of a strong French military contingent that the Holy Alliance had sent to help Ferdinand VII reestablish absolute monarchy was felt everywhere. Equally conspicuous for the young traveler was the existence of a sizable religious class about which he could not stifle his anger: "They form more than two per cent of the entire population. Two men in a hundred, who, neither sow, nor reap, nor labour; and who, nevertheless, eat, drink, and luxuriate!" (YS, 1:40). His first weeks in Spain, then, tended to confirm all the usual prejudices of Spanish corruption and despotism, as well as the anti-Catholicism that he had brought with him. His trip from Barcelona to Madrid revealed to him the poverty of the Spanish peasantry. Moreover, it abruptly introduced him to travel insecurity, another endemic problem of early nineteenth-century Spain. As he was crossing the province of Tarragona, Mackenzie noted the poor aspect of the local peasantry, which made him conclude, exasperated, that they "must be toiling to pay the pageantry of some degenerate noble in Madrid, or to fatten and sensualize the monks I had seen rolling along the rambla of Barcelona" (YS, 1:60). In the same province, near the Ebro river, a gang of robbers held up the stagecoach in which Mackenzie was traveling, brutally murdering the coachman and postillion. As a result, the rest of the journey to Madrid had to take place under the escort of dragoons and other regular soldiers. Finally, traveling across Valencia and the barren plains of La Mancha, Mackenzie arrived in Madrid in the late fall of 1826.

In the capital Mackenzie associated with the American group lingering around the Everetts, the Richs, and Washington and Peter Irving, and thus put his project of immersion in Spanish culture to rest for a few months. "Of my own mode of life and occupations in Madrid," he tries to justify in *A Year in Spain*, "it is unnecessary to speak, since they had little connexion [sic] with the customs of the country" (YS, 1:149). Mackenzie, however, experienced indeed a close rapport with the Spanish people, especially through his friendship with his landlord, Don Valentín Todohueso, and his family. The house where he lived was the same to which Longfellow, who had just arrived, moved when Mackenzie left. In Madrid Mackenzie began an enduring friendship with the future scholar from Maine, and made a short trip with him to Segovia, El Escorial, and Aranjuez.

Mackenzie finally set out for Andalusia on 11 April 1827 on a trip that proved to be as eventful as the one across Catalonia. Not long after his departure from the capital his diligence was robbed.[3] Still intent on his travel plans, Mackenzie proceeded to Cordova, Seville, Cádiz, and finally Gibraltar. In the British colony Mackenzie gave up the possibility of a speedy return to New York on board an American battleship. He wanted to visit old Granada: "There was, however, a long-cherished desire still unfulfilled, which attracted me in a different direction. I was within a few days' ride of Granada, and in that name, so full of touching and heroic associations, there was a charm too strong even for my homeward yearnings" (YS, 3:7). After an unsuccessful attempt to sail from Gibraltar to Málaga, Mackenzie had no other choice than traveling overland to Granada. He finally reached it, all in all lingering there for a fortnight that was, according to him, "one of the most pleasing of my life" (YS, 3:43). In fact, unlike other travelers who stubbornly clung to the past, Mackenzie found the Granada of the present to be just as beautiful as the city of his boyhood dreams. He moved on to Ronda across the sierra, and guided by Juan Cañestro, whose wagons were carrying ice from the sierra for the coffeehouses of Algeciras, he returned to Gibraltar. He had completed his Spanish tour and was ready to sail back to New York to write his account of it.

European travel and travel writing afforded many aspiring young writers a chance to fashion in their own terms not only a literary career but also a public image. Mackenzie, like many of his contemporaries, did not miss that opportunity. He wrote his travelogue of Spain promptly and, as he recalls in The American in England, "with the same enthusiasm which attended the travels it described," but found it particularly difficult to convince a publisher to trust a dilettante in belles lettres like him.[4] In October of 1828 Irving, by then in Andalusia, wrote encouraging him in his efforts to find a publisher, and advised that, if necessary, Mackenzie himself should bring out the book.[5] At last, however, in 1829 Hilliard, Gray, Little & Wilkins of Boston undertook the first edition of A Year in

"The padre complied with becoming resignation." This robbery scene, engraved by A. Dick after a drawing by J. G. Chapman, appeared in the title page of volume 2 of *A Year In Spain* (1836). The cross, a further memento of roadside violence, reminded readers of the insecurity of Spain, which Mackenzie saw as a corollary of its disgraceful political situation. Courtesy of the Harvard College Library.

Spain, by a Young American, which met a small yet favorable reception. In the *North American Review*, for example, Willard Philips termed its author "a sprightly, sensible, well informed traveller, with great activity of observation, a good talent at narration, and not deficient in the power of presenting scenes and objects to the reader's imagination."[6] But Philips remarked, too—anticipating an objection of later reviewers—that at times Mackenzie sounded too bookish and that consequently he wrote at his best whenever he related personal occurrences. Longfellow, to whom Mackenzie had personally given a copy of the book, also commented on it. Writing to his friend at the beginning of January 1830 from Bowdoin College, the aspiring scholar revealed, "Your work has a great celebrity in these parts, and my copy—which, by the way, is the only one in town, is in great demand. People are curious about the author" (LL, 1:333).

The second edition of *A Year in Spain* came out the following year with renewed favorable comments, and soon the popularity of the book crossed the Atlantic.[7] In England John Murray decided to publish *A Year in Spain* provided that Irving edited it for the British public gratis. Irving agreed, and after revising it during the late months of 1830 he had it ready for publication in March 1831. According to Ben Harris McClary, Irving changed "a book intended for the American public into a form palatable to the developing British Victorian taste." Thus, apart from revising the work with an eye for style and toning down Mackenzie's effusive language, Irving deleted all the unnecessary encyclopedic information, removed all references that might offend British pride, and avoided passages that could be interpreted as immoral. Mackenzie in general was satisfied with the revisions.[8] If the book encountered a favorable reception in England, it was partly because its most devoted champion was Irving. "Here it is quite the fashionable book of the day, and spoken of in the highest terms in the highest circles," he wrote from the British capital. "If the Lieutenant were in London at present he would be quite a lion."[9] Likewise, in his review of the book for Murray's *Quarterly Review* Irving called *A Year in Spain* "one of the most amusing books of travels that we have read for a long time." He observed that Mackenzie rendered his descriptions of Spanish life "with the microscopic minuteness, the persevering and conscientious fidelity of a Flemish painter," yet at the same time maintained "a graphic touch, and a lively colouring about them that prevents their ever becoming tedious."[10] Not all the British critics, however, referred to the style of the book as Irving did.

Part of the critical attention to the book also focused on its fresh treatment of the subject matter, which considerably differed from the previous travel accounts of genteel travelers. Instead of merely "othering" Spain, the traveler-narrator in *A Year in Spain* shows that he is able to take on his own otherness and even share in some of the Spanish mores. "He is no pretender to high and fashionable intercourse; and does not bore us with accounts of the fêtes to which he was invited, the fine folks whom he met, or the extraordinary distinctions he received," said the reviewer in the *Literary Gazette*, who also noted Mackenzie's resolution "to make himself acquainted with Spain, and the manners and customs of its population."[11] A similar view was expressed in the pages of *Fraser's Magazine*: "National prejudices are treated with deference—national faults with commiseration—the virtues of the people he acknowledges in manful terms of commendation—he takes nothing for granted, but examines into every matter himself, and, what is not general with tourists, has a reason for every conclusion."[12] But if the good reception of *A Year in Spain* in England surely helped to boost Mackenzie's fame in the United States, there is still another factor that perhaps contributed to that even more. Following up on the success of the British edition, Ferdinand VII issued a royal edict banning *A Year in Spain* and its author from the country on the grounds that it "contained injurious expressions concerning the king and royal family in Spain, and sacrilegious mockery of her institutions and law" (SR, 1:13–14). The subversive quality of Mackenzie's account had begun to make itself manifest.

After this early acclaim, Mackenzie tried to enlarge the book with an account of his trip to Granada. The task proved more difficult than expected, but finally in 1836 Harper & Brothers issued what became the definitive three-volume third edition of *A Year in Spain*, an edition that soon generated new reactions in the United States.[13] Most reviewers, like that in the *Southern Literary Messenger*, welcomed the addition of the new volume dealing with a place that Irving's *Tales of the Alhambra* had turned into a romantic landmark.[14] But whereas the *Knickerbocker* once again focused on Mackenzie's style, especially his "graphic power and a grave humor," the *New Yorker* affirmed, "we do not hesitate to assert that no work of equal value on the institutions, manners, physical, moral, and intellectual features of the Spanish peninsula has appeared since the opening of the Nineteenth Century," concluding that if all aspiring writers wrote like him people would complain much less about the poor quality of American literature.[15] Fortunately, the *American Monthly Magazine* noted, Mackenzie's volumes on Spain had been evaluated on their own and had withstood "attempts to foist a prolific and promising writer into the same rank with Washington Irving and other established models of literature."[16] At any rate, the recognition of this promising writer did not stop, and in 1836 *A Year in Spain* was even translated into Swedish.[17] It was a demonstration that travel writing, like other literary genres from the United States, was considered good enough to stand on its own in the foreign literary marketplace.

II

In the early nineteenth century the travel book suffered from a certain lack of definition as a genre, wavering between the encyclopedic travelogues of previous decades and the impressionistic books of the new period. Mackenzie did not shape his travel account as an offshoot of Irving's sketchbook, but rather patterned it

as a travelogue that, at least formally, owed more to the didactic
tradition of the preceding century than to the rising touristic conventions of his own. While maintaining a certain descriptive detachment between subject and object typical of eighteenth-century
travel accounts, Mackenzie constantly allows room in his narrative
for his moral response as spectator. In so doing, however, he does
not succumb to the empty superficiality of overused picturesque
conventions. His informative aim is unmistakable from the beginning, as he asserts his book "originated in a desire to convey some
notion of the manners and customs of the Spanish nation" for
homebound American readers "without abandoning the comforts
and security of the fireside" (YS, 1:vii). Mackenzie transmits whatever information he may obtain about the mores, arts, and politics
of Spain, to name a few subjects, through chapters resembling formal essays that he intersperses with actual episodes of travel. Moreover, he constantly cites the observations of other travelers such as
Antillon, Laborde, and Bourgoing. These three travel books were
almost complete travel guides in themselves, including atlases,
road maps, lists of post roads, and so on. Jean François Bourgoing's
Noveau Voyage en Espagne (Paris, 1789) was translated as *Modern
State of Spain* (London, 1808) from a French edition of 1807. Alexandre de Laborde's *Itinéraire descriptif de l'Espagne* (Paris, 1808)
was translated as *A View of Spain* (London, 1809). Isidoro de Antil-
lón's *Elementos de la geografía astronómica, natural y política de
España y Portugal* (Madrid, 1808) was available in German (1815)
and French (1823) editions.

The presentation of or allusion to other texts is no doubt one of
the most important rhetorical conventions of travel writing that
Mackenzie does not disregard. Even so, his accumulation of encyclopedic information and his display of the many readings he had
done before and after his journey to Spain do not serve to analyze
Spain as a social or political theorist nor as a *philosophe*, for Mackenzie seldom engages in a dialogue with the sources he cites. Allusions to background readings simply become a strategy that
Mackenzie employs, as a beginning travel writer, to endow himself
with more authorial value before his readers. His analysis comes
from his own observations and is presented in his own voice. By
doing this, he positions himself more as participant in things Spanish and less as a passive raconteur of them. Moreover, as his
account developed toward a romanticized representation it demonstrates that the enlightened American perception of Spain had as
much to do with the revolutionary zeal still alive in travelers like

Mackenzie himself as with the rational inquisitive methods of travelers like Noah and Ticknor.

The two cities of Spain about which Mackenzie writes most extensively are Madrid and Granada, preferring the eighteenth-century encyclopedic approach employed by Ticknor rather than the impressionistic voyeurism to be used by Longfellow in *Outre-Mer*. Of the six full chapters on Madrid, for example, one is devoted to its history, architecture, institutions, and location, while another deals with its amusements. Two chapters could stand on their own as separate essay pieces. The first, on the bullfights, resembles the essay that Ticknor had published on that spectacle in the *North American Review* a few years earlier. The second, describing an execution of two criminals, adduces, as we shall see later, new evidence on the rampant violence existing in early nineteenth-century Spain as well as on the governmental way of deterring it. Mackenzie's account of his visit to Granada also employs the culturalist rhetoric of eighteenth-century travel writing and rejects romanticism. Though Mackenzie affirms that through his romantic readings on Granada he "abandoned [his] boyish imaginations to the creations of the romancer" and "contracted a desire to see that Granada which [his] fancy had been taught to picture to itself in colours so captivating," the reality he finally reproduces to his readers is far from the ideal of romance (YS, 3:37). During his visit to the palace of the Alhambra he seems more concerned with the repairs, situation, structure, quality, and materials of each hall than with their romantic associations. Like Thomas Paine in "The Crisis," Mackenzie's aim is to offer his readers "no vapours of the imagination."[18] In sum, he does not represent his trip to Granada as a romancelike experience so much as an eighteenth-century fact-gathering tour.

The essayistic chapter that offers the best example of travel writing in the intellectual discursive mode of the Enlightenment is entitled "General View of Spain," which served in both the short and enlarged editions of the book as a concluding *summa hispanica*. Using this type of generalist chapter, Mackenzie demonstrates his skillful use of major textual conventions of his genre. There, in a gesture similar to Noah's parting remarks from the Spanish border, and anticipating Caleb Cushing's reflections at the end of *Reminiscences of Spain*, Mackenzie recapitulates the different subjects discussed throughout his journey across Spain with an encyclopedic wholeness characteristic of a fireside library. The chapter contains information on geography, history, population, economy, class, gender, and race, among many other topics, but more than its breadth, I think, its importance lies in its premonitory role. Mackenzie, by way of a somewhat homilectic prose reflecting his Enlightenment views, comments on the importance of freedom for the Spanish people, and stresses the necessity of a revolution in that country to escape from the anomie in which it was enmeshed. These concluding remarks, then, not only indirectly foster revolutionary thought and present the traveler-narrator as a sort of Byronic hero; they also foreshadow the Civil War that was to shake Spain in the years immediately after his journey.

Mackenzie's representation of Spain is then an example of late Enlightenment or preromantic travel account. His representation of that nation, however, comes closer to a Painesque or Byronic revolutionary stance than to the encyclopedic, fact-gathering version of the Enlightenment of the accounts left by Noah and Ticknor. Mackenzie's standpoint demonstrates that the Enlightenment was not only about Reason, but also about republican or democratic revolutions. Accordingly, he seems to have those principles constantly in mind as he travels across the peninsula, observes its inhabitants, and reminisces about its past. It is no coincidence that many of the Spanish historical figures mentioned in *A Year in Spain* exemplify either enlightened leadership or revolutionary ideas. King Wamba, for example, was an honest sovereign for the Visigoths, and so was Abderahman III to the Arabs "for the enlightened protection [he] extended . . . to learned men" (YS, 2:127–29). Likewise, Mackenzie praises the fallen heroes Juan de Padilla and Pablo de Olavide. The former embodied the ambitions of the average Spaniards and the rising bourgeoisie against the privileges of the nobility during the reign of Charles I, while the latter represented the anticlericalism of the Age of Reason during the reign of Charles III. Despite his brief forays into past history, Mackenzie's real concern in *A Year in Spain* lies with the contemporary history of Spain that was creating and sometimes unraveling itself violently before his eyes.

The relationship that *A Year in Spain* formally manifests with the preceding generation of travel writing in the mode of Noah and Ticknor also places this book as a kind of bridge between them and the romantic representations of Irving and Longfellow. At key moments its adventurousness and exoticism intensify the imaginary component of the travel narrative and thus contribute to its reading as a popular romance of foreign lands. The Spanish settings Mackenzie presents, though generally focused on the sublimity of barren and treeless open spaces, often have touches of exoticism and pastoralism as well. Take, for instance, his description of the valley of the Manzanares, one of the summer resorts for the inhabitants of Madrid:

> Here, on the afternoon of a feast-day, entire families come out to taste the joys of the country. Seating themselves in circles under the trees, they spread in the midst such provisions as they may have brought with them, and then make a joyous repast, with the earth for a table and the sky for a canopy. This over, they dance to the music of the voice, the guitar, and the castanet, mingled with the murmurs of the rushing river; and at a late hour each seeks with a lighter heart the shelter of his habitation. (YS, 2:12–13)

In a scene reminiscent of Ticknor's repast on the spot overlooking the Guadalquivir near Cordova, Mackenzie's picturesque portrait of the merry Spaniards no doubt calls attention to a romantic view of a benign landscape in essential harmony with its inhabitants. The scene also parallels the idyllic compositions of life around Madrid—best exemplified by *La merienda a orillas del Manzanares*—that Francisco de Goya had painted in the 1780s. Mackenzie keenly captured, like the Spanish master, the delightful and repulsive facets of Spanish life in those days. Mackenzie, too, travels across Spain with a keen eye on anthropological differences between its diverse regions, thus anticipating Irving's ethnographic fascination with the Spanish Other. In addition to this, the traveler's adventures presented in *A Year in Spain* are some of the most grisly and violent in the early American representation of Spain, probably only rivaled by the anonymous *Scenes in Spain* (1837). The account Mackenzie hears about the assassination of the Bishop of Vic at the hands of the constitutionalists, the robbery of the diligence he lives through, and the execution he witnesses in Madrid are but a few of the episodes in this travelogue with embedded codes of popular fiction and romance.

Surely American travel writers felt at ease to experiment with or depart from established literary conventions and genres, including their own, once they found themselves away from home. But most important for them, as Terry Caesar has noted, is the fact that they "can appear to be on an ideological holiday" in a foreign land.[19] This is true of Mackenzie's narrative, for along with the traveler's incidents and the geographical and anthropological exoticism, probably the most important aspect of his representation of Spain is the subversive role that his travel book intended to play in both Spain and the United States during the early nineteenth-century. As it was pointed out earlier in this study, travel writers could fashion themselves in their texts and adopt new personas along different parameters of race, gender, class, and even nation. Mackenzie adopts this rhetorical strategy and thus neither appears before the reader as a genteel Ticknorite hobnobbing wealthy and influential personages nor represents himself as an amateur ethnographer or religious pilgrim, as years later Irving and Longfellow respectively did in their Spanish travelogues. Instead, during his sojourn in Spain Mackenzie nearly takes up the role of a young Byronic hero who, Carwin-like, roams the bridle roads of the Iberian Peninsula glad to have assumed a new Spanish identity. In that period, as James Buzard has noted, Byronic gestures became a rhetorical convention, a trademark of antitourism whereby travelers could endow the roads beaten by other travelers with new experiences. Furthermore, with the demise of the aristocratic Grand Tour, being Byron also had a democratizing effect because it was feeling rather than class that made travelers feel exclusive.[20] According to the recommendation that Mackenzie makes in the preface, all prospective travelers to Spain should erase their identity. They must go native and temporarily adopt the religion and customs of the local people, stifling whenever necessary the feelings of disgust they might experience. Noting Mackenzie's openness to mingle, unprejudiced, with all social classes in Spain, the *Southern Review* in its review of *A Year in Spain* affirmed that "a traveller of this character is precisely the one to give us a fair account."[21] The skillful use of several rhetorical conventions thus suggests that the epistemological contact Mackenzie proposes surely came to be considered, at least at the textual level, as an equitable representation halfway between history and romance.

The realization of an ideological period bracketed off from the rest of the travel writer's existence proves, however, rather difficult, as cultural and political discourses, constraints, and allegiances from home continue exerting their influence upon the traveler. Whereas on the one hand Mackenzie's assumed nativism sometimes appears to be a source of humor as the Spaniards mistake him for a Catholic Irishman, on the other hand it is also a threat to cultural purity. For a representative of the American republic in a foreign country the denial of one's own identity and the temporal appropriation of foreign mores might in itself be seen by some readers as an act that could disturbingly result in cultural dissidence. To counter a misreading of his nativist strategy, Mackenzie therefore highlights the Americanness of his travel narrative at key points. From the Catalonian coast, for example, he descries with pride a ship "displaying the stars and stripes of that banner which has never been branded with dishonour, nor sullied by strong-handed injustice" (YS, 1:33). Similarly, he finishes book 2 describing an American battleship moored in Gibraltar that makes the other vessels in the port look minuscule. For a traveler as imbued with revolutionary impetus as Mackenzie, there was indeed no fear of cultural and political degradation, for common sense clearly dictated which political system was more perfect. As another compatriot traveler who was equally subversive expressed it, the American traveling in Spain was "in little danger of losing his republican notions by breathing a despotic atmosphere; on the contrary, the misery and misrule constantly before his eyes, make him thank God more and more every day that he was born a freeman" (SS, 122). The American exceptionalist discourse embedded in these travel writings was thus a sound platform from which travel writers could assert their national identity as well as their cultural authority.

Mackenzie's travel book apears to be still more politically subversive when regarded within the context of Spain itself. While its criticism of the crown and the altar exhibits the type of Enlightenment rhetoric used by his predecessors Noah and Ticknor to uphold liberal values in their travel writings, Mackenzie stretches the decorum of Enlightenment belles lettres beyond these authors and, with Painesque acerbity, comes close to personal diatribe. To do that, for example, Mackenzie overturns one of the conventions of the Enlightenment travel book, the author's dedication.[22] At the beginning of the book he mocks Ferdinand VII as "His Satanic Majesty," and later terms him a "bigot and besotted son of sensuality" (YS, 3:115).[23] Similarly, he portrays the heir apparent, Don Carlos, as a creepy figure whose "ghastly grin" frightens the multitudes (YS, 2:13). These and other comments, as I mentioned earlier, turned Mackenzie into a persona non grata in Spain, but he did not take these intimidations seriously and even returned to the peninsula in 1834. In *Spain Revisited* he even reproduced the royal decree banning his book (SR, 1:375–76). By and large, this was a Byronic gesture expressing defiance toward the Spanish authorities and pride in his own militancy. Mackenzie's *A Year in Spain*, whether in its role as a political instrument denouncing the ancien régime or perhaps as a text attempting to reform the course of events in Spain, emerged as a transgressive book whose high-flown anti-absolutist attacks must have made the domestic republican reader nod in affirmation with its author.

III

No doubt Mackenzie entered Spain with his share of republican prejudices regarding the political system of Spain, but no doubt, too, it was only when he traveled within the kingdom that he came to realize fully the pernicious consequences of such a system. Centuries of royal despotism, national isolation, and economic mismanagement, together with the recent Napoleonic invasion of the peninsula and the later repression of the liberal opposition to the ancien régime, had produced a state of political disintegration whose most clear manifestation was violence. Many travel books on Spain contain several icons pointing to the existence of violence in that country, the most noticeable being the numerous roadside wooden crosses erected as mementos. Mackenzie, however, whether unsatisfied with those symbols, or eager for a more hyperbolic description of violence, added another powerful icon to the representation of Spain: the gallows. By describing execution scenes carefully, he not only augmented the existing myth of Spanish lawlessness and insecurity but emphasized that these took their toll on the bodies of real Spaniards. Violence in Spain was not anonymous; it had names and faces, and went far beyond the bones Noah and Ticknor had unearthed in the Spanish fields.

The representation of scaffold scenes, political violence, and roadside bloodshed is not the chief objective of A Year in Spain but rather a theme that Mackenzie subordinates to his more important strategies of political subversion. The book describes many instances of both political and common violence that Mackenzie either witnessed or heard about. There is a naturalistic quality to these scenes that makes them a gripping means to bring home a strong political message to his audience. Mackenzie listens to the first macabre crime story in Spain during his journey from Barcelona to Valencia. A fellow traveler, a former constitutional militiaman who had been exiled in Marseilles for a year, relates the assassination of the Bishop of Vic. This prelate, who allegedly was a liberal but in fact always remained a royalist, could not be openly executed by the constitutionalists, and thus they sent a band of armed robbers to seize and slay him by the road. The story constitutes for Mackenzie a clear example of the brutalization of the Spaniards, and, more importantly, of their continuous reversal of roles. There the upholders of democracy commit the same abhorrent political crimes of their absolutist opponents, and thus Mackenzie concludes his comments on the episode with an enlightened maxim: "I am unwilling to believe that the happiness of a nation, any more than that of an individual, can be promoted by crime" (YS, 1:55). However opposed he might be to absolute monarchy and its repressive politics, Mackenzie realized—as Thomas Paine did after witnessing the horrors of the postrevolutionary terror in France—that the violent overthrow of the ancien régime by the revengeful masses would not be enough to restore order and peace in Spain.

Mackenzie not only denounced the religious and political persecution of those in office; he also focused, in an indirect manner, on how the effects of the unconstitutional situation of Spain impinged upon the powerless common citizen. While he did not directly indoctrinate his American readers on the evils of European despotism, he indirectly made them feel it in their bones through his allusion to the lack of law and order in Spain. The robbery of the stagecoach in which he was traveling became for Mackenzie, to use Frederick Douglass's term, a sort of "blood-stained gate"[24] to several other painful scenes he was to witness in Spain. This incident opens as a very anticlimactic contretemps for Mackenzie, who, lulled into sleep by the movement of the diligence during his overnight journey to Valencia, had begun to fancy himself close to New York. No sooner, however, had the highwaymen stopped the coach than he was abruptly returned to the desolate road in the outskirts of Amposta where the robbery was taking place. Mackenzie narrates that from the window of the cabriolet he could record all the particulars of the robbery, and especially the way in which the coachman and Pepe, the young postillion, were picked to be murdered in cold blood because they had recognized some of their assailants. This ghastly scene that the traveler's gaze encounters is far more ironic and bitter than the picturesque views Irving and Longfellow are later to represent from their balconies in Granada and Madrid, respectively. The latter represent, in a sense, the progressive retreat from the cruel realities of Spain occurring in the American representation of Spain. The sour testimony of the subversive traveler will shift slowly toward the hedonistic voyeurism and quest for pleasure of the romantic tourist.

Mackenzie describes the whole episode with an iconography drawn from gothic fiction and popular criminal literature. The late time of the day, the lonely milieu, and the conjecture that the robbers might have been spying on the travelers during their last stop at an inn intensify the suspense. This was emphasized, incidentally, in the 1836 edition of *A Year in Spain*, which includes an engraving of the robbers as the frontispiece of book 1. The tragic development of the event, too, escalates by degrees. First, deaf to the coachman's pleadings for mercy, one of the robbers hits him in the head with a huge stone until he lies agonizing. Then, the robbers plunder the passengers, sparing only by chance the cabriolet that Mackenzie was sharing with a priest. Finally, another member of the gang stabs the young postillion several times:

> My own eyes seemed spell-bound, for I could not withdraw them from the cruel spectacle, and my ears were more sensible than ever. Though the windows at the front and sides were still closed, I could distinctly hear each stroke of the murderous knife, as it entered its victim; it was not a blunt sound, as of a weapon that meets with positive resistance, but a hissing noise . . . This moment was the unhappiest of my life. (YS, 1:76)

The interpolation of the aggressors' hollerings with the sobs and screams of the two victims, all related by a petrified peeping traveler, create an eerie atmosphere of gothic romance that nevertheless cannot displace the realism of the account.

Mackenzie concentrates extensively upon the description of this episode as it is not only the first robbery to which he fell prey but the one displaying the most vicious brutality he had ever seen. So meticulously does he dwell on the crudity of this incident that in comparing it to his account in book 2 of the holdup of his diligence outside Madrid months later, the latter nearly strikes the reader as a piece of comic relief. For one thing, on that occasion there are no victims, and for another Mackenzie is, no doubt, trying to tone down a much too negative representation of a country he liked despite its misfortunes. In that case he even finds some justification for the criminal activities of Felipe Cano, the leader of the robbers, who seems to epitomize the fortunes of many men in Spain. A former guerrilla soldier, constitutionalist, and Freemason escaped from a penitentiary, Cano can only exist outside the law and against it. The violent Spain he represents, Mackenzie seems to suggest, is but another side of the political degeneration of the country.

The narration of the first robbery surely generated multiple responses from the fireside American audiences Mackenzie was addressing, which must have ranged from sympathy for the murdered boy to anger at the political system that permitted so cruel an act to happen. To produce these effects, Mackenzie stretched his account and remarked that none of the travelers who subsequently passed by the scene of the crime stopped to succor any of the victims for fear of being questioned about the murder. Likewise, several chapters later he resumes where he left off and mentions that the coachman finally died after many days in agony. His appeal to republican audiences to understand the seriousness of the political situation in Spain is thus accomplished not only by appealing to their enlightened reason—which, as I have already mentioned, he also does—but by calling upon their sentiments.

Thus, the narration of the nocturnal robbery near Amposta and its bloody dénouement, appearing as early as in the third chapter of the book, sets the tone strongly for a representation of Spain where sheer physicality seems to be the dominant key. By this sheer physicality I do not refer, however, to the traveler's manful endurance of certain trials in the peninsular roads nor to his fulfillment of hedonistic wishes in medieval Spanish locales. Granted, these conventions of travel writing contribute in a noticeable manner to gendering Mackenzie's Spanish narrative as well, but what I nevertheless consider to be more appreciable in A Year in Spain, especially since it strengthens its subversiveness, is the physicality of pain written on the body of the Spaniards. Mackenzie, who had been used to the rigors of the Navy for more than a decade when he traveled in Spain, evinces a sensitive eye for all aspects of pain, and thus not only focuses on murdered people, but also on other Spaniards who suffer, ranging from the beggars and the blind in Madrid to the convicts carrying out their life sentences under abject conditions in the penitentiary in Málaga.

Whether he was politically motivated by sentimental or reformist impulses, or attracted by morbid drives toward violence and bloodshed, Mackenzie turns the representation of the body being subjected to violence into the most salient aspect of his travel narrative. In many respects, it is not implausible even to suggest that his strategy shares into the emerging interest and discussion of corporal discipline in antebellum America that Richard Brodhead has cogently examined.[25] Later texts like Richard Henry Dana's Two Years Before the Mast (1840), Frederick Douglass's Narrative of the Life of Frederick Douglass (1845), and Melville's White-Jacket (1850) publicized the issue more and in specifically American contexts. A Year in Spain, though situating it in a non-American context, becomes however no less participant in this debate over disciplinary measures. Besides, we should not forget that the third edition of the book appeared in 1836, a date closer to the above-mentioned texts, and also that in 1842 Mackenzie found himself involved in one of the most notorious cases of corporal discipline in the Navy, in the light of which the punishments in A Year in Spain surely gain new significance.

Just as he does with the robberies and roadside assassinations,

Mackenzie deliberately presents the scaffold scenes as instances of depictions of violence that are illustrative of the subversive and political charge of his work. It is no coincidence that book I of *A Year in Spain* concludes quite significantly with a chapter fully devoted to the most conspicuous spectacle of physical punishment: a public execution. Mackenzie, almost as if trying to offer a closing statement about the dismal state of affairs in Spain, describes the hanging of two criminals at the Plaza de la Cebada in Madrid with the same exhaustiveness he employs in his narration of the robbery near Amposta. He had already been present at a public execution in southern France that, as he observes, filled him wih a "feeling of oppression and abasement, of utter disgust," but the realization that "a scene of such powerful excitement could not fail to elicit the unrestrained feelings of the multitude, and to bring the national character into strong relief" compels him to linger there (YS, 1:250). On this occasion, the gloominess of the climate—the execution takes place on a sunless and chilly winter day—together with the symbolic quality of the actual setting of the hangings—the square is the usual butchers' market with slaughterhouses nearby—mesmerize the traveler's gaze and contribute to presenting the gallows scene at the Plaza de la Cebada almost as a locale of gothic romance that in many respects bears strong similarities with "The Market-Place" chapter in Nathaniel Hawthorne's *The Scarlet Letter* (1850).

It is of course difficult to discern to what degree the introduction of such gothic elements is a rhetorical or perhaps a marketing convention. What seems certain, however, is that the inclusion of this episode, in addition to enhacing the gothicism in the book, gives Mackenzie the chance to comment on the grandiose machinery of absolutist power and retribution that Michel Foucault has so poignantly dissected in *Discipline and Punish*. Public corporal punishments and executions, Foucault has shown us, did not redress crimes, but rather exercised terror and asserted royal authority by means of a visible and complex ritual that effectively displayed power relations to the population.[26] Mackenzie describes in detail all the paraphernalia of this ritual, beginning with the variegated multitude, continuing with the numerous soldiers, and finally focusing one by one on the culprits as they approach the gallows accompanied by many monks.

For Mackenzie the most dramatic aspect of the execution is not the capital punishment itself, for in fact he seems to approve of it as a just retribution for crimes. What baffles him is the bestial manner in which the discipline is effected, with the executioner sitting

The execution of Doña Mariana de Pineda in Granada, engraving by R. Hinshel-wood after a drawing by J. G. Chapman for the frontispiece to the anonymous *Scenes in Spain* (1837). The executioner, and above all the figure of the priest charge this gallows scene with a lurid atmosphere of gothic romance similar to that manifest in the hangings that Alexander Slidell Mackenzie narrated in *A Year in Spain*. Courtesy Biblioteca, Universitat Pompeu Fabra (Barcelona).

on the shoulders of each malefactor to precipitate the hanging. To all of this, the curious observers respond, as was expected from them, in awe. "The conduct of the crowd was singularly solemn. As each victim plunged downward from the gallows," Mackenzie observes, "there was a tremulous murmur upon every lip, ejaculating a short prayer for the peace of the guilty soul which was then entering upon eternity" (YS, 1:261). But the aftermath of the execution is the most melancholy. As the crowd disperses, Mackenzie abandons the square "in a state of mind which none need envy," adding,

> I experienced a return of the same sickly feeling of disgust with mankind and myself with which I had once risen from the reading of Rousseau's *Confessions*. Surely there can be nothing in such a spectacle to promote morality, nothing to make us either better or happier: a spectacle which serves but to create despondency, and to array man in enmity with his condition. (YS, 1:261)

With the inclusion of his trip to Granada in book 3 of *A Year in Spain*, Mackenzie again touched upon the issue of capital punishment. Although in that city he was not a spectator of the whole machinery of power at the actual moment of punishment, he saw the result of another hanging a few hours after its conclusion, and tried to convey his own impressions by highlighting the four interrelated motifs that, according to James Buzard, constitute the "authenticity effect" of travel writing.[27] Mackenzie describes the Square of Elvira as he found it empty of crowds, onlookers, and sentinels:

> Nothing interrupted the solitude of the place except the triumphal column that commemorated some exploit of the conquest, and the heavy upright posts and cross-bar whence depended the fatal cords by which the criminals were suspended; being fastened close together, two for each victim, the bodies touched and displaced each other at each instant, yielding as the breeze swept by. Their dress was the ordinary garb of the peasant, put on and buttoned as if to go forth to labour; the feet of one were partly concealed by a sandal; the other had heavy shoes, the nails of which were still bright; their hands, bound tightly beside them, were horny and toil-worn; and their faces, though livid and blackened, wore no peculiar expression of malignity. This singular blending of associations of ordinary life with the repose and still silence of death, overcame the mind with gloom and confusion. (YS, 3:135)

This passage, paradoxical as it may seem, tries to evoke the sublime "stillness" experienced by the traveler, while reinforcing the "nonutility" of the sight, which seems to be rather accentuated for its inspirational purposes. Moreover, the excerpt also stresses the scene's "saturation" with political and social significance, and at the same time reveals its inherent "picturesqueness" by composing a whole out of all the different parts in it. With certain irony, Mackenzie indirectly calls attention to the juxtaposition of the past glories of Spain—symbolized by the monument—with the present evils afflicting the country—personified by the robbers. The tilting corpses hanging from the beam under the gray sky of Granada become icons of dispossession and powerlessness, and at the same time seem to reiterate visually the lifeless state of the country. These dead bodies create a somber, quasi-Poesque scenario which finds a correlate in Goya's series of etchings begun in 1810 and entitled *Los Desastres de la Guerra*, where the Spanish master represented the body submitted to the most grueling torments and mutilations.

There is, moreover, an important implication to be drawn from the two executions that Mackenzie describes in his Spanish travelogue, for just as those executions allow him to represent the sway of royal power over common criminals, so they help him to introduce the issue of the punishment of political culprits. In other words, Mackenzie showed to his readers that in Spain the execution of liberals and criminals had no boundary whatsoever, both being united by the same scaffold, even sometimes by the same executioner. Thus, for example, he mentions that the dead malefactors he saw in Granada were hanging from the same spot where some Freemasons had been executed several months before. Likewise, in the Plaza de la Cebada in Madrid he observes that "along this very street the purest and bravest of Spanish patriots had been drawn to execution on a hurdle," and that he had probably seen "the very executioner who had ridden upon the shoulders of Riego!" (YS, 1:262).

As the examples discussed so far illustrate, in *A Year in Spain* Mackenzie shows to what degree the body in Spain can be punished, destroyed, and literally disposed of. Indirectly, too, he suggests to his readers that on seeing the hanged and murdered bodies they stand before historical beings, before people who make of Spanish history something palpable and known of which neither they nor the traveler can escape. He is reluctant to escape from this ugly contemporary scene into the romantic impressionism that the later travelogues of Irving and Longfellow displayed as those authors embarked upon transcendental epiphanies in the Alhambra. Thus, aware that there is no retreat into a historicized representation of Spain, Mackenzie is more willing to see its sadness, evil, and tragedy.

IV

The historical discourse Mackenzie highlights in *A Year in Spain*, then, is not about the lessons of the past, as it was in Noah and Ticknor, nor a flight to the glorious medieval past or a stay in an eternal primitivistic present, as it will be in Irving, nor again a retreat into idealistic subjectivity as Longfellow will make it. The emphasis on the body in *A Year in Spain* is important in so far as it underscores the fact that the traveler is seeing history in the making. Accordingly, rather than furnishing his readers a glamorized conception of Spanish history that highlighted its past glory, Mackenzie prefers to stress to them its stark contemporaneity. Drawing on the evils of Spain, this seemingly pragmatic appraisal of things Spanish adumbrated the decay of Spanish imperialism and the rise of Anglo-American rule that certain historical discourses of the time were spreading. The transcendental optimism of Longfellow and Irving eventually was to supersede this historical, negative, and pessimistic romantic view of Spain given by Mackenzie, and instead of inscribing bodies upon which suffering, repression, and violence are written in a noticeable manner, Longfellow and Irving were to capture subjects denoting difference and picturesqueness.

But just as Mackenzie conceptualizes the body as a locus of a great deal of corporal suffering, so he represents it as a place under constant surveillance. The violent expression of royal power he saw taking shape on the gallows becomes in those cases a more subtle domestication of the soul through what Foucault has termed "technologies of power." With the demise of the liberal revolution in Spain and the reinstatement of the ancien régime, the repressive apparatus of the absolutists sent many constitutionalists to exile in England, America, France, and North Africa. Those who remained in the peninsula had to submit to a broad program of political cleansing and policing, regardless of their political or nonpolitical activities, after which they were considered ideologically fit. Once a citizen was "purified," he could become "indefinite" and be able to hold a public office. The problem with that, Mackenzie explains, voicing the concerns of some of the people he met, was that these people were in fact never to be offered nor given a public job, and thus they would remain for years in a sort of existential limbo.

Describing several of these office holders, Mackenzie suggests that this state of indefiniteness to which the crown exposes many of its subjects is even worse than death itself. To begin with, many "unpurified" never attained the status of *indefinidos* because they could not afford to bribe the corrupt tribunals who evaluated their cases. In short, these tribunals too often would try to find some type of impediment as a pretext to hold some control over the citizens. Consequently, for Mackenzie these victims of the technology of power whose social status was not defined represented very nearly what Orwell in our century was to call unpersons, a group of disenfranchised and disempowered bodies. Indeed, the shift from tragedy to comedy that Foucault sees as inherent to the technologizing of power is true of all of these people that Mackenzie encountered. The way in which Mackenzie describes how his landlord, Don Valentín Todohueso, and his language professor, Don Diego Redondo, live and make ends meet, reiterates the drollness and grotesqueness, at the same time, of this horde of nondefined people whose plight Mackenzie was trying to make visible to his audience. And if perhaps there is nothing comic in their representation, at least we could say that Mackenzie presents them as tragicomic figures trying to dodge the disciplinary rules that constantly maintain them in a rut.

In Seville Mackenzie meets another of these individuals kept in this state of political purgatory, an army officer whose "cheekbones and mustaches of black and gray . . . were quite as hollow and as crestfallen as those of Don Quijote" (YS, 2:189). In spite of having remained loyal to the crown throughout the last political events of Spain, Mackenzie notes, this man had been declared *indefinido* and left unable to sustain his family economically. Mackenzie pitifully concludes, "He was evidently a poor officer, a very poor officer" (YS, 2:189). There is, however, a comic note verging the grotesque in the account, since in a nearly Kafkaesque situation, the officer is waiting for orders that never come, and in the meantime he and his wife and children have to live off the charity of local convents. Quite symbolically, too, Mackenzie places the representation of this man after his own return from a visit to the Roman ruins of Itálica. The destitution he saw in the dilapidated Roman ruins finds a correlate in "the threadbare dress of the veteran, his meager countenance, the contending sense of pride and poverty there expressed, and the tearful eye that proclaimed the triumph of the last" (YS, 2:189).

Mackenzie's appeal to sentimentality in his portrayal of Spaniards like this hunger-stricken officer, however, seems to be at odds with the bodily realism that he employs in other sections of the book. It situates, in fact, his representation of Spain in a paradox, for whereas on the one hand the Spaniards are nearly seen as bodies, as Others circumscribed to their physical state—and therefore impossible to commune with the traveler's self—on the other hand, especially in the description of the indefinite citizens, he presents them as people not only of flesh and bones but also with their own voices and concerns. By sympathizing with them, Mackenzie attempts to transcend the boundary between the Other and the traveler's self. Albeit perhaps somewhat condescendingly, he does advocate a shared humanity beyond cultural differences, for a connection between people suffering both in Spain and the United States. The story of José, the twelve-year-old orphan who carries the traveler's luggage in Aranjuez, is a further illustration of his sentimental appeal for political ends, for he explains that the young boy never knew who his father was, and his mother was killed before his eyes by paramilitary royalist volunteers. Mackenzie, however, carries his point home in a final assessment: "Jose could not tell whether this murder had been instigated by religious or political fanaticism, or by revengeful jealousy; it was enough for him that they had killed his mother" (YS, 2:54).

Mackenzie's sentimental project, then, is in a sense a universalizing one, for he is denying otherness through making subjective sentimental contact with others. In its own way *A Year in Spain* was strengthening the social feelings between Spaniards and Americans during a period in which neither nation knew much about the other. Mackenzie was using sentimentality not only as an appeal to the reason and feelings of his domestic readers but as a political tool that might bring about social change. Just as the abolitionists were beginning to combat slavery through sentimentalism, Mackenzie perhaps was hopeful that his book could play a similar role against the human bondage brought about by absolutism. The sentimentalism of *A Year in Spain* is then politically motivated, and posits views that Mackenzie reinforced in *Spain Revisited*. In his second Spanish book he continued portraying the violence in which the country was immersed, except that in that case the cause of it was not Ferdinand VII, but the factional dispute between Carlists and Cristinos.

In fact, in the postscript to his "General View of Spain" added to the enlarged edition of *A Year in Spain*, it seems as though Mackenzie astonishingly reverses all the liberal political views he had manifested in the first edition, as he expresses his predilection for Don Carlos's cause in the Civil War. At the time he was writing the postscript, Don Carlos's followers had been waging war on the liberals for three years, and the fate of their campaign seemed favorable. Thus, Mackenzie affirms, "In the interests of humanity we desire the triumph of the only party under which Spain may again become tranquil" (YS, 3:311). This statement, which at a first reading might seem to be an enlightened rational maxim, is rather a more practical thought motivated by sentimentalism and by having in mind all the victims with a name he had seen falling during his travels in Spain. The subversive Painesque stance toward the problems of Spain that I described before as characteristic of *A Year in Spain* continues to be present, yet with an undercurrent of revolutionary disenchantment through the realization that neither a long civil war nor a bloody revolution would contribute to the well-being of the Spaniards.

When the Duyckincks observed, some time after Mackenzie's death, that in his two Spanish travel books "Spain, always a theme fruitful in the picturesque, loses nothing of its peculiar attractiveness in his hands," they may have had in mind Mackenzie's poignant representation of Spain. Instead, however, they preferred to emphasize that he traveled "as Irving, Inglis, Ford, and many others have done, with a constant eye to Gil Blas and Don Quixote."[28] And while this view of Mackenzie's representation of Spain is partially true, it neglects, I think, the fact that he also kept a constant eye on the violent side of the country and that one of his intentions was to re-create it in front of the domestic reader's hearth. It is possible, I think, to speculate that Mackenzie's *A Year in Spain* was successful in appealing strongly to the sentiment of its readers, even though perhaps it did not attain its subversive goal. At any rate, Mackenzie's account certainly was an indirect contribution to the mythology of the romantic voyage to Spain and thus, even though the banditti and the highway murders were soon to become things of the past, many later American travelers in Spain kept writing about them for a long time as quintessential elements of the Spanish tour.

5

Between Oriental Past and Ethnographic Present: Washington Irving and the Romancing of Tattered Spaniards

OF ALL THE ANTEBELLUM AMERICAN TRAVEL WRITERS IN SPAIN, WASH-ington Irving enjoyed the longest and most fruitful stay in that country. It was the longest because his two sojourns, from February 1826 until August 1829 and from July 1842 until August 1846, amounted to nearly seven years. It was the most prolific because its resulting materials virtually monopolized the fictional and nonfictional representation of Spain in the United States for nearly the rest of the century. Compared to Washington Irving, the other American travel writers examined in this study may seem to have had short-lived outbursts of interest in Spain. None stayed in the country for more than a year, and in terms of literary output only Mackenzie rivaled Irving with his two voluminous Spanish travelogues. Yet, these other authors' representations of Spain should not be approached as texts inevitably overshadowed by Irving's production, but rather ought to be regarded as texts that helped contemporary readers prefigure, contextualize, complement, and sometimes even challenge the contents of Irving's Spanish books.

No doubt Irving's literary achievement stands out quantitatively among his other compatriots who also sought inspiration in things Spanish. "Altogether on Spain Irving wrote some three thousand pages and approximately one million words, amounting to about one third of his total writings," Stanley Williams has computed, adding that "although he is still known as the traditional interpreter in American literature of old England, he devoted far more space and effort to his books on Spain."[1] Between his entering the Iberian Peninsula at nearly age forty-three and his death at Sunnyside at seventy-six, Irving's involvement with things Spanish produced, in addition to miscellaneous contributions to newspapers and magazines, *Life and Voyages of Christopher Columbus* (1828),

A Chronicle of the Conquest of Granada (1829), *Voyages and Discoveries of the Companions of Columbus* (1831), *Tales of the Alhambra* (1832), *Legends of the Conquest of Spain* (1835), *Wolfert's Roost* (1855), and the posthumous *Spanish Papers and Other Miscellanies* (1866).[2] With *The Alhambra*, Spain became once and for all subject to a popular romantic vision in American travel writing, but Irving's was a reactionary rather than a radical romanticism. As he began writing his Spanish travel book he had to confront the dilemma of whether to voice the appalling truths he had discovered there, or ignore them. He chose to ignore them by constructing Spain in terms of a grandiose medieval past bound to a permanently primitive present peopled with tattered hidalgos in the timeless setting of the Alhambra. The choice gave him and his readers a far prettier image of the country than the grim one of former travel books. Spain became a textualized paradise to which one could pleasantly flee.

Irving's representation of Spain can be conceived as a progressive attempt to articulate his romantic, ethnographic, touristic, and historical view of that country through such diverse genres as travel book, biography, mock epic, and sketchbook. Here I will not endeavor to discuss, however, whether the cycle of Irving's Spanish works, and more specifically those written before his return to the United States in 1832, manifests a self-conscious turn to romance and to the romantic exploration of the self, as Jeffrey Rubin-Dorsky sees it, or whether it constitutes, according to William L. Hedges, "the gradual stifling of imagination in one single stock response."[3] Instead, the main concern of this chapter will be the culmination of Irving's personal involvement with Spain in his emblematic Spanish travel book, *The Alhambra*, where, by posing as an amateur ethnographer-folklorist, he valorizes and historicizes his narration of the Other in a way that permits him to escape a direct confrontation with the here-and-now that travelers before him had faced. Indeed, to approach *The Alhambra* as an ethnography can tell us something different about Irving's representation of Spain from the usual psychobiographical interpretations focused on his personal anxieties. In this chapter I will argue that Geoffrey Crayon, the traveling storyteller, fashions himself as a cultural anthropologist doing ethnographic fieldwork in a subculture of the Spanish society, among the "ragged community" inhabiting the Moorish palace, and that the final result of his stay in that pre-Malinowskian period was not, of course, the type of objective ethnographic monograph we are accustomed to today, but an androgynous travel book that represented a permanently primitive part of the country and elevated it to the category of romantic retreat. Wavering between history and romance in a text liable to be read as an ethnographic account, Irving makes the palace of the Alhambra stand for the whole country, and thus implies that Spain—or at least Andalusia—is a domain where one may seek refuge from the forces of reform and change.

Like the other texts discussed in *Between History and Romance*, Irving's travel account touches upon issues of representation that encroach public and private matters such as the construction of the traveler's self and the narration of the foreign nation. Irving carefully capitalized on the mystique of a last—and almost geographically lost—community of individuals frozen in time not only to render a textually mediated representation of Spain but also to explore the idea of a pleasurable site of exile for a romantic artist like himself. This chapter will therefore comprise several sections that account for the interrelation of such issues. It explores the biographical and literary factors that triggered Irving's interest in things Spanish; likewise, it also focuses on the rationale of his travel itinerary as well as on the process of composition and reception of *The Alhambra*. Furthermore, it outlines the rhetorical conventions of travel writing that Irving employed to charge his text with the discourse of romance, a discourse that resorts to exotic and gothic elements as much as to the gendering of travel, and yet becomes truly engaging when Irving presents himself carrying out tasks similar to today's ethnographic fieldwork in Granada. Irving's strategy gave him the image of a diligent folklorist, and also helped him to construct an ethnographic romance that represents a timeless community virtually untouched by the changes of contemporary political and economic history. I will argue, howewer, that despite the apparent neglect of contemporary issues, some of them indeed surface in the narrative, albeit rather abstrusely and, when they do, are treated with doses of humor and mild satire. Irving indeed blended the discourses of history and romance, although he gave much more emphasis to the latter; he did so under strong personal motivations, in a cathartic manner, for he never intended to pry into Spanish affairs as deeply and crudely as other travelers.

I

Travel writers often approach otherness through a subtle textualization of the geography and people they encounter. Their textual appropriation of otherness, however, begins on many occasions long before the journey proper, and thereby it eventually causes a feeling of belatedness. Irving had been interested in Spain before he traveled there and implanted its romantic representation in the United States with *The Alhambra*. He had been familiar with its history and literature for many years. In his childhood he had been mesmerized by the tales in *The Arabian Nights* and by narratives of Spanish discovery abridged for children in popular anthologies.[4] Likewise, in *The Alhambra* he reminisces that during his boyhood "on the banks of the Hudson" he "pored over the pages of old Gines Pérez de Hyta's apocryphal but chivalresque history of the civil wars of Granada" (A, 39).[5] No doubt the belatedness one experienced before setting out might be a genuine, almost childlike emotion, but no doubt, too, it had a potential rhetorical force that in the long run travel writers like Irving knew how to harness. For the American traveler therefore to write about Spain meant rewriting one's own readings on that country.

Even though Irving received some romantic notions of Spain through childhood readings and foreign authors like Lesage and Florian, he seriously began to dig the rich ores of Spanish Golden Age literature when he was in France in 1824. There he became very fond of the comedies of contemporary dramatist Leandro Fernández de Moratín, but his favorite authors were the playwright Calderón de la Barca and Miguel de Cervantes (JIII, 692–707). The latter, in particular, as we saw in chapter 2, became later a major source of his ideas about Spain. Irving admired Cervantes so much that he even considered writing a biography of him. Moreover, during his Spanish travels Irving likened himself to Cervantes's knighthero. It was in Spain, however, where Irving undertook a working textualization of otherness by way of reading Spanish and Moslem history *in situ*. Once he had settled in Madrid, Irving read and collected—assisted by his brother Peter—a great deal of material on the history of the Moorish kingdom at the library of Obadiah Rich and in other institutions of the capital.[6] Moreover, after the completion of *Life and Voyages of Christopher Columbus*, for which he had to rummage various libraries in Madrid, he began to have spare time to do more readings. Finally, in Granada he paid sporadic visits to the Jesuits' library to read old parchment-bound chronicles. Like an ethnographer on the field, Irving did as much research as he could, left Madrid with many notes in his saddlebags, and continued jotting down information from occasional readings done throughout his southern tour. His textual construction of Spain thus became a cumulative process where history and romance mingled with the descriptive and inscriptive discourse of the amateur anthropologist.

Not all of Irving's prior notions of Spain, however, were strictly based on the rhetoric of history and romance. They were also indebted to other travelers, their narratives, and even their advice. He read at least two standard travel books on Spain, Henry Swinburne's *Travels Through Spain in the Years 1775 and 1776* (London, 1787) and Alexandre de Laborde's *A View of Spain* (London, 1809), that described the country in the discourses of the Age of Reason. Moreover, in April 1819 he met Ticknor in London. The future scholar had just arrived from Portugal, and it is quite probable that he exchanged with his compatriot his general views on Spain, and on Granada in particular. Thus, before going to Spain Irving was more aware of its past through romances, novels, and poetry, than of its present through contemporary accounts. His representation of Spain then arguably constitutes a fresh start, for on the one hand he was virtually unaware of what other American travel writers had published before him, and on the other hand he refused whatever little he knew. Ticknor might have influenced him, but there are no traces of that in *The Alhambra*. Likewise, if he later on enjoyed reading and editing Mackenzie's *A Year in Spain* during 1830 and 1831, the ugly scenes it contained certainly did not make him change his mind about the charming Spain he depicted in his Spanish sketchbook of 1832. If anything, Mackenzie's book must have motivated him to create a counterimage where otherness would be seen through the eyes of the historian-romancer turned amateur ethnographer. That is, a counterimage that consisted in romancing the picturesqueness of the ragged Spaniards in order to create a representation of Spain placed beyond the pressures of contemporary history.

The early textual connections that travel writers allegedly hold with the countries they visit become more often than not a rhetorical convention behind which the true motivations of travel lie hidden. Irving's first visit to Spain was in fact motivated more by personal circumstances than by strict belletristic interests. He traveled there at the invitation of Alexander Everett, then American Minister plenipotentiary in Madrid, to serve as diplomatic attaché in the American legation. Everett commissioned him to translate the first volume of a collection of Columbian papers that Martín Fernández de Navarrete had recently published. For the first time, a Spanish scholar had been granted royal permission to consult and transcribe original documents related to the discovery of the New World unknown until then, and Everett felt that those documents should be made available to the American public. Irving, worried in those days by the grim pecuniary situation into which some bad investments and the negative critical reception of *Tales of a Traveller* (1824) had plunged him, calculated that the benefits from this hack work would produce temporary economic relief. Moreover, he knew that as attaché to the diplomatic legation he would be allowed to do historical research in Spanish libraries where he might find new sources of inspiration with which to rekindle a literary career that many considered exhausted. Finally, and perhaps most importantly, he moved to Madrid prompted by the possibility of traveling in southern Spain with his brother Peter, and thus fulfilling his romantic interest in folklore, history, and picturesque scenery and characters. Consequently, rather than becoming a platform to launch his career, the journey to Spain breathed new life into Irving's used-up literary imagination.

The journals and letters that Irving kept help us to reconstruct his itinerary, activities, and moods to a greater extent. Irving and his brother arrived in Madrid on 15 February 1826, finding the country relatively calm despite the current royalist repression and staunch policy of enlightened despotism. The political situation was not, in principle, Irving's main preoccupation. What captivated him at once was the social and physical condition of the country; the picturesqueness of the common people and the Oriental atmosphere that, as he saw it, still lingered in the capital were a good prelude of what he could encounter southward. In Madrid he stayed at Obadiah Rich's house and soon began to work on his translation using the consul's excellent library of Hispanic-Americana. His goal, expressed in many letters, was to conclude his translation and carry on with his peninsular tour as quickly as possible. He wrote almost without a pause and completed a rough draft of *Life and Voyages of Christopher Columbus* promptly, but subsequent revisions of the manuscript and his simultaneous dedication to other projects delayed his departure for two years (JIV, 82–132). Many single-line entries in his "Spanish Journal, 1827–1828: Madrid" reveal that for months Irving was exclusively and busily devoted to the Columbus project. This journal also attests that as early as August 1826 he was working on "Granada." In the fall of 1827, for example, in addition to working on *Life and Voyages of Christopher Columbus* he was gathering information for three future projects: *Chronicle of the Conquest of Granada*, *Mahomet*, and *Legends of the Conquest of Spain*. It is plausible to believe, if we approach the journal as a literary construct as much as any other published accounts, that Irving was consciously constructing a nearly Franklinesque self-image in which constancy and hard work emerged as the chief values.

The same journals, however, also reveal that during his laborious years in Madrid Irving, like Ticknor in the previous decade, interrupted his routine to enjoy such local amusements as bullfights, operas, and Spanish plays. He attended the soirées of foreign diplomats and local worthies—who took him for Fenimore Cooper[7]—and likewise he kept strong ties with the American circle formed by his brother Peter, the Everetts, the Richs, and enlarged by visitors like his nephews Pierre Munro Irving and Theodore Irving. Alexander Slidell Mackenzie and Henry W. Longfellow paid homage to the famous Geoffrey Crayon, too.[8] During those two years Irving interrupted his busy writing schedule only three times to visit the outskirts of Madrid: first, in August 1826, to make an excursion to Segovia and La Granja, and on the other two occasions, in October of the following year, to see El Escorial, Toledo, and Aranjuez. Naturally, Irving rejoiced when he was finally ready to set out on the Andalusian tour he had been announcing and postponing in innumerable letters to friends and family since his arrival. Irving was beginning a trip that reflected more than his personal need to escape two years of intense work in Madrid; he was embarking on a symbolic journey turned pilgrimage whose ultimate goal was Granada and the paradisiacal enclosure of the Alhambra. It was the last expedition of his many years of romantic wandering in Europe in quest, as Jeffrey Rubin-Dorsky observes, of an earthly paradise.[9] But he was traveling, too, across significant cultural and political postcolonial boundaries. He was leaving the center of a fallen empire for the capital of the one that preceded it; he was moving from the politically powerful capital to the historically rich albeit economically disenfranchised Andalusia that he commodified as the epitome of Spanishness. In short, he was restoring the ancient Moorish toponym of Al-Andalus, once embracing the whole of Spain, to its original signified, and in so doing he was stressing the synechdochical representation of Spain—taking the part (Andalusia) for the whole (Spain)—for which he is remembered.

The trek to southern Spain was one of the conventional travel itineraries that, with Byron as one of its most visible figures, the rhetoric of travel writing had for long charged with poetical associations. Apart from what this trip meant to Irving at the personal level, the account he was to devise out of it exerted an important influence on subsequent American travel writing on Spain. Irving at last departed on his long-wished tour on 1 March 1828 with two fellow diplomats, yet without his brother, who had to travel to Paris due to an illness. Irving's party reached Cordova, former capital of the western caliphate, after several days across the plains of Castile and the Sierra Morena. Despite this being their first important stop, they hurried on to Granada and the famed Alhambra, which at first sight disappointed Irving slightly. "The Alhambra differs in many respects from the picture that had been formed by my imagination," Irving wrote to Thomas W. Storrow on 10 March 1828, "yet it equals my expectations, high as they were wrought" (LII, 279). Little could he imagine that the fictional Alhambra he was to construct indeed was going to form pictures in the imagination of many American travelers who followed after him. Irving's spell was in fact so gripping that many experienced the "Romantic dilemma of 'belatedness' " which, as James Buzard notes, travel writers feel when they find it impossible to achieve uniqueness abroad.[10] In the same decade the anonymous author of *Scenes in Spain* (1837) specifically refused to describe the palace because it was difficult to be more thorough than Irving's book (SS, 98–99). Three decades later, William Cullen Bryant experienced the same frustration: "I am not about to describe Grenada [sic]. After what Irving has written of it, I should as soon think of attempting a poem on the wrath of Achilles in competition of Homer."[11] All in all, the frustration travelers felt in describing Granada almost became a commonplace, another convention of the genre, yet one that attests to Irving's powerful image-making capacity.

Even though Irving's textualization of Spanish traveling symbolically presented Granada as the traveler's ultimate destination, the actual conventional route continued. From Granada Irving carried on with his journey across the towns and geographical landmarks that later constituted the background of *Chronicle of the Conquest of Granada*. He and his friends crossed the Alpujarras, reached Málaga, and then proceeded to Gibraltar across the rough mountains of Ronda.[12] After spending some days in the English garrison, they continued to Cádiz and Seville, where Irving reunited with his friend David Wilkie. His journey, however, came to a halt due to a new outbreak of literary productivity. The revisions he had to make to *Life and Voyages of Christopher Columbus*, for which he needed the Biblioteca Colombina and the Archives of the Indies, made him remain in Seville for several months. He interrupted that stay only with an excursion to the Columbian sites of Palos, Moguer, and La Rábida.[13] When he finished his corrections Irving moved temporarily to Puerto de Santa Maria, where, undisturbed in a solitary cottage, he wrote *Chronicle of the Conquest of Granada*. In April 1829 he returned to Seville to meet Prince Dolgorouki, the friend who in May accompanied him in his second journey to Granada.

Irving carefully manipulated the chronology of his travels in order to make them suit his artistic purposes. His second stay in that city was longer and also, from a literary perspective, more profitable than the previous one, for he enjoyed a great deal of freedom to roam around the palace annotating his impressions of it and its inhabitants. Still, in order to provide a sense of unity and at the same time combine the impressions of his first trip with his later perambulations, in *The Alhambra* he collapsed both visits into one. Irving's solitude was possible because not long after their arrival in Granada diplomatic duties recalled Dolgorouki to London, and consequently he remained alone to linger and write in the palace with the sole company of its residents. Whereas on the one hand during his stay he established a productive daily routine of data collection similar to ethnographic fieldwork, on the other hand he almost involuntarily fell prey to the voluptuousness of the place. Judging from the tone of some of the letters he sent from there, it seemed as though he was negotiating or resisting, half-willingly and half-regretfully, his surrender to desire.

One of the chief ideological characteristics of American travel writing, as Terry Caesar has recently argued, lies in its continuous capacity to problematize the American writer's "experience of homelessness."[14] Irving's stay at the Alhambra enacts quite significantly the uneasiness of the American traveler's quest for a home away from home. While Irving was searching for a space that could provide him with security, in several of his letters he phrased his stay as though he had been involuntarily made to remain, succumbing to the snares of self-indulgence. "I am so pleasantly fixed here," he wrote his sister on 12 May 1829, "that I think I shall be induced to linger a little while and employ myself tranquilly in literary occupation; after which I shall bid adieu to this country" (LII, 417). To his friend Everett four days later he said the Alhambra was "one of the most delightful solitudes in the world" and he would be "tempted to linger in it" (LII, 422). A week later he also confessed Henry Brevoort he was "nestled in one of the most remarkable, romantic and delicious spots in the world" dreaming or "spellbound in some fairy palace" (LII, 424). Pleasure, inducement, delight, and temptation are but some of the words he used to summarize the reasons for his sojourn. Similarly, by mid-June he told his brother Peter:

> I am determined to linger here until I get some writings under way connected with the place . . . that shall bear the stamp of real intimacy with

Portrait of Washington Irving by David Wilkie, dated Seville, 23 April 1828. Courtesy of John Murray.

the charming scenes described. . . . It is a singular good fortune to be thrown into this most romantic and historical place, which has such sway over the imaginations of readers in all parts of the world, and I think it worth while departing from my original plan and remaining here a little while to profit by it. (LII, 436)

Irving originally planned to sail to France to join his brother as soon as possible; the allure of the Alhambra, however, prolonged his stay. Despite complaints that the voluptuousness of the place deprived him from working consistently and bringing his literary plans to an end, in Andalusia Irving surrendered to the same forces of desire that almost seduced Ticknor. Consequently, he regarded his unexpected appointment as first secretary of the American legation in London as a godsend, even if that entailed a confrontation with what he called the "business and bustle of the world." Postponing his departure several times, Irving finally resumed his course along the Mediterranean coast through Alicante, Valencia, and Catalonia. He left Spain with great regret on 23 August 1829. "A residence of between three and four years in it," he acknowledged to Henry Brevoort, "has reconciled me to many of its inconveniences and defects, and I have learned more and more to like both the country and the people" (LII, 462).

Busy at first with diplomatic work in London, Irving did not publish his "Spanish sketchbook" until 1832. His usual publisher, John Murray II, refused to acquiesce to his terms of publication, and thus *Tales of the Alhambra* finally came out in London and Philadelphia published by Colburn and Bentley and by Carey and Leah respectively.[15] Its publication raised a great deal of critical interest, being inevitably compared with Irving's former productions, especially with *The Sketch Book*.[16] The *Eclectic Review*, for example, affirmed that Irving used "the same quiet humour, the same easy and happy style, the same talent for rich and beautiful, though unexaggerated description," and the *Westminster Review* called it an excellent example of poetical prose.[17] Most reviewers, however, like one in the *New England Magazine*, agreed that by and large this new sketchbook did not surpass the original.[18] Along with its polished Crayonesque style, another characteristic of the book they praised was its didacticism. "To those of us who know little of the interior of Spain, of the domestic state of things there, and of the speech, habits, and notions of the common people," added one reviewer, "Mr. Irving's book will give some information, at least as regards a part of the country."[19]

Some reviewers found the realistic sketches in the book by far superior to the romantic tales and legends. Everett, for example, affirmed that "the best articles are those, in which the author gives a description of scenes and persons that have come directly within his own observation: such as the Journey, the Balcony, the Haunted Tower, the Author's Chamber, and the Visitors."[20] Similarly, the *Westminster Review* praised the introductory approach to Granada because "in a very few lines the pencil of Irving conveys the general effect of Spanish landscape with more force and vividness than whole volumes of preceding travellers."[21] The *New York Mirror* in its turn lauded Irving's capacity to transport the reader to the actual locale of the book, and mentioned that the first sketches of travel and customs in Granada were "impressed in every page, every line, every word, with the reality of truth and the glow of nature."[22] Yet, seeing Irving's massive output of Spanish materials, others were beginning to regard with irony his capacity to represent Spain ad nauseam:

> In how many more tomes his tour through the Peninsula is to be described, we have not the least idea. Neither have we the means of calculating the number of volumes which he may be even now meditating upon the literature, antiquities, mountains, manufactures, laws, and wines of that romantic land, for he seems to have the art of splitting into a thousand forms a collection of matter, which other travellers would be contented with cramming into one journal.[23]

Apart from these reviews, the favorable reception of Irving's Spanish sketchbook can also be specially measured by the numerous editions that followed after the original one of 1832. *The Alhambra* remained in print throughout the century and its tales were celebrated in Spain as well. It was soon translated and no doubt it has become one of the most reprinted American literary pieces ever since.

In studying the cultural work of this book, however, it is necessary to distinguish between the *Tales of the Alhambra* of 1832 and the more elaborated revised edition of 1851 that Irving retitled *The Alhambra*.[24] In the latter Irving not only substantially revised some of the original sketches and incorporated new ones, but also he definitively abjured the Crayonesque persona—whose real identity everybody knew—and associated himself with the romantic figure of Boabdil.[25] The travel writing quality of the revised edition became thus more enhanced, so that, as Suzan J. Fakahani observes, it went beyond a mere collection of folklore to become "a unified, well-documented study of the history, quality of life, folklore, and tales of the palace."[26] Notwithstanding the diversification of characters and themes that Irving brings into the *Tales of the Alhambra* of 1832, it is still possible to consider this book as a piece of travel writing. The legends and tales remain virtually untouched, the voice of the travel writer presides over the narrative structure of the book, and finally the sketch "The Journey" connects the reader to Granada. James Buzard, in tracing the development of travel writing as a genre throughout the nineteenth century, has acknowledged the importance of poems, novels, sketches, stories, and other works that "tended to supply some blend of mimetic and diegetic," that is, provided objective information and at the same time gave cues on how to react to the objects seen.[27] With its open form, Irving's *The Alhambra* also performed a similar task, as it provided subsequent visitors to Granada not only with information about the palace and the city but also Irvingesque cues on how to react to those sights as well as a masculinized itinerary to reach them.

II

The rhetoric of romance present in *The Alhambra* and most of the other early American travel accounts on Spain often depended on a touristic discourse charged with masculine elements. In Irving's narrative the contingencies of his journey constitute, as they did to Noah and Ticknor, an important source of romance for the domestic American readership. Irving described his itinerary and captured his readers' enthusiasm for the romance of travel in the opening sketch entitled "The Journey," where the list of toponyms—Alcalá de Guadaira, Alcalá de los Panaderos, Gandul, Arahal, Osuna, Antequera, Archidona, and Loja, to name a few—is in itself a catalogue of exotica. The allusion to places with sensuous names appears as a literary convention that connects Irving to the textual antics of Poe and other romantic writers who likewise reveled in the sonorous gothic and Oriental place names they invented. Yet, apart from its idealization of the land and the people of Spain, "The Journey" is also an eulogy of rough traveling anticipating the glorification of manhood later found in such travel classics as Richard Henry Dana's *Two Years Before the Mast* (1840) and Francis Parkman's *The Oregon Trail* (1849). Clearly, both the male republican reader perusing the two-volume Geoffrey Crayon edition of 1832, and, decades later, the Victorian male reader browsing the 1851 revised edition could fancy themselves trekking strenuously across the Andalusian mountains with Irving. The

American myth of exploring a virgin land or a feminized geography that yielded itself to the pioneers, transforms itself in this and other travel writings into a mixed fantasy of surrender and dominance for male travelers.

While many travel accounts employed the feminine pronoun whenever they referred to Spain as an entity, on seeing its craggy, weatherbeaten aspect male travelers found it difficult to gender the geography of Spain with precise traits. It was not easy to assign feminine attributes to that country, but it definitely became useful for travelers to adopt the discourse of masculinity. From time to time the rough masculine milieu where these writings were set enjoyed the pleasures of places conveniently bracketed off for the male traveler. Terry Caesar has argued that this rhetorical convention of travel writing, which consisted in opening private "nooks" and "gaps" for the traveler's solace, came into being especially at the turn of the century as travelers sought "private" places off the beaten path. Caesar regards these places as gendered, domestic spaces occupied by women travelers escaping from the male hordes.[28] While Irving was not escaping this problem, he nevertheless created a definite gendered space. He and his companions, as Ticknor and Mackenzie had done before them, were determined "to travel in true contrabandista style; taking things as we found them, rough or smooth, and mingling with all classes and conditions in a kind of vagabond companionship" (A, 7). The rewards for these explorers traveling Don Quixote–like in such a rugged male domain were to be found within the walls of a local inn or in the feminized domestic interiors of the Alhambra. Irving's party, like the knight of the woeful countenance, sojourns at several inns such as those at Arahal, where they are serenaded by the local people at night, and Loja, where Irving sat "until a late hour listening to the varied themes of this motley group, who mingled together with the unreserve of a Spanish posada" and offered "contrabandista songs, stories of robbers, guerrilla exploits, and Moorish legends" (A, 20). The travelers do not receive blows and insults, like Cervantes's hero, but a pleasurable reward that no doubt delighted the domestic reader as well.

Along with this discourse of pleasure, one of the strongest rhetorical conventions of romantic travel writing present in Irving's text is the use of gothic and exotic elements. To construct his romance of travel more imaginatively, Irving combines the traveler's episodes with the gothicism and orientalism of the Moorish palace. First of all, he tints his own walks with a poetical tone that requires the readers' suspension of disbelief. He advises them to "remember the nature of the place, and make due allowances," for in the "haunted ground" of the palace do not operate "the same laws of probability that govern commonplace scenes and every-day life" (A, 104). In the light of this, what he wrote years later from Sunnyside seems difficult to believe: "The account of my midnight rambles about the old palace is literally true. Everything in the work relating to the actual inhabitants of the Alhambra is unexaggerated fact: it was only [in] the legends that I indulged in romancing."[29] His saunterings in the palace have the glamour of romance and are as likely to be a traveler's yarn as any one of the tales and legends.

The gothicism and orientalism of *The Alhambra*, however, arise not only from the embedded Oriental and medieval tales but also from the architectural setting itself. It is not surprising that one of the genre conventions Irving plays up deliberately is the influence that gothic settings exert on their dwellers. In "The Court of Lions," for example, Irving says the palace has the "power of calling up vague reveries and picturings of the past, and thus clothing naked realities with the illusions of memory and the imagination," and consequently it is for that very reason he seeks "those parts of the Alhambra which are most favorable to this phantasmagoria of the mind" (A, 79). Irving imagines himself in the Hall of Justice seeing the Catholic Monarchs celebrating their victory over the Moslems while Columbus stands anonymously in a corner of the room. With this historical picture he makes his readers feel the thrill of armchair travel, which stems from the congruence between thing seen and imagination fed by predecessor texts. It is a situation akin to the experience that, as Dean MacCannell observes, modern tourists live through when they match a touristic sight with the marker that signaled its existence.[30] Thus, in *The Alhambra* the supernatural setting of the palace permits Irving to travel across different ages; he willingly surrenders to the flowing yet suspended quality of ancient time and in so doing he presents to his readers the romance of time travel. Moreover, he tries to recreate the touristic idea of authenticity by often picturing himself roaming around the half-deserted palace. The solitude of the place is a gift for the privileged sojourner from abroad as well as for the audience for which his tales are intended.

Whether it was a dilapidated castle, a shabby inn, or a ruinous palace, the influence exerted by gothic settings sometimes provided American travel writers with insights into their own being. One of the best examples of Irving's self-presentation as a romantic traveler in a mysterious setting where this insight is triggered undoubtedly is "The Mysterious Chambers." Having resolved to move to the rooms originally occupied by Lindaraxa and centuries later by Queen Elizabetta Farnese, Irving begins his nocturnal reconaissance of the palace. During his first night in those apartments he begins to imagine things and hear frightening sounds (which he later discovers to be the paroxysms of a madman) that make him return to his chamber, but the following nights of full moon he resumes his nocturnal explorations of the palace more self-assured. "Who can do justice to a moonlight night in such a climate and such a place?" he asks. "The temperature of a summer night in Andalusia is perfectly ethereal. We seem lifted up into a purer atmosphere; we feel a serenity of soul, a buoyancy of spirits, an elasticity of frame, which render mere existence happiness" (A, 61). This weightlessness in the palace, this harmony and sense of union with his surroundings anticipate some exclamations made by later American romantics. His physical and spiritual ductility, for example, recalls the Emersonian notion of the transparent eyeball, of becoming one with everything around yourself. Likewise, the changes effected under the moonlight bear some resemblance to Hawthorne's explanation in "The Custom-House" of how things in his room change and lose substance under the moonlight, and the writer enters the "neutral territory" that links reality and imagination. Irving's Spanish writings significantly seem to indicate that Spain is this neutral territory, and more particularly within Spain the palace of the Alhambra.

The search for cultural reservoirs, for anthropological terrestrial paradises like the neutral territory of the Alhambra, was a rhetorical convention that enjoyed great vigor in American travel writing, and so did one of its adjacent discourses, the romantic cult of the noble savage. Eighteenth-century writers and editors of travel literature, Percy Adams reminds us, had cemented the myth of the noble savage so much that it became "largely a fireside creation and, as a result, assumed many forms, depending on the nation, the time, and the literary school of the man of letters involved."[31] In Irving's travel narrative, the noble savage is to be found among the tattered Spaniards that form the community of Alhambrans, and particularly in the figure of Irving's valet Mateo Ximenez. Indeed, the generic conventions of travel literature hitherto discussed infused doses of romance into Irving's narration, but his anthropological romancing of otherness was to be even more productive.

Irving found an untapped source of romance for his travel book in the study of the ordinary Spaniard. His edenic view of the Alhambra in fact connected his representation of Spain with the literary tradition of portraying noble savages in pastoral New World settings, a tradition which stretched further back to sixteenth-century European accounts of discovery and colonization. His interest in Spanish customs, however, stemmed in the first place from his general attraction to folk tales cherished in his New York Dutch background and continued during his travels in Europe. Furthermore, it also arose from his enthusiasm for picturesque tourism. His fondness for the pictorial representation of national characters dated from his early years in Italy when, through his friendship with Washington Allston, he had considered becoming himself a painter. It is not surprising, then, that in Spain Irving was constantly captivated by picturesque people, about whom he particularly liked to write in letters to such painters as David Wilkie and Charles Leslie. Writing from Madrid on 23 February 1826, he confessed to the latter: "Indeed the Spaniards seem to surpass the even the italians [sic] in picturesqueness; every mothers [sic] son of them is a subject for the pencil" (LII, 178). Finally, Irving's study of the common Spaniard also had a correlate in the half-sentimental, half-Rousseaunistic ethnographic curiosity he had already exhibited in his earlier representations of American Indians. He represented the people of southern Spain using the same paternalistic discourse of "Traits of Indian Character" or of his descriptions of the Caribbean Indians in *Life and Voyages of Christopher Columbus*. They were representatives of an immutable pastoral primitivism that had almost ceased to exist in the bustling Anglo-Saxon countries from which he came.

III

Nineteenth-century American travel writing often deployed an ethnographic discourse that hinged upon an anthropologic present where the Other never changes and lives in an orderly world. Irving adopted this discourse and accentuated his ethnographic curiosity more in *The Alhambra* than in any other of his Spanish texts. Even though many travel writers attempted to pin down, more or less successfully, the general traits of what they took to be the unchanging Spanish character, Irving was the first antebellum American traveler in Spain to fashion himself as a cultural anthropologist doing fieldwork and mapping a distinct social group in a methodical manner. Doubtlessly, his construction of himself as a folklorist crossing gender, class, and national boundaries offers an additional perspective to the romance of travel because it adds the idea of an extended, on-site process of writing-in-residence not found in other travel writers. James Boon defines ethnographic fieldwork as "a prolonged episode, ideally (since Malinowski), during which a lone researcher visits a remote population. The experience . . . must be hauntingly personal and richly particular."[32] Irving rhetorically constructed his travel account as a personal experience that not only no other contemporary traveler could emulate but also as an anthropological secret reserved for the discovery of his own readers alone.

The anthropological romancing of the Spaniards that Irving carries out in *The Alhambra* is a carefully wrought rhetorical process that follows, *mutatis mutandis,* the different steps of modern ethnographic fieldwork. I have already mentioned that Irving collapsed his two stays in Granada to provide the semblance of a protracted stay or what Boon terms "a prolonged episode." Moreover, I have also called atention to Irving's readings and archival research, which remind us of the process whereby an anthropologist reads all the available literature on the close community he is to study and live with. Yet, apart from these two aspects, Irving followed other steps of ethnographic fieldwork to overcome cultural differences. He carried out a territorial survey of the Other's community, found a niche for himself in the community through linguistic affiliation, engaged in participant observation, interviewed native subjects, collected data, and finally processed it away from the fieldwork site. Unlike modern ethnographers, Irving was unable to consult census information, did not find reliable newspapers in a country with no freedom of the press, and had neither photographs nor recordings in a period predating the mechanical reproduction of sound and image. Moreover, he did not collect ethnographic artifacts save the stories culled in his books. He nevertheless managed to measure population and register in his own idiom the identity of the Other, so that rather than aiming at a quantitative appraisal of the culture he was analyzing, he seems to point toward the type of semiotic anthropological interpretation Clifford Geertz has termed "thick description."[33] Irving constructed a notion of Spanishness based above all on the invisible threads that constituted national character.

One of the genre conventions that the ethnographic account and the travel book share is the description of the locale where the narrative is set. Irving starts his sojourn among the community of the Alhambra, like most ethnographers, surveying the territory and demarcating the geographical area of his study. By placing "The Journey" at the beginning of his travel book he accomplishes the same

effect of the first chapter in Ticknor's *History of Spanish Litera-*
ture; that is, he describes the geography of the peninsula and
strengthens the relationship between ethnic and geographical
traits, between landscape and people. In this sketch Irving delin-
eates the rugged orography of the kingdom of Granada as he and
his companions approach it: the sierras are criss-crossed with precipices and defiles, stone crosses by the road mark the scene of ominous crimes, and solitary castles and churches dot the barren and
empty landscape. Spain appears not as a "soft southern region" like
Italy, but rough and treeless (A, 3). Irving explicitly demonstrates
that the scenery becomes the local character, so that the arid lands
they are crossing remind him of the Africanness inherent in the
Spaniard.

Irving's territorial survey, however, does not conclude with his
approach to Granada. Once in the city, he shares a new demarca-
tion of the local geography with his reader in the sketch "Panorama
from the Tower of Comares." In the morning Irving invites him to
go along with him to the summit of the tower and from there both
enjoy a bird's-eye view of the landscape with the Darro, the Gener-
alife, the Sierra Nevada, the vega, the city of Santa Fe, and other
landmarks. Unlike Ticknor, Noah, and the other early travelers
who observed the landscape not with the eye of someone enrap-
tured by its beauty but as someone only interested in its utilitarian
possibilities, Irving, a pictorial landscapist, asserts that Spain in-
spires feelings of sublimity. His view from atop, however, may not
be as innocent as it purports to be, for it reproduces the conventional use of panoramic views in travel writing that, according to
Mary Louise Pratt, denotes a fantasy of dominance typical of colonial subjects in a position of power. The landscape is empty and
unfolds itself to the conquering hero and his invisible eye.[34] Irving
had already used this view of Granada and its environs from the
palace in chapter I of *Chronicle of the Conquest of Granada*, a work
that coincidentally enacts the clash of two colonial empires. There
the initial sweeping cinematographic view of the city and the vega
or plain surrounding it already sets the pattern for the series of
landscape and city descriptions that occur later.

Leaving aside Irving's covert fantasies of dominance, his scan-
ning of the landscape, apart from enhancing the exotic romanticism encapsulated in the travel book, concomitantly entails his
traveling across space in time, further back to pre-1492 Spain. It
was in *Chronicle of the Conquest of Granada* where Irving began
exploring the rugged topography of the south that later constituted
the physical background of *The Alhambra*. The geographical partic-

ularities with which Irving ornaments the numerous inroads and sallies taking place in this mock chronicle undoubtedly prove his firsthand knowledge of many parts of Andalusia. In his account of the siege of Ronda in chapter XXX Irving manifests his familiarity with not only the rocks and precipices on which that city was located but also of its fortifications and water supplies. Likewise, his account of the siege of Málaga in chapters LIV–LXIV evinces details that only someone familiar with the area could have employed.

The first letters Irving sent to friends from Granada and Málaga in March 1828 already reveal his sensitivity to the irregular Andalusian landscape, which he often described employing the aesthetic vocabulary of the Picturesque and the Sublime. For example, in a letter to Antoinette Bolviller he explained he had crossed the spectacular pass of Despeñaperros in the Sierra Morena "winding along the the brinks of precipices, overhung with cragged and fantastic rocks," noting that the scenery resembled the pictorial compositions of Salvatore Rosa (LII, 281). Likewise, he confessed Prince Dolgorouki that during his trip to Málaga through the Alpujarras the sublime scenery instilled in him "that feeling of severe grandeur which I have experienced in reading the pages of Dante" (LII, 288). The sketches and pencil drawings of some parts of Andalusia that he interspersed in his journals and diaries also show the link between the picturesque tourist's constant inscription of the exotic and the ethnographer's notetaking routine. The survey of the territory that Irving's travel writing deploys by means of his ethnographic discourse appears, in short, counterpointed by the subjective appreciation of his touristic discourse.

Irving also found it easy to fit in the new community because he had one of the most important keys to otherness: language. He had begun to study the Spanish language in 1824, when he found himself idle in Paris after the failure of *Tales of a Traveller*.[35] A few months later, in March 1825, he wrote his nephew that he found the Spanish language to be "full of power, magnificence, and melody," also adding:

I do not know anything that delights me more than the old Spanish literature. You will find some splendid histories in the language, and then its poetry is full of animation, pathos, humor, beauty, sublimity. The old literature of Spain partakes of the character of its history and its people; there is an oriental splendor about it. The mixture of Arabic fervor, magnificence, and romance, with old Castilian pride and punctilio; the chivalrous heroism, and immaculate virtue; the sublimated notions of honor and courtesy. (LII, 236)

In addition to showing a close similarity to Ticknor's ideas on language and literature, Irving's linguistic judgments, clearly tinted by romantic coloring, suggest too some affinity to the notion of *Völkersprache* postulated by some nineteenth-century philosophers and grammarians like Johann Gottlieb von Fichte, Jakob Grimm, and Wilhelm von Humboldt. Through language one was simultaneously crossing the borders of nationhood as well as of otherness, since language and nation were one indivisible unit.

Irving reiterated his romantic views of the Spanish language and its reflection of popular character in another letter sent to Thomas Storrow on 5 May 1827, where he echoed the aesthetic phraseology of painting:

> The more I am familiarized with the language the more I admire it. There is an energy, a beauty, a melody and richness in it surpassing in their combined proportions all other languages that I am acquainted with. . . . It is characteristic of the nation; for with all its faults, and in spite of the state into which it has fallen, this is a noble people, naturally full of high and generous qualities. All the fine qualities of this nation, however, grow wild. You do not find them most in those cultivated classes where you look for them in other countries . . . but you find them among the common people, who have been brought up without care and almost without education. There are more natural gentlemen among the common people of Spain than among any people I have ever known, excepting our Indians. (LII, 233–34)

Irving's ethnographic romanticization of the Spanish people through language entailed, however, a paradox. On the one hand, as traveler-turned-anthropologist, Irving communed through language with the Other he was representing, and even adopted the speech of otherness for self-expression once he left Spain. But on the other hand, as traveler-diplomat, decades later he employed his good language skills in a less innocent and more politically committed task. Irving, the "transculturated subject," to borrow Mary Louise Pratt's term,[36] who lamented his commonplace days in London with the Spanish poem "¡Ay Dios de mi alma!" is, culturally speaking, a great deal apart from the Minister to Spain who in 1842 used his expertise of the Spanish language to negotiate and to wield power from his diplomatic vantage point.[37] With this shift Irving not only exposed the political and cultural biases embedded in ethnographic writing, but once again demonstrated the uneasiness with which early nineteenth-century American travel writers represented Spain both as setting for male romantic wanderers and as training ground for upstart agents of American expansionism.

Covering the nationalistic agenda of American travel writing under the thin veil of history and exoticism, the ethnographic romancing of Spain in *The Alhambra* resides, as I have been arguing, in Irving's fashioning himself as an amateur folklorist collecting data by means of different techniques. No doubt the writer's territorial survey and linguistic expertise are relevant steps in the fieldwork process, but no doubt, too, the most important of these techniques is participant observation because by presenting his journey to Granada as the authentic testimony of a cultural expedition it was possible for Irving to legitimize the verisimilitude of his travel book. The sketches relating his direct observations of the daily life of the people connected with the palace result particularly interesting because they reinforce the image of Irving as a folklorist doing fieldwork. Moreover, these sketches concomitantly focus attention on the operations of the ethnographer's gaze during the course of the day. No other part of *The Alhambra* offers a clearer insight into the folklorist's cultural curiosity than "The Balcony," and ironically no other part undermines it so strongly with the self-deception implicit in his voyeurism. Irving from his balcony observes a church-going procession where the central character, a young maiden, is followed by friars and several family members. Assuming that she is being forced to take the vows, Irving becomes enraged, but his local informant interrupts him to destroy his imaginative flight and tell him that in fact the young lady became a nun of free will, something which, according to Irving, goes against the rules of romance. In this case, as in many others, his guide's common sense brings Irving back to reality, yet always to a mild reality circumscribed to the Moorish palace or to the city of Granada.

In addition to participant observation, another ethnographic technique that Irving practices is in-depth interviewing of key informants. His typical method of composition, as Fakahani observes, entails, first, his listening to Mateo Ximenez's—or someone else's—story associated with a traditional place, and, second, his revitalization of that story.[38] In the palace Irving relied above all on informants like Doña Antonia Molina, or Tía Antonia, her niece Dolores, and María Antonia Sabonea, also known as la Reina Coquina. Irving also gathered considerable information from conversations on romantic history and folklore with local aristocrats and intellectuals. In Puerto de Santa María, for example, Irving met with Johann Nikolaus Böhl von Faber and his daughter Cecilia, known as a novelist under the penname of Fernán Caballero. She discussed several points of Spanish customs and folklore with Irving, and shared with him her own views on the poetical manipulation of literary materials. In Granada, Irving met Mauricio Alvarez de Bohorques, Duke of Gor, who gave him access to his library and to other local libraries.

His chief informant among the "sons of the Alhambra" was Mateo Ximenez, a sort of archetypal noble savage or primitive man. Irving invariably dubbed him "gossiping squire," "learned Theban," "whilom philosopher," and "historiographic squire." These and other epithets were trying to epitomize the main traits of Spanish character—particularly a gifted poetic imagination, a strong common sense, and a vivid historical consciousness—which Irving felt Mateo Ximenez embodied. The sketch that illustrates quite well Irving's fieldwork routine as well as his affable relationship with his informant is "A Ramble Among the Hills." During the walks he and Mateo used to take in the environs of the palace, the latter related to Irving all the different stories associated with each promontory, river, and physical peculiarity in the area, evincing "the sensibility of the common people of Spain to the charms of natural objects" (A, 155). Irving's ear becomes attuned to the way in which his informant tells him stories, but Irving's voice nevertheless remains dominant. If, as Stanley Williams notes, Mateo Ximenez "was, in a sense, the anonymous author of The Alhambra,"[39] why does he not share authorship along with Crayon/Irving?

The interplay of all the informants' different voices in the narrative structure of The Alhambra in a sort of Bakhtinian dialogism orchestrated by the traveler-narrator poses a crucial question that none of the previous travelers had taken into account. How can a traveler represent the Other and at the same time empower them, or how can the Other gain control of accounts made of them? James Clifford has suggested different ways whereby ethnographers are trying to give more authority to their informants. Using straight renderings of the Other's voice with no additional editing, or interpolating the ethnographer's voice with that of the interviewed native are some of the methods he proposes, none of which, however, remains totally effective.[40] Irving's representation of the Spaniard is caught in this paradox of modern anthropological descriptions of otherness because despite giving credit to each one of his informants, either in The Alhambra or in his journals, his voice ultimately supersedes that of the Other, places it in a subordinate position, and employs a rather paternalistic tone. This is precisely the type of anthropological stance that Clifford has termed "salvage, or redemptive, ethnography," whereby "the other is lost in disintegrating time and space, but saved in the text."[41] In the community that Irving is describing, the past counts more than the present, and it seems as though its cultural values can be saved only by the superior traveler/writer from outside acting as amateur ethnographer.

Irving's textualization of the foreign culture may have failed to empower the native subjects, but his logocentric inscription of otherness indeed boosted his literary career. The effort of collecting data and the subsequent step of revising it manifest the inherent rhetorical nature of both travel writing and ethnographic writing. The last step of Irving's ethnographic romance was to process all the observations he had garnered during his months in the south and to draw his own conclusions on the community of people he had met. Irving processed the data he had collected partly in Spain and partly in London, where he continued writing on his project of a Spanish sketchbook whenever his diplomatic duties allowed him to do so. His journals attest, for example, that by January 1829 he had already drafted such tales as the "The Legend of the Enchanted Soldier" and "Legend of the Three Beautiful Princesses," but in fact it took him until early May 1832 to bring to the press the two volumes of *Tales of the Alhambra*. These volumes, however, as he later recalled in the preface to the revised edition, "were put together somewhat hastily and in rather a crude and chaotic manner."[42] That is probably why instead of packaging and closing off his representation of Spain with the 1832 edition, Irving continued his anthropological interest with several contributions to magazines that later on he incorporated to the 1851 edition. In the revised edition, for example, the people's "oriental passion for story-telling" and gusto for the marvellous (A, 103) that Irving had discussed in "Local Traditions" were emphasized in the new essays "Spanish Romance" and "Poets and Poetry of Moslem Andalus." Likewise, Irving continued reiterating the fusion of Arabic and Gothic elements in the Spaniard as well as stressing the Africanness of the Andalusians and their otherness when compared to the balance of Europeans. This anthropological interest, however, was one that could not escape a clear rhetorical goal as well as the increasing demands of a cultural marketplace in which exoticism, otherness, and even Spanishness were a literary asset.

IV

Leaving aside the constraints Irving might have felt before the generic conventions of travel writing and before an antebellum public avid for the exotic, his rhetorical construction of himself as an anthropologist in residence romancing the tattered Spaniard is closely connected to his own views on history and its relation with romance. These views are particularly relevant because they rhetorically manipulate the class system of Spain so as to render a pastoral view of the country. Moreover, they tackle the recent Napoleonic Wars, the ruinous state of many sites, and the contemporary monarchy of Ferdinand VII so obliquely that Irving's vague allusions to them allot virtually no space to criticism. Even the clergy, the target of many travelers' incisive judgments, appear in *The Alhambra* as likeable cartoon villains. Irving treated his representation of Spain with humor and mild satire, romanticizing it so much that it reads as a bland text alongside such realistic accounts as Mackenzie's *A Year in Spain* or Caroline Cushing's *Letters*.

The first impression the reader receives from Irving's blending of history and romance within the arena of travel narrative is his tendency to erase the humdrum actualities of the present—such as, for example, the poverty of the Alhambrans—and highlight the romantic medieval past. For Irving, as for many other romantics, the deeds and ideals of both Christians and Moslems during the Middle Ages were loftier than those he was witnessing in the reign of Ferdinand VII. Consequently, he closed the latter period off and concentrated all his narrative energy on a dignified medieval past that he had described very carefully in *Chronicle of the Conquest of Granada*. From that medieval past Irving chose the losers, which he emblematized in the figure of Boabdil, and in so doing he cast himself as a corollary of the ethnographer in a closed community: a romantic writer in exile trying to exonerate the guilt of Western expansionism.

Irving's first self-conscious essay in the fusion of history and romance was *Chronicle of the Conquest of Granada*, which adumbrated the later interplay of both genres in *The Alhambra*. As Irving manifested in several letters preceding the publication of his mock chronicle, the genre identity of this work remained dubious. In the summer of 1828 he sent the manuscript to Colonel Aspinwall, his literary agent in London, and told him it was "an attempt, not at an historical romance, but a romantic history" (LII, 331). Toward the end of October he expanded on this notion in a letter to Alexander Everett where he clarified that the work was "tinted by the imagination so as to have a romantic air, without destroying the historical basis or the chronological order of events" (LII, 347). Still, several months later he remarked to Prince Dolgorouki that he had "been hazarding a kind of experiment in literature" of unpredictable success, an experiment whose romance had less to do with amours between knights and damsels than with actual warfare (LII, 375). Finally, not long before the publication of the work, he reiterated this to Aspinwall on 4 April 1829: "The Chronicle, I am aware, is something of an experiment, and all experiments in literature as in any thing else are doubtful. . . . But I have made a work out of the old chronicles, embellished, as well as I was able, by the imagination, and adapted to the romantic taste of the day. Something that was to be between a history and a romance" (LII, 396). Despite his claims to literary experimentation, the truth is that Irving was capable throughout of maintaining a high degree of historical credibility, so much so that his book won the encomiums of Prescott.[43] Like Fray Antonio Agapida's chronicle, Geoffrey Crayon's *The Alhambra* became a literary hybrid, a travel book standing also halfway between a history and a romance. If, according to John Frey, in his mock chronicle Irving practiced "the romance of history," that is, "an aesthetic appreciation of what truly took place" requiring virtually no imaginative expansions on the part of the author,[44] then in *The Alhambra* history became the subject matter upon which the traveler could construct, if he wanted, a nonhistorical discourse using romance.

Michael D. Bell claims that the conservative theory of romance reconciled "historical fact" and "romantic fiction" only in the "misty past."[45] Irving's antiquarianism attracted him more to the Middle Ages than to his own late 1820s and early 1830s. Granted, his primitivistic fancies also connected him somehow with the present, but it was a timeless present that had little to do with the present his friend Mackenzie had narrated three years before him. Irving treated the Spanish medieval history in a twofold manner, first through the romantic tales and legends set in the Moorish past of Granada, and second through such essays as "The Hall of the Ambassadors," "Alhamar, the Founder of the Alhambra," "Yusef Abul Hagig, the Finisher of the Alhambra," "The Mysterious Chambers," "The Abencerrages," "Poets and Poetry of Moslem Andalus," and "Palace of the Alhambra" whose historical accuracy he emphasized in the revised edition by means of footnotes and references. But unlike earlier American travel writers in the peninsula, Irving did not use the historical component of the travel book as an arena for explicit social commentary nor as a sphere for open comparisons between Spain and the United States. If Irving's apparently otherwordly romance parallels contemporary events in Spain, it does it in a subtle manner, and since only today's critics can perceive what Irving might be getting at, we can assume that the cultural work of *The Alhambra* prompted more the evasive rather than the subversive response of antebellum American readerships.

If the ethnographic focus of the book provided an evasive representation of Spain, the same was true of its reactionary comments on the class system of the community in the Alhambra. For instance, in "Inhabitants of the Alhambra" Irving views the poverty of the local people not as a burden or as an affliction, but as a virtue: "There are two classes of people to whom life seems one long holiday, the very rich, and the very poor; one because they need do nothing, the other because they have nothing to do; but there are none who understand the art of doing nothing and living upon nothing, better than the poor classes of Spain. Climate does one half, and temperament the rest" (A, 42). For Irving the sons of the Alhambra illustrated this dictum, living in what seemed to be a terrestrial paradise where everything was taken care of. Besides, that indolent view of the Spaniards inherently contributed to Irving's ideal romantic representation of Spain as a country that provided plentifully for its offspring. The reactionary politics of Irving's romancing of Spain is also attested by Irving's biographer Stanley Williams, who notes that when the Duke of Gor made some disquisitions on the egalitarianism of the Spaniards Irving was impressed by his notions, but "never confronted his host with apothegms on American democracy, or by pointing out Granada's bitter squalor."[46] In short, it was in the arena of history, one he often romanticized too much as well, that Irving tried to find answers to the apparent arcadian façade of Spain.

Early American travel writing created a discourse about things Spanish that probably stuck more permanently in the readers' imagination than the facts and news printed in gazettes and newspapers, and Irving's contribution to that discourse was effected by means of humor and satire. Even though in general traits *The Alhambra* works as a piece of escapist travel writing, it can be said to embed, at least partially, a satirical undertone voicing Irving's preoccupation with certain current Spanish topics. In the Spanish sketchbook Irving employs a type of humorous satire similar to that he had employed in *Knickerbocker's History of New York* (1809) and *The Sketch Book* (1819–20) to deal obliquely with some of the problems of the postcolonial United States. Noah and Ticknor had represented nineteenth-century Spain as the direct consequence of a series of historical episodes that brought about political instability, economic stagnation, and cultural poverty. Mackenzie refused such an analytical method and confronted the Spanish problems with a stark realism of the here-and-now. In contrast to the empirical cause-and-effect analysis of the former and the revolutionary representation of the latter, Irving, in his Spanish travel writings, retreated into a historical and ethnographic account of Spain that rejected former enlightened allegorical readings of the nation and stressed its aesthetic and symbolic quality. By doing this to many of the characters and settings in his tales and sketches, Irving found a pretext for a reactionary revision of history.

His account of the Napoleonic invasion of Spain and its politically turbulent aftermath offers, I think, a good example of Irving's literary historicization through characters that become symbols. Unlike Noah, Ticknor, and Mackenzie, who, as we saw in the previous chapters, made explicit references to the consequences of the French invasion, Irving scarcely alluded to it. In *The Alhambra* Irving mentions that during "the recent troubles in Spain" the French saved the Moorish palace from neglect and also laments that they burned many books in the Jesuit's library of Granada. With so little information, it would be difficult to tell that Spain had lived through such a conflagration. However, the issue of the Peninsular War surfaces again in the sketch "The Veteran," where, focusing on an old soldier—"a kind of walking monument of the troubles of Spain, on which there was a scar for every battle and broil" (A, 205)—Irving offers a better portrait of the vicissitudes experienced by many Spaniards who fought in the war against the French and were subsequently neglected by their government.

Another case of Irving's departure from the enlightened analysis of previous authors is the different manner in which he treats such an important romantic topic as ruins. Whereas for Noah and Ticknor the dilapidated buildings they encountered gave a pretext to mull over contemporary issues and their connection to past historical events, for Irving the architectural remains of the Moors in Spain became, on the one hand, visible icons where romance and history coalesced, and on the other hand symbols of lost bliss and security. The palace of the Alhambra—a terrestrial version of the fabled Garden of Irem which old king Aben Habuz commands to build in "Legend of the Arabian Astrologer"—seems with its fortified walls a bulwark protecting the blissful people luxuriating within against the forces of progress prowling without. Irving turns the palace into a paradise almost lost, and creates the illusion that the solid walls of the Alhambra protect the romantic traveler's *locus amoenus* from the invasion of the hostile world lurking outside.[47] In "Important Negotiations," he has to abandon the "region of poetry and romance to descend to the city and return to the forlorn realities of a Spanish posada" (A, 35). The poetic space encircled by the palace is thus set apart from the prosaic exterior, notwith-standing his having attached a great deal of romance, as we have seen, to the commonplace realities of the Spanish inns. The archi-tectural boundaries of the palace do not solely regulate the appor-tionment of work and pleasure, but also of past and present. Jeffrey Rubin-Dorsky observes, for example, that the palace offered Irving a timelessness that set him off from the real world outside, a time-lessness which is narratively patent in his change to the present tense not long after his arrival.[48] When Irving crosses the threshold, then, he walks into the past and travels across time, therefore bringing together supernatural romance with history.

Through his focus on old Arab-Spanish history Irving could at the same time avoid and draw subtle parallelisms with the crude realities of contemporary Spain. As Mary W. Bowden observes, in *Chronicle of the Conquest of Granada* Irving satirized the reign of Ferdinand VII in such a similar way as he had ridiculed the Jeffer-sonian administration in his Knickerbocker burlesque of New York. Thus, the holy war undertaken by Ferdinand and Isabella to rid the country of infidels is paralleled in contemporary history by the cam-paign of terror and repression fostered by Ferdinand VII to drive the Spanish liberals into exile. Likewise, the courtly intrigues for the accession of Boabdil to the throne occupied by Muley Abul Has-san have an equivalent in Ferdinand VII's machinations to succeed his father, Charles IV, dominated by his minister Manuel de Godoy.[49] All in all, it seems as though Irving was infusing history with romance to make more palatable a series of conflicts much more severe in real life than they appeared to be in fiction.[50] Once again it was Irving's strategy to counter the real Spain his friend Mackenzie had not avoided.

There was, however, more than just old Arab-Spanish history in Irving's subtle allusions to some political issues of contemporary Spain and in his evasion of them. Bowden notes, for example, that "The Legend of the Rose of the Alhambra" is prophetic of Ferdi-nand VII's abolition of the Salic Law, which would have barred the accession to the throne of his daughter Isabella II.[51] Yet, a more frightening key is touched in "The Governor and the Notary," a tale that could be said to echo the public executions that, as we saw in the previous chapter, Mackenzie witnessed in Madrid and Gra-nada. Irving's portraits of the punctilious governor of the palace and the captain-general of the city, continuously disputing with each other whose rights prevail first, offer a good satire against local administrators. But when their rivalries get so much out of hand that they are about to bring about the hanging of a corporal in the

THE ALHAMBRA

BY WASHINGTON IRVING

G. P. PUTNAM'S SONS.

Title page from a late edition of Washington Irving's *The Alhambra* (New York: Putnam's, 1887). The arabesques and the central, eye-catching perspective in this circular engraving convey respectively the exoticism and escapism that imbue Irving's romantic travel book. From the author's collection.

Plaza Nueva of Granada and of a notary in the garrison, Irving makes the reader realize the absurdity of their petty grievances. The difference between Irving's tale and the contemporary executions, however, lies in Irving's happy ending, another symptom of his escapist stance. The notary's wife, accompanied by her progeny, implores the pardon from the captain-general and finally manages to win her husband's release.

The open criticisms of the corrupt clergy of Spain that, as we saw in previous chapters, other Americans did not hesitate to make, appear in Irving's travel writings not in a direct form, but in an oblique, fictionalized manner. Since his first days in Madrid, Irving had regarded the role of the clergy suspiciously. He recorded in his journal, for example, that from his room at Obadiah Rich's home he used to contemplate the friars at the convent of Atocha leading what truly seemed a not too strenuous life. It is quite probable, then, that from his observations in Madrid as well as from stock literary representations Irving came up with the cartoonlike Roman Catholic friars and monks in such stories as "The Legend of the Two Discreet Statues," "Governor Manco and the Soldier," and "The Adventure of the Mason."

In "The Legend of the Two Discreet Statues" Fray Simon, a covetous Franciscan friar, extorts the family of Lope Sánchez, a poor dweller of the Alhambra who has discovered a Moorish treasure. As the confessor of Sánchez's wife, no sooner does Fray Simon hear the news of their new wealth than he unscrupulously violates the secret of confession to extract money from them, doing it so many times that the only alternative for Lope and his family is to leave Granada secretly. The friar's avarice desperately drives him to stalk the Sánchez the night of their departure, except that on that occasion the unexpected apparition of the goblin horse Belludo and seven hellhounds sends him packing. The supernatural ending of this tale, which cuts off the friar's escalating greed, represents Irving's laugh at many a cleric who under a pious guise acted on pure self-interest. Thus, of Fray Simon he ironically notes that even the dogs could smell his sanctity.

Irving portrayed another greedy Franciscan confessor in "Governor Manco and the Soldier." This fat cleric, Irving notes, "twinkled and flashed at sight of the rosaries and crosses" that the unknown soldier brought to the governor's presence claims to have found in the leathern sack of an old Arabian steed. Irving does not describe this friar as carefully as the previous one, but significantly notes that he promptly reported what he had seen to the Holy Office, thus starting an argument between the governor and the religious order about who should own those ancient spoils of war. The avarice of the individual clergyman takes greater proportions as it reflects the institutional greed. Irving's criticism of friars, however, does not constitute his only attack against the cupidity of the Roman Catholic church, for he also mocked the figure of the priest in "The Adventure of the Mason." There he portrays a miserly priest who hires a poor bricklayer to bury four jars full of gold in a vault. When the priest died other "priests and friars thronged to take possession of his wealth; but nothing could they find but a few ducats in a leathern purse" (A, 78). This scene reminiscent of Jonson's *Volpone* evinces Irving's criticism of money-grabbing clergymen who not only preyed on other people but upon each other. Using these caricatures of Roman Catholicism in the framework of supernatural and fantastic tales, Irving showed that romance could be blended with and embed a criticism of certain aspects of contemporary Spain.

Still, if Irving's British and American Protestant audiences detected the criticism implicit in these stories, it was surely owing to two important reasons. First, because Irving certainly knew that his Anglo-American readers shared a clear bias against Roman Catholicism, and second because in those stories he not only criticizes a particular religion but such universal traits as laziness, cupidity, and ambition. That being the case, the universalizing fairy-tale quality endowed to these stories of clerics does reiterate Irving's avoidance of concrete sociopolitical moments in favor of eternal, easy-to-accept truths. His readers considered him strictly a romancer and an evasive historian. His satire loses all its usefulness as a biting critique of Spain if only today's scholars can perceive its subtlety. His comments on Spain being no more than insinuations, the cultural work of *The Alhambra* must have been far from that of the preceding American travel writings on Spain clearly intent to enlighten their readers.

Irving's flight from time and his seeking refuge inside an elaborate domestic interior might have appealed to audiences more and more accustomed to romantic descriptions with Oriental and dreamlike scenarios. But for late representatives of the previous Common Sense philosophy like Alexander Everett, Irving was errant. Everett, thinking that Irving was demonstrating a clear lack of historical sensibility, argued in his review of *The Alhambra* that the tone of the book did not befit the Moorish ruins, which, he believed, "lead more naturally to grave meditations on the fall of empires, and melancholy musings on the frailty of human greatness." These were precisely the type of reflections that Noah and Ticknor favored, and thus Everett lamented that such "a patriotic citizen of the great and flourishing Republic of the Western world" as Irving

> while wandering through the splendid royal halls, whose present dilapidated condition serves as a memorial of one of the political movements that have changed the face of society, instead of turning his thoughts upon the high concerns of Church and State, should be chiefly occupied with the personal characters and little domestic arrangements of the house-keeper's family [and] the humors of honest Mateo Ximenez.[52]

Everett seemed to forget, however, that chronologically and sometimes even ideologically Irving was as much a by-product of the eighteenth-century philosophical tradition as he was, and that under his guise of humorous, romantic time-traveler and paternalistic ethnographer he occasionally shared similar intellectual concerns with the former American travelers in Spain. Irving, a sketcher rather than an heroic painter, might actually be seen to be doing a little counter history of his own sort.

In "The Hall of Ambassadors" Irving offers his own philosophical reflection on the fate of the Moslems in Spain. He explains that at dusk, while comparing the Alhambra with the Gothic architecture without, he "fell into a course of musing"—just as he had done years before, in *The Sketch Book*, upon entering the dark halls in "Westminster Abbey"—that made him contrast the Gothic walls outside with the ornate Moorish tracery inside, two architectural styles symbolizing "the opposite and irreconcilable natures of the two warlike people who so long battled here for the mastery of the peninsula" (A, 44). At that point Irving does not reveal his preference for either one, and instead, in a tone similar to William Cullen Bryant's description of the Illinois mound builders in "The Prairies," he resignedly utters: "Such is the Alhambra. A Moslem pile in the midst of a Christian land; an oriental palace amidst the gothic edifices of the West; an elegant memento of a brave, intelligent, and graceful people, who conquered, ruled, flourished, and passed away" (A, 46). The tenor of the whole book, however, implicitly manifests his preference for the past Moorish culture.

V

Irving's romancing of history and his positioning himself in both the geographical and historical margins carry, however, mixed overtones. As this chapter has been arguing so far, Irving was, on the one hand, employing his marginal stance as cultural anthropologist to retreat from the ugly realities of Spain into its prettified past or, for that matter, its eternal ethnographic present. But, on the other hand, if in his actual travels Irving moved geographically toward the fringes of the nation, then in his writings he was ideologically moving in that direction as well. It is quite significant that he chose the fate of the Moors, embodied in the romancelike tragic figure of Boabdil, as one of the most prevalent themes in *The Alhambra*. And even more significant is the fact that Irving seems to suggest parallelisms between Boabdil, with whom Irving sympathized and identified himself strongly, and the Indian King Philip, whom Irving described in *The Sketch Book* in a chapter entitled "Philip of Pokanoket." Irving, however, strengthened his empathy with Boabdil in the revised edition of 1851, many decades after his return to the United States.

Having in mind the date of Irving's revision, it could be argued that the comparison between both monarchs permitted Irving to comment subtly on contemporary American politics. His insinuated comments on American topics by way of highlighting the Philip-Boabdil duality, however, must have passed as unnoticed as those on Spanish issues. In *The Sketch Book* Irving portrayed Philip with a full list of republican virtues: "proud of heart and with an untamable love of natural liberty," as well as "a patriot attached to his native soil—a prince true to his subjects, and indignant of their wrongs."[53] Similarly, in *The Alhambra* the king of Granada is equally depicted as a monarch loyal and fair to his subjects, following on the positive portrait of him that Irving had produced in *Chronicle of the Conquest of Granada*. Irving, too, had sympathized with the Indian king descrying his former dominions from his exile in Mount Hope, and in his Spanish sketchbook he was pitying even more the tragic figure of Boabdil abandoning Granada bound to his banishment in the Alpujarras. With these two unjust banishments, so heroically endured by their sufferers, Irving seems to attempt to transcend personal empathy to obtain exoneration of Western cultural guilt. His siding in *The Alhambra* with the losers of one of the most important conflicts in Western history—the downfall of the last Moslem foothold in Western Europe—can thus be replicated, in the broader context of antebellum American letters and politics, with his siding with the victims of Anglo-Saxon expansionism in the American continent.

Not many years later than the publication of *The Alhambra*, Irving's friend Prescott and other New England historians narrated in their histories the rise of modern Spain above all as a single Christian, unified nation, linking it thus to the justifiable cultural and economic expansionism of Christendom across the globe. Irving, on the contrary, seems to go against the grain by focusing on Spain as a medieval divided state almost more prosperous under the Moorish than under the Christian yoke. Granted, in *The Alhambra* he is legitimazing, like the other historians, the idea of empire, for his sojourn takes place in the seat of a former kingdom that once kept at bay the forces of Christianity. But the empire he is immortalizing is measured by different standards. In his gendered geography and architectural symbolism, Irving embraces the feminine side of the defeated Moslems, represented by the Alhambra, and casts off the victors, symbolized by their dark cathedral, as the forces of darkness.

More importantly, however, for Irving's reactionary stance is the fact that the comparison between King Philip and Boabdil allowed him to reflect upon the plight of the romantic artist exiled from his paradise or source of inspiration. It was Mount Hope for the Indian leader, and Granada for the Moorish monarch. Exile for a romantic dreamer like Irving signified his detachment from the palace of the Alhambra, yet a palace that he could recreate in his travel book. Irving could not restore the past grandeur and harmony of the kingdom of Granada, but at least his book could call attention to the city and to the palace that symbolized its glories. Almost immediately after the publication of his travel book "alhambraism" became a fashion in England and the United States, and his name became attached to the palace.[54] For subsequent nineteenth-century American travelers the trip to Granada was to become not only a visit to Boabdil's royal palace but also to Washington Irving's "enchanted pile."

Irving returned to Spain from 1842 until 1846, but his second residence had a different tenor. Despite being unanimously appointed Minister Plenipotentiary to the Court of Isabella II by the United States Senate, and received with open arms in Spain, Irving found his return far from pleasurable.[55] In the first place, as Claude Bowers suggests, he had accepted his diplomatic post with hopes of having enough leisure to begin his biography of George Washington, which he expected would culminate his career in letters.[56] Yet he did not have much spare time for literary pursuits; apart from jotting down notes for his future project, his writing became relegated to diplomatic letters describing the situation of Spain. It is said that Secretary of State Webster used to put away all his correspondence to read Irving's dispatches as soon as they arrived.[57] Irving found that the country had changed politically, socially and economically, losing its aura of romance. Rather than retracing his own steps of 1826–29 he was in Spain, in Mary A. Weatherspoon's phrase, "with an American frame of mind" as his many leaves of absence to Paris and London demonstrate.[58] For the first time, then, Irving had to put aside the romantic Spain of the 1820s and face the realpolitik, intervening in courtly intrigues between the Queen and her opponents, and gathering information on United States expansionist interests in former Spanish territories. The middle-aged man who, arriving in Madrid in the mid-1820s to write his biography of Columbus, had managed to avoid political strife ultimately became not a self-fashioned amateur ethnographer one more time but rather a self-fashioned amateur politician in his sixties working de facto as an agent of expansionism.

6

Fireside Travel Writing: Henry Wadsworth Longfellow's Sentimental Pilgrimage across Spain

Except for a few lyrics in the ever-shrinking portion allotted to him in anthologies, Longfellow's works are nearly absent from today's canon. Dana Gioia, in a vindicatory essay that explains this neglect, has made a strong call for a reassessment of the poet's career on its own terms instead of by the aesthetic standards imposed by modernist poets and New Critics.[1] Gioia argues that the disparagement of Longfellow's aristocratic lifestyle at Craigie House, his penchant for narrative poetry, and his combination of bourgeois didacticism with Christian moralism should give way to a conscientious evaluation of his contributions to modern American poetry. We cannot forget, Gioia observes, that as a cosmopolitan litterateur and adapter of new prosodies from abroad Longfellow prefigured certain characteristics of Pound, Williams, and Stevens. However, if the cultural significance of Longfellow's oeuvre is to be recovered and reevaluated in different historical and cultural terms, then it is also necessary to include his travel writings in this project, for they play an important part not only as adumbrations of his later poetic achievements but as significant texts in the tradition of nineteenth-century American traveling abroad. Longfellow wrote two prose books employing the framework of travel narrative. The first, *Outre-Mer: A Pilgrimage Beyond the Sea* (1835), the sketchbook that started his creative literary career, recounted in a poetical manner his first visit to Europe; the second, *Hyperion* (1839), was a romance based on his second visit to the Old World.

Using a narrator who describes himself as a pilgrim and his transatlantic journey as a pilgrimage, in *Outre-Mer* Longfellow produced his view of France, Spain, and Italy through a potpourri of tales, travel anecdotes, translations, character sketches, and learned essays. The fact, however, that the book narrates the nation in an erratic manner and has neither apparent thematic unity, like Irving's *The Alhambra*, nor narrative linearity, like Mackenzie's *A Year in Spain*, does not mean that Longfellow's project necessarily lacks cultural coherence or that his objectives were totally diffuse. With his sketches Longfellow created a text that underneath its apparent sentimental simplicity resisted the readers and demanded that they make sense out of a hodgepodge of topics. *Outre-Mer* was, in a sense, a romantic departure from the cultural narrative tradition of the Enlightenment. It contains twelve chapters devoted to France and four to Italy, and between them seven dealing with the representation of Spain: "The Journey into Spain," "Spain," "A Tailor's Drawer," "Ancient Spanish Ballads," "The Village of El Pardillo," "The Devotional Poetry of Spain," and "The Pilgrim's Breviary."

Admittedly, because of the diverse topics he chose for, and the broad scope he gave to, his representation of Spain, and because of the resistance to dry touristic discourse he manifested there, Longfellow's narrative seems less defined than those I have already examined. He strove to do something similar to what Caleb Cushing announced at the beginning of *Reminiscences of Spain* (1833), that is, "to communicate an idea of the country" by means of "detached pictures" (RS, 1:v), but, sandwiched between sketches of France and Italy, Longfellow's representation of Spain had to compete, as it were, for cultural salience in *Outre-Mer*. Moreover, the literary genre and model he looked to played a significant role in the manner in which his representation of the foreign nation was to be perceived. To a certain degree the fortunes of Longfellow's *Outre-Mer* have been similar to those of his poetry, except that the yardstick used to measure this European travelogue has not been Modernism but Irving's *The Sketch Book* (1819–20), which Longfellow read eagerly during his undergraduate years at Bowdoin College and later adopted as a model. This decision, according to some critics, marred it. Newton Arvin, for example, notes that *Outre-Mer* "suffers of course from being much too consciously and directly the imitation of another book. . . . Irving is a disturbing presence."[2] Stanley Williams, in a remark of ironic disapproval, observes on the other hand, "The disciple excelled the master; that is, in his sentimentalization of Spain Longfellow went far beyond Irving."[3]

This chapter, however, does not attempt to establish how much this and other travel writings by the author of *Evangeline* are indebted to Irving, but rather to focus on the representation of Spain he produced in the late 1820s with his travel writings, and in 1835 with the definitive edition of *Outre-Mer*. Longfellow's book reinforced the romantic representation of Spain that Irving had recently disseminated, but instead of retreating into a historical or ethnographic image of that country, Longfellow escaped into a more spiritual view. The romance of Spanish travel thus resided not so much in its capacity to reenact Spanish history as in its power to foster a wide range of spiritual moods and emotions in both the reader and the writer. Even though Longfellow was an aspiring man of letters, he surely knew that he could reap benefits from a European travelogue saturated with sentiment. James Buzard has noted that the new romantic models of travel writing that had appeared before and especially after the Napoleonic War were "well suited to a competitive cultural market" in which genteel travelers were losing ground to hordes of plebeian tourists. The heirs of the Grand Tour tradition felt that little by little the experience of European travel was turning itself into a philistine rather than a cultural activity, and only if they stressed "the inchoate standard of 'enthusiasm' or power of feeling" they could make "travel seem at once open and exclusive."[4] The search for cultural exclusiveness and literary fame may then partly help us to account for the significance of a spiritual view of foreign lands and peoples in Longfellow's travel writings. No other evidence supports that more strongly than the ascending course that his literary career took after the publication of *Outre-Mer*.

I

The textual manipulation of on-site travel writings like letters and journals into a crafted travel book demonstrates that, as a travel writer, Longfellow early on became familiar with the major rhetorical conventions of the genre he was cultivating. While in his journals he did show the other side of Spain that Mackenzie and the previous pre-romantic travelers had depicted, in *Outre-Mer* he preferred to sentimentalize it. Like Ticknor in the previous decade, during his three years in Europe Longfellow kept several journals and diaries that he duly filled with information for others to read. "You will remember," his father advised him before his first departure for Europe, "that a description of the wonders of the world will always be interesting to us, who are so far removed from you and them."[5] Accordingly, in addition to one diary in English and another written in both Spanish and French, Longfellow kept two journals in Spain, one of them significantly titled "Brother Jonathan in Spain."[6] In the pages of his Spanish journal he was carefully inscribing the voice of a self-appointed quintessential New Englander, and thus he was creating a new persona for himself.

These notebooks and the letters that Longfellow regularly sent home furnished him with a quick and direct source of materials for *Outre-Mer* after his return. "Often his first notations were sketches, incomplete fragments of sentences, which were expanded with care and with increasingly self-conscious, archaic, and ornate phrasings, in the long letter-journals which he sent home," Lawrance Thompson has observed. "These letters . . . later grew very simply into the chapters on Spain when *Outre-Mer* was compiled. Entire passages will be found in the letters which are identical with sentences in *Outre-Mer,* except for changes of a few words."[7] Still, he did not always render a straight transcription of these personal travel writings. The representation of Spain he produced in *Outre-Mer* and, to a certain degree, in *The Spanish Student* (1843)— which Whitman terms "the dramatic form of *Outre-Mer,* or the dramatization of his letters home and his diaries"[8]—reveals that Longfellow carefully selected and manipulated his travel materials, and that even on certain occasions he did not employ them at all. The effect that he wished to achieve in his Spanish travel book sometimes was at odds with the experiences he narrated in his travel notes.

The textual spontaneity and the fragmentation that Longfellow uses in his account evince that he wished to depart from some rhetorical conventions of the previous tradition of travel writing. Moreover, his narrative voice foreshadows the spiritual Transcendentalist inner view of travel that Emerson and Thoreau were to express a few years later. Whereas his letters and journals were more or less straightforward, *Outre-Mer*'s representation of Spain was desultory, pieced from bits of touristic experiences. Despite this apparent disconnectedness, however, Longfellow conveyed a view of Spain as a melancholic as well as moral domain where the traveler could attain a deeper insight into his spirituality. Longfellow was not as attracted as Irving to the primitivistic or ethnographic side of Spain, but to its spiritual side. For one thing, he did not stay in the Iberian Peninsula long enough to have undertaken intense fieldwork in a Spanish community. His spiritual transcendentalizing denied, in a sense, the otherness of the Other, but placed him in a sentimental universalizing project that shared, *mutatis mutandis*, similar goals with Mackenzie's appeal for justice and liberty in Spain. Unlike his friend, though, Longfellow did not conceive Spain as a battleground between the forces of progress and reaction, nor his travel book as a vessel for revolutionary rhetoric. Longfellow's Spain is not what Emerson might have called "a fool's paradise." It is rather a spiritual retreat where the aspiring romantic artist can find not only inspiration, but also an insight into his future life.

Clearly the spiritual reading that Longfellow's European tour offers attests the importance that William W. Stowe has given to the pervasive rhetoric of religion on the American traveler abroad. Stowe remarks that, particularly in the antebellum period, religion helped Americans to articulate European travel as a ritual with fossilized itineraries and fixed attitudes that many travelers on the Continent followed earnestly.[9] With its spiritual scope, Longfellow's view of Spain markedly differed from what had been presented to readers in the United States until then. In previous chapters it has been pointed out that for the enlightened Americans who had traveled in the peninsula Spain epitomized poverty, political disorder, and the lessons of the past. Ticknor, though mainly representing Spain along these lines, somewhat changed this depiction as he felt and expressed the lure of empire along with the lure of desire. To this desire Irving surrendered completely, to be rescued only by a diplomatic appointment that sent him away to London. Longfellow, while acknowledging the lure of desire, nevertheless represented Spain much as he did with the other nations described in *Outre-Mer*, that is, as a stage in a nonsecular pilgrimage to the Old World.

Besides its aura of pilgrimage, however, Longfellow's first voyage to Europe also contained aspects of an educational grand tour, business trip, and romantic escape all in one. The trustees of Bowdoin College, his alma mater, had offered their nineteen-year-old graduate a newly endowed professorship in modern languages for which he was not sufficiently prepared at that time, and for which, consequently, he was advised to travel abroad. Stephen Longfellow, who would have liked his son to study Divinity or Law yet finally acquiesced to his plans to gain eminence in the field of belles lettres, treated this European journey with Calvinist zeal from the very beginning. Indeed, it represented not only an extraordinary educational opportunity for his son, but an investment that had to be carefully planned if it was to return academic dividends in the future years. Helped by friends knowledgeable on matters of European instruction, father and son devised a tentative course of studies that eventually, once far from provincial Maine, the would-be professor did not follow to the letter. Instead he explored and discovered the delectations of the romantic European wanderlust.

Having collected letters of recommendation from several New

England notables, among them Ticknor—whom he found "a little Spanish-looking man"—Longfellow sailed for Havre aboard the packet *Cadmus* on 15 May 1826. His initial goal was to master the French language, and, accordingly, he spent the first nine months in France. However, when the time came to continue with his academic plans he grew confused. Cogswell, Ticknor, and Bancroft had advised him to attend lectures at a German university, whereas he wished to visit southern Europe first. The political situation in that area, though, especially in Spain, did not make the trip very safe. "I think indeed that I must give up the Spanish; at all events I must give up the idea of visiting Spain," he replied from Paris to a paternal suggestion that he travel there to learn Spanish. "The country is filled with all the horrors of a civil war. It is as much as one's life is worth to visit it. We get most terrible accounts from every quarter" (LL, 1:187). But at length, convinced by Pierre Munro Irving that there was no danger in traveling there, he departed for Spain, reaching "the very heart of the empire—without falling among thieves" on 6 March 1827.[10]

In the first decades of the nineteenth century, epistolary communication between genteel hosts and traveling guests still remained as one of the prevailing social conventions inherited from the eighteenth-century Grand Tour. The letters of recommendation Longfellow carried from the United States and Paris easily introduced him to the American circle in Madrid. In the capital of Spain he felt much better situated and treated than in France. "With Madrid I am much delighted. I have not seen a city in Europe which has pleased my fancy so much, as a place of residence," he wrote to his father soon after his arrival (LL, 1:217). He immediately became a good friend of Mackenzie, with whom he made a trip to Segovia, La Granja, and El Escorial. Likewise, he almost felt at home with the Everetts and the Richs. Of all these compatriots in Madrid, however, the one who made the greatest impression upon him was Washington Irving, the author he had revered for so long, whom he thus described to his parents:

> He is one of those men who put you at ease with them in a moment. He makes no ceremony whatever with one—and of course is a very fine man in society—all mirth and good humor. He has a most beautiful countenance—and at the same time a very intellectual one—but he has some halting and hesitating in his conversation—and says very pleasant, agreable things in a husky—weak—peculiar voice. He has a dark complexion—dark hair: whiskers already a little grey. (LL, 1:222)

Thanks to him Longfellow also enjoyed the "opportunity of a peep or two into good Spanish society," which otherwise would have remained a restricted social ground for the twenty-year-old traveler. But however he may have enjoyed the experience, he still preferred to associate himself with the locals and go with them to bullfights and other popular entertainments.

The consumption and acquisition of cultural goods stood out for many nineteenth-century American tourists among the principal goals of their European tour, and Longfellow was no exception. As it has been pointed out in previous chapters, while some travelers were to use this cultural luster obtained abroad to achieve social distinction at home, others employed it to propel their professional careers. Any type of cultural good became valuable as long as it could bear the token of exoticism or otherness. Of course, the most apparent cultural value available to young Longfellow, as it also is to today's students enrolled in study abroad programs, was the language of the country he was visiting. In order to study the language and mores of the Spaniards better, Longfellow lived with the local family of Valentín González during his stay in Madrid. They not only made his residence more pleasant, but also constituted an unofficial and direct access into otherness that no formal lessons could provide him. With them he paid a short visit to the village of Villanueva del Pardillo in late May and early June that afforded him a glimpse of rural Spain. During this excursion Longfellow met one of Mina's guerrilla veterans from the Napoleonic War, pitied the toilsome existence of Galician laborers away from their region, and joined in the local peasant dances. Significantly, on his last day in that Castilian village he recorded in his diary, "I like to see things in reality—not in paintings—to study men—not books."[11] It was certainly an ironic statement for a bookish figure on the way to make a profit with the circulation of irreality, with the romancing and commodification of otherness in the genre of the travel book.

If the educational goal of European travel helped Longfellow to legitimize his sojourn in Madrid, it also provided him with a reasonable excuse to hide other impulses to go abroad that travelers verbalize with more difficulty. In that city, unlike Ticknor, Longfellow did not disclose much information about his studies, except for occasional justifications that the capital was the only place to learn proper Spanish. In several letters he even had to demonstrate to his father he was not wasting time and money. Lawrance Thompson, in his study of Longfellow's early career, emphasizes this view of the would-be author's disposition to have a good time at the expense of more serious literary studies. According to this critic,

> in all his journal passages and scores of letter-pages, written from Spain, Longfellow made no reference to any Spanish author except

Cervantes and no reference to any Spanish literature except ballads which he had found translated by Byron or Lockhart. This is important in that it reveals a point zealously concealed by Samuel Longfellow: during this first European visit, Longfellow was *not* primarily interested in study and scholarship.[12]

For a young romantic in Spain with little historical and literary background to draw on for associations, and probably with little eagerness and opportunity to hobnob with the upper crust, the objectives of his peninsular quest acquired a different, more spiritual tenor.

After his studies in Madrid, Longfellow set out on the classic tour of the south. He departed on 2 September with ten other passengers in a *galera*, or large mule-drawn covered wagon bound for Seville.[13] For five days they traveled across the Quixotic "classic ground" of La Mancha, where windmills and inns reminded him of all the Cervantesque characters, and where also the signs of poverty and houses still dilapidated from the Napoleonic War brought fears of robbery to his mind. In *Outre-Mer* he was to record with sadness the aspect of this part of the countryside:

> The villages you pass through are poverty-stricken and half-depopulated; and the squalid inhabitants wear a look of misery that makes the heart ache. Every league or two the ruins of a post house, or a roofless cottage with shattered windows and blackened walls, tells a sad tale of the last war. It was there that a little band of peasantry made a desperate stand against the French, and perished by the bullet, the sword, or the bayonet. (OM, 2:111)

Apart from the threat of robbery, the long journey in the uncomfortable *galera* also took its toll in the young traveler's resilience, for, as he confessed in a letter to Irving, "I was parched by the sun; choked by the dust:—torn to atoms by the motion of the vehicle:—and finally reached Seville with a fever that lingered about me all the time I was there" (LL, 1:242). Clearly this vocabulary of pain, whether true or exaggerated, brings the reader back to the rhetorical stratagems employed in the previous century by what Charles Batten dubs "splenetic travelers."[14] Just as in the Enlightenment, so in Longfellow's days complaints about one's trip carried on drawing attention to the veracity of the travel account.

The connection between travel and reading, so important in the formation of a textualized version of abroad, does not play as important a role in Longfellow's journals and travel letters as it does in other authors' accounts. He turns to other topics in the representa-

Self-portrait of Henry Wadsworth Longfellow on his way from Málaga to Granada in November 1827 [bMS Am 1340 (172)]. The caption ("To horse—to horse—he quits, forever quits / A scene of peace though soothing to his soul") evinces the magnetism that Byron's poetry exerted on the male American traveler in Spain. By permission of the Houghton Library, Harvard University.

tion of Spain. We have already seen how Cervantes instilled in him vague literary recollections. Likewise, he visited Seville with echoes of Byron's *Don Juan* in his mind, but left it without regret. Even though he was comfortably surprised by the disposition of the houses, with their refreshing inner courtyards, the cathedral did not impress him, and neither did the beauty of the women, of whom he had heard so much. He found Cádiz equally depressing because behind its architectural pulchritude he perceived the decay of its once bold fortifications and witnessed the existence of numerous beggars on the streets. Longfellow proceeded from Cádiz to Gibraltar, where he expected to find passage for Italy and thus finish his visit to Andalusia, but lack of vessels detained him in the British fortification for about a month. At last, tired of waiting, he traveled to Málaga, where he pressed on for an unplanned excursion to Granada. His journals intimate that his approach to Granada was an expedition into the world of fantasy. He recalls that "the lights of the city glimmering in the distance and the sound of the evening bells called my thoughts away from the realities of life to the musings of romance." But even in such otherwordly retreat, Longfellow realized that the imagination could not match the spiritual rewards of the traveler. "There are moments in our lives to which we feel that romance could add nothing, and which poetry itself could not beautify," he wrote in Granada. "Such were those I passed lingering about the Alhambra and dreaming over the warlike deeds of other days."[15] On 15 November he abandoned those scenes of romance and returned to Malaga, where a week later he embarked on a Swedish ship bound for Marseilles.

II

Longfellow's Spanish sojourn of eight months had concluded, and with it, judging from his letters and journals, his desire to travel and see the world. From now on he was to textualize Spain rather than visit it. "I am travelling through Italy without enthusiasm—and just curiosity enough to keep me awake! I feel no excitement—no—nothing of that romantic feeling which everybody else has—or pretends to have," he complained to his mother from Florence in late January 1828. And he continued: "The fact is I am homesick for Spain. I want to go back there again. The recollections of it completely ruin Italy for me: and next to going home—let me go to Spain" (LL, 1:255). Perhaps, as Longfellow himself suggests in *Outre-Mer*, it was more a case of plain homesickness than just of romantic longing for Spain, but, according to his brother, he "was thrice in Europe in after years, but never again visited Spain. He was unwilling to break the spell of that early time."[16] However this might be, the liminal state of traveler had to give way to that of young scholar. After his European Grand Tour Longfellow finally returned to Maine in August 1829 to assume academic responsibilities at Bowdoin College, where he taught until 1835. During his first years in that institution Longfellow worked intensively preparing translations, scholarly essays, and textbooks, even though these were activities, as he confessed to his friend Greene, that did not require the same courage that creative writing did.[17] Moreover, he attempted to produce his first full-blown nonscholarly work in a series of European sketches published as "The Schoolmaster" in the *New England Magazine* between 1831 and 1833. Longfellow lost interest in this project and never completed it, though later he recycled some of it in *Outre-Mer*. He had conceived both projects during his residence in Europe and they shared certain traits.

The rather long process of composition of *Outre-Mer* evinces not only Longfellow's ambivalent thoughts as to the scope of his creation but also, and perhaps more importantly, certain doubts about his own literary authority. Longfellow's first mention of *Outre-Mer* appears in a letter from Göttingen dated 15 May 1829 where he told his father he was working on "a kind of Sketch-Book of scenes in France, Spain, and Italy" (LL, 1:309–10). The project remained stagnant, even after a letter that his friend Everett sent him from Boston on 27 April 1832 where he encouraged him to write: "Our friend Irving is coming out with a new Sketch Book for which I expect great things. Cannot you give us something in the form of travels or sketches in prose or verse about Spain? The subject is excellent and almost new. Your recollections are now more fresh than they will ever be hereafter" (PP, 227–28). There is no further mention of Longfellow's travel writings until 9 March 1833 when he confided to his friend Greene that he was at work with "a kind of Sketch Book of France, Spain, Germany, and Italy;—composed of descriptions—sketches of character—tales, illustrating manners and customs, and tales illustrating nothing in particular. Whether the book will ever see the light is yet uncertain. If I finally conclude to publish it, I think I shall put it out in Nos. or parts" (LL, 1:408). He finally did put it out in numbers, and thus in 1833 Hilliard, Gray & Company of Boston published *Outre-Mer* No. I, composed of sketches of France. Only the sketch "The Journey into Spain" contained some Spanish materials. By mid-July, writing to Alexander H. Everett apropos this number, Longfellow said: "I fear they may strike you as rather too trivial in their character. My object is to give variety, and in the next no. which will appear in the Fall, I shall endeavor to give something of a different shade and hue" (LL, 1:419). Despite his fears of seeming artlessness, Longfellow was nevertheless confident in the successful completion of his European travelogue, as he told to George Ticknor later in December of that year: "What I shall finally make out [of] this book I hardly know; as it is not yet fully written out. If I can complete my plan satisfactorily, I hope the work will not be without its merits" (LL, 1:427).

Outre-Mer No. II, the number that contained his sketches on Spain, was published in 1834 by Lilly, Wait & Company of Boston. As soon as the manuscript was nearly finished, towards the end of October Longfellow wrote his friend George W. Greene to outline its contents for him:

> The No. on Spain is finished. Its papers are; I. Spain; being a general introduction. 2. El Cajon de Sastre;—a collection of sketches in Madrid. 3. The village of El Pardillo. 4. The Ancient Spanish Ballads. 5. Leaves from my Journal; embracing my journey to Andalusia, and sketches of Cordova, Cadiz, Seville, and Granada. A thousand topics are touched upon; and I think this No. far superior to either of the preceding. The style is more spirited and vigorous,—and the subjects less familiar to most people. (LL, 1:455)

The representation of the country that Longfellow rendered in that number did not vary considerably from what appeared in the subsequent 1835 two-volume edition, published in the United States by Harper's and by Bentley in England. In that edition he expanded the section on Spain with translations and a scholarly essay on devotional Spanish poetry previously published in the *North American Review*.[18] The letters to his editors prior to the preparation of the book reveal that he was quite particular about terms of publication, copyright, profits, and anonymity. Under no circumstance did he want to mar his starting literary career with a youthful travelogue of apparent inconsequence. Still, as George Rice Carpenter observes, this minor travelogue showed American audiences that "the author knew not only books, but men; not only languages, but life," and also demonstrated that he "had caught the subtle essence of Old World romance which Ticknor, with all of his philosophic questionings had missed."[19]

Although, in general, one can agree with Newton Arvin that *Outre-Mer* "seems to have made no very great stir either among reviewers or readers," on the whole the critical reception of the book turned out to be auspicious for the neophyte author.[20] In July 1834, Longfellow wrote about it to George W. Greene in high spirits: "Outre-Mer No. 2 seems to succeed admirably. The critics say he is a fine boy, and looks very much like his *pa*" (LL, 1:443). In a letter from Boston, dated 20 July 1833, Everett sent him his "best acknowledgments for it" and promised to make it known in the next number of the *North American Review* (PP, 229). It was in that periodical that William Peabody called *Outre-Mer* "the production of a writer of talent, and of cultivated taste," and applauded its author's openness to things foreign.[21] Similarly, while acknowledging that the book was not especially exciting as a travelogue, the *American Monthly Magazine* nevertheless praised its style and emphasized its being the product of a poet, for its descriptions have "a tranquilizing and subduing influence, which steals insensibly into the heart and captivates the soul with its soothing spell."[22] The *Knickerbocker*, in the most laudatory of the reviews, prophesied that the author had "a glorious career before him" and enumerated the merits of the work, namely "a quiet sweetness of thought, forcible pathos, the most accurate observation of men and things, a quick perception of the burlesque, and moving appeals to the affections." But most important, perhaps, was the fact that this review paid close attention to Longfellow's mood in the Spanish chapters: "In Spain, our author seems to have been impressed with the different moods of Cervantes and Manrique; sometimes gay and merry, at others sad and didactic."[23] In short, Longfellow's first literary venture received the public support that, in a flattering manner, his pilgrim of Outre-Mer had requested from readers in "The Epistle Dedicatory."

By and large it could be argued that Longfellow was trying to accomplish in one travel book what Irving had fulfilled with many, that is, to offer a cultural interpretation of the Old World distilled through the eyes of a wandering American litterateur. The task was difficult, especially since early in the book the traveler-narrator seems to strike a note of pride in his remembrance of things done in Europe: "I have traversed France from Normandy to Navarre; smoked my pipe in a Flemish inn; floated through Holland in a Trekschuit; trimmed my midnight lamp in a German university; wandered and mused amid the classic scenes of Italy; and listened to the gay guitar and merry castanet on the borders of the blue Guadalquiver [sic]" (OM, I: 9). This catalogue of place names and things usually associated with them reveals that in *Outre-Mer* Longfellow tended toward a broader general understanding of Europe—unlike Irving, who with his British and Spanish sketchbooks had striven toward cultural specificity. His chief goal was to render an account and spiritual exploration of Catholic Europe in which Spain assumed a central position. That Longfellow was not interested in the representation of a single European nation can be derived as well from what he confided to his father from Trieste in December 1829: "Whoever first makes a Sketch Book of Spain will necessarily make a very interesting book" (LL, 1:287). Irving had just published *Chronicle of the Conquest of Granada* and the only full American record of travel in Spain was Mackenzie's *A Year in Spain*. Had Longfellow been extremely attracted to the project, perhaps he might have written his Spanish sketchbook before *The Alhambra* (1832), but he never did. He had his own plans for a travel book of Europe.

III

The avoidance of a straightforward narrative line is probably the most noticeable departure from the previous eighteenth-century travel-writing tradition in Longfellow's representation. The chapter that marks the first part of his Spanish tour, "The Journey into Spain," details the traveler's movement from France to Madrid. Yet once he has settled in the capital the narrative shifts its focus toward miscellaneous themes discussed in the chapters "Spain," "A Tailor's Drawer," and "Ancient Spanish Ballads." At that point, what would seem a resumption of the account of the journey—the visit to an adjacent village described in "The Village of Pardillo"—is interrupted by another disconnected essay ("The Devotional Poetry of Spain"), so that it becomes difficult to discern the narrator's intentions. The narrator finally proceeds with "The Pilgrim's Breviary," the last sketch on Spain, which relates his journey to the south. Through this meandering narration the pilgrim-narrator manages to convey a sense of cultural rather than geographical movement. Apparently interspersing miscellaneous information without a purpose, he is striving to communicate a more transcendent message than simply his motion from place to place.

This sort of mixed bag containing essays on culture interwoven with narrative is characteristic of the hybrid and conventional nature of travel writing. In this anti-narrative discourse the pilgrim narrator vacillates, stops, changes subject abruptly, and again picks up where he left off his account. Edward Wagenknecht observes, for instance, that "the travel sketches are frequently broken in upon however by character studies and occasionally by stories."[24] On certain occasions even the stories are interrupted or not reported at all. In a scene reminiscent of Irving, for example, Longfellow explains that during an excursion to the old Moorish alcazar near the village of Villanueva del Pardillo the different members of the party told legends of the past related to the ruin. But unlike Irving, for whom that would have probably meant a cue to open a new chapter retelling, at least, one of the tales, Longfellow cancels that option arguing that "upon reflection, they [the tales] seem too frivolous, and must therefore give place to a more serious theme" (OM, 2:44). Still, the following chapter cannot be more significantly anticlimactic, for it discusses religious Spanish poetry. The shift to something less frivolous may thus be part of the travel writer's belatedness, that is, of his difficulty in writing about his travels once the travel experience itself is terminated and its textualization begins.

While the textual indefinition of travel writing as a genre is one of the rhetorical conventions that Longfellow seems to be exploiting quite intentionally in *Outre-Mer*, another one that also operates strongly in it is the implied orality of the text. As Terry Caesar observes, American travel writing was not meant to be completely textual, since quite often the travel writers' addresses to their readers remind us of the lectures given by travelers on the Lyceum circuit.[25] Longfellow was probably aware of this rhetorical practice. If on the one hand the haphazard representation of Spain may have led readers to conclude that the pilgrim was not making a clear point, on the other hand his aimless narrative performance concomitantly reiterated, in a paradoxical manner, the verisimilitude and the romance of the account by stressing its oral quality. Longfellow's raconteur introduces the issue of orality as early as in the second chapter of the book, entitled "The Pilgrim of Outre-Mer," where he recalls how in the past travelers and pilgrims alike invited listeners to take a seat by the fireside and receive in exchange a few travel yarns. Aware that in the nineteenth century readers have become "wiser and less credulous," he nevertheless acknowledges they still retain "the same curiosity—the same love of novelty—the same fondness for romance, and tales by the chimney-corner" (OM, 2:8). Thus, the narrator also imbues his representation throughout with the romance of fireside oral culture.

In the light of the structural orality of *Outre-Mer*, one could even suggest that Longfellow came up with the first fireside representation of Spain. Indeed it is a representation, as Stanley Williams suggests, especially suited for youngsters: "The Spanish chapters resemble a child's guide to the geography and literature of the Peninsula."[26] There are instances in *Outre-Mer* where the narrator fashions himself as a fireside traveler, but Longfellow's pilgrim is not trying to delude anybody with his yarns. In a cozy environment like that of his later "The Fire of Drift-Wood," Longfellow attempts to construct an honest, sympathetic rapport between traveler/writer and listener/reader. Irving's Crayon had invited the reader to accompany him in his rambles within the Alhambra, and he had highlighted, too, his very writing and narrating from inside the Moorish palace. Longfellow's pilgrim, on the other hand, emphasizes less his *being* in Spain than his *having been* in Spain. This rhetorical strategy allows him to transcend the otherness of the Spaniards and engage in a sentimental project whereby he can join his audiences almost as if to deliver them a tale of survival and reassurance. In short, he demonstrates that a young American could wander in the Catholic Old World and still return home safe and sound to tell the fireside story of his own pilgrimage. The final pages of the book, in particular, make this issue of orality and textuality coalesce in the construction of personal experiences: "My pilgrimage is finished. I have come home to rest; and recording the time passed, I have fulfilled these things and written them in this book, as it would come into my mind,—for the most part, when the duties of the day were over and the world around me was hushed in sleep" (OM, 2:251). Here Longfellow reiterates the orality of the travel account, emphasizing the first-person pronoun, and stresses its constructed nature, stating that it becomes a sort of Wordsworthian "emotion recollected in tranquility" late at night in the travel writer's chamber. Moreover, as the sentences he uses come partly from Sir John de Mandeville's *Travels*—a paradigmatic work of fireside travel writing—and partly from Wordsworth, he extratextually connects *Outre-Mer* both to its ancient roots of medieval pilgrimage writings and its more recent conventions of romantic travel writing.

The rise of a clearly articulated antitouristic discourse that attempts to separate genuine travelers from spurious tourists constitutes, as James Buzard has demonstrated, one of the most important rhetorical conventions of early nineteenth-century travel writing. Longfellow, however, made use of this discourse just as much as he disregarded it, and with its anti-touristic and antididactic stance *Outre-Mer* became precisely the opposite of what the Enlightenment travel book had stood for. During his brief stop in the northern town of Vitoria, for example, the narrator begins a typical description of the local landmarks, but decides not to continue it because "descriptions of churches and public squares are dull

and tedious matters for those readers who are in search of amusement, and not of instruction" (OM, 2:194). Likewise, he refuses to
provide a meticulous depiction of the bullfight, one of the quintessential commonplaces of travel books on Spain. In the travel writings he sent home he assumed a similar position. His description
of the cathedral of Seville, for example, is broken off abruptly: "I
was never born to write a guide-book; I have no patience in describing churches, palaces, cities, so I have left a blank to be filled up
with engravings."[27] This attitude was no doubt a response to several
factors. First, his criticism of touristic discourse constituted a reaction against the constraints and weaknesses thus far imposed by
matter-of-fact Enlightenment travel books. Secondly, his anti-intellectual stance, as Thomas Pauly suggests, was a strategy Longfellow
used to reconcile himself with the general public and at the same
time get rid of the stigma of boring scholar he had received from
Alexander Everett, editor of the *North American Review*.[28] Paradoxically, though, nothing could be in fact further from anti-intel-
lectualism than the three literary essays he included in *Outre-Mer*.
Finally, there is the romantic feeling of individualism that sets the
traveler apart from the rest of ever-growing participants in the collective cultural practice of European travel.

Longfellow particularly voices the antitouristic discourse of early
nineteenth-century travel writing in "The Journey to Italy," where
he humorously describes two tourists he met. One of them was an
American

> who made it a point to see everything which was mentioned in the
> guide-books, and boasted how much he could accomplish in a day. He
> would despatch a city in an incredibly short space of time. A Roman
> aqueduct, a Gothic cathedral, two or three modern churches, and an
> ancient ruin or so were only a breakfast for him. . . . Every object
> seemed of equal magnitude and importance. He saw them all; they
> were all wonderful. (OM, 2:145)

On seeing this prototype of Twainian innocent abroad, Longfellow
concludes, "Life is short, and art is long; yet spare me from thus
travelling with the speed of thought; and trotting from daylight
until dark, at the heels of a cicerone, with an umbrella in one hand
and a guide-book and plan of the city in the other" (OM, 2:145).
The obvious target in these lines is, apart from the philistine tourist, the genre of the guide book. With its facts and realistic information, it was located at the antipodes of the impressionistic
representation Longfellow was trying to carry out, and thus received the scorn of the romantic traveler's antitouristic discourse.

Longfellow's refusal in *Outre-Mer* to represent the geographical setting of his peninsular travels realistically is also symptomatic of the turn to the romantic in the early American representation of Spain. Longfellow was aware of the new literary preferences of his readers, and to satisfy their fondness of romance, one of the strategies he followed was to select and excise very carefully what he had inscribed during his sojourn. In the personal writings he sent home he tried to bring his family close to all that he was seeing, often making geographical similes that compared areas of Spain with parts of their native New England. He was, as it were, Americanizing the Iberian landscape in a way that no other American traveler in Spain had so far done so overtly, even though, like them, Longfellow compares and contrasts always to the advantage of his own nation. He told them, *mutatis mutandis,* that the rough sea he gazed from the Basque coast reminded him of the seashore in Maine, that the mountains of Despeñaperros bore some resemblance to the White Mountains, and that the Guadalquivir called to his mind the Delaware River. Moreover, the cart he took to go to Segovia looked like a westward pioneer's wagon, and the smoky inn-kitchens, with their badly ventilated conical hearths, reminded him of a wigwam.

In contrast to the familiarization and detail he purveyed to the readers in his family circle, for the general readers of *Outre-Mer* Longfellow represented the peninsular landscape as a distant, unfamiliar locale. It was a strategy characteristic of the romance that he used to make his account palatable and thus ingratiate himself again with his readers. This genre, as Gillian Beer observes, by bringing this dissociation between reader and subject matter to the forefront of the narration, distances audiences from the contrarily palpable realism of the account. What would otherwise appear to be close to home or similar to things at home is viewed as exotic and remote.[29] As a travel writer, paradoxical as this may be, Longfellow thus defamiliarizes his audiences rather than acquaints them with the actual setting of the journey. This was never true of earlier Enlightenment travel accounts, which, though highlighting the exoticism of Spain here and there, constantly remind the reader the actual state of the country: barren, solitary, treeless, and uncommunicative.

IV

Shunning the assumed objectivity of Enlightenment travel writing, the textual construction of Spain that the early nineteenth-

Interior of an inn in the Kingdom of Valencia, featuring some of the elements that Longfellow Americanized in the writings he sent home. The local carts, for example, reminded him of pioneer wagons whereas the conical hearths of the kitchens looked like wigwams. From volume 1 of the folio edition of Alexandre de Laborde's *Voyage pittoresque et historique de l'Espagne* (Paris: Didot, 1806–20). Courtesy of Arxiu Històric de la Ciutat de Barcelona.

century American travelers produced wavered between the romance of history and the romance of literature. Since historical topics, as we will see, were not Longfellow's forte, he leaned toward literary allusions to instil romance into his narration of Spain. This authorial attitude demonstrates once again the constructedness of the Spanish text, as Longfellow relied on information he either did not know or was not much interested in during his first journey. It has already been mentioned that, while in Spain, the young Longfellow's knowledge of Spanish literature was not too broad, but even so *Outre-Mer* strives to transmit a different impression. As he prepares for his excursion to Villanueva del Pardillo, for example, he says he is eager not only "to see the peasantry of the land in their native homes" but also "to see how far the shepherds of Castile resemble those who sigh and sing in the pastoral romance of Montemayor and Gaspar Gil Polo" (OM, 2:29). Similarly, as he crosses the region of La Mancha he is quick to remind that this is the same plain where Don Quixote wandered. The crossover from life to literature, from past to present, and vice versa can take place in such a bookish region. "A few years pass away, and history becomes romance, and romance, history," he affirms. "To the peasantry of Spain, Don Quixote and his Squire are historic personages" (OM, 2:104). No doubt, in representing this land of pastoralism and chivalric romance as a land of living history, Longfellow's pilgrim was inviting readers to travel with him two centuries backwards. It was an invitation similar to that which Irving's Geoffrey Crayon extended to readers, to perambulate with him the interiors of the Alhambra and fancy themselves in fifteenth-century Spain. This evasive pastoralism and escapist literary historicism place Longfellow's account, no doubt, far from the tangible country his colleague Mackenzie narrated in *A Year in Spain*, or away from the realism displayed in Caroline Cushing's *Letters*. They nevertheless iterate once again the constructedness of the Spanish text, contrived after a long information-gathering process away from the country and the people being represented.

The promise of distant blissful lands publicized by many a travel book must have been an appealing topic for many antebellum readers. The romantic retreat into an arcadian setting that the sketch "The Village of Pardillo" promises is, however, a slight failure, as Longfellow debunks romance just as much as he champions it. To begin with, he shows that the pastoral ideal is deceiving, for even though the setting is picturesque, the village turns out to be only "a cluster of stone hovels roofed with red tiles and basking in the hot sun, without a single tree to lend . . . shade or shelter" (OM, 2:31–32). The local church, unlike the clean, whitewashed building he compels readers to imagine, becomes another fiasco, for it is simply "a gloomy little edifice, standing upon the outskirts of the village, and built of dark and unhewn stone, with a spire like a sugar-loaf" (OM, 2:34). Moreover, the "little great men of El Pardillo," as he affectionately yet sarcastically dubs the priest, the mayor, the surgeon, the sacristan, and the notary public of that village, constitute a grotesque gallery of characters. The mayor, for example, he terms "a most potent, grave, and reverend personage, with a long beak of a nose, and a pouch under his chin, like a pelican" (OM, 2:39). The notary public, on the other hand, is "a poor man with a large family, who would make a paper cigar last half an hour, and who kept up his respectability in the village by keeping a horse" (OM, 2:40). Compared to the list of ministers, monarchs, and potentates often displayed in the travel accounts of the Enlightenment, as for example in Ticknor's writings, one cannot help noticing an ironic turn in Longfellow's description of these local personages. But even as he discovers that the reality of the country is far from the ideal *locus amoenus* of literature, Longfellow clings to the idyllic idea of rural Spain and even tries to replicate it himself.

In the ideology of the pastoral, Raymond Williams observes in *The Country and the City*, the relations of production, the exploitation of the poor, and many more serious problems are consciously absent.[30] These concerns are absent, too, from Longfellow's representation of rural Spain. His account of what he did there during his stay, especially his description of himself leisurely reading the pastoral poetry of Garcilaso de la Vega under the shade of a tree, supports it. The only pastoral elements Longfellow found lay in the different amusements with which the villagers spent their free time after mass on Sunday, when

> the time was devoted to sports and recreation; and the day passed off in social visiting, and athletic exercises, such as running, leaping, wrestling, pitching quoits, and heaving the bar. When evening came, the merry sound of the guitar summoned to the dance; then every nook and alley poured forth its youthful company,—light of heart and heel, and decked out in all the holyday finery of flowers, and ribands, and crimson sashes. (OM, 2:41)

Longfellow rejoices, with a certain degree of condescension, in the fact that the poor peasants have a good time after a long week of hard toil, but his retreat into a bucolic Spain ignores the real issues that the popular classes there had to face. "Longfellow cared not a fig for looking beyond the picturesque; for concerning himself with those social and historic causes which had made Spain a prey for lawbreakers and bandits," writes Lawrance Thompson, who also affirms that "the young romantic, whose vision was blurred by his love of the bizarre, could not work up any interest in the age-old struggle between the oppressed and the powerful."[31] Longfellow does not, like Mackenzie, excoriate with acerbity those who caused these problems. On the contrary, like Irving, he also seeks refuge from the ugly contemporary scene. Yet rather than retrenching into the timeless primitivism or perennial past of Spain, like Irving, Longfellow seeks security in a sentimentalized religious retreat.

Irving and Longfellow were both romantics, but romantics of different kinds. Irving's kind of romanticism was much more historically based while Longfellow's adopted a much more subjective spiritual stance. Moreover, Irving was much more influenced by Walter Scott's kind of historicism, or by historicism more generally, than was Longfellow, whose concerns were more sentimental and transcendent. Although he knew something of Spanish history, Longfellow was far less informed than Noah, Ticknor, Mackenzie, Irving, or Cushing. In general, the historical discourse that he blends with romance comes precisely from the medieval literature that he began to study after his residence in the country. His meager knowledge of or lack of interest in Spanish history is evident in the chapter entitled "Spain," which voices his sorrow for the current condition of the country. "My mind instinctively reverts from the degradation of the present to the glory of the past," the pilgrim observes, yet what he considers to be glory is left untold (OM, 1:205). It is, most likely, the Christian, masculine feats of arms that his fellow New England historians admired so much and which, seeing the state of the country, he wished could return. "The dust of the Cid lies mingling with the dust of Old Castile," he comments, "but his spirit is not buried with his ashes. It sleeps, but is not dead. The day will come when the foot of the tyrant shall be shaken from the neck of Spain." Significantly, though, the young traveler finishes his tirade with a telling coda that chokes any emerging radical politics: "But I am no political seer—I will dwell no longer on this theme" (OM, 1:206). Dutiful to his paternal recommendation,[32] he tried not to intervene in local politics at all.

The difference between the letters and the journals and the published text once again sheds light on the condition of travel writing as a rhetorical construct. Longfellow employed the estrangement necessary to create romance not only for his geographical representation of Spain but also for his account of the travel episodes themselves and, in particular, of everything connected to the state of civil unrest reigning in the country. This was not true, however, of the letters he sent to his family, where more than once it is possible to sense young Longfellow's anguished voice. For rhetorical reasons the text obfuscates or ignores the problem of terror. The "truth" is more likely to be found in the more immediate letters than in the more retrospective published text. To his mother, for example, he declared that he had entered Spanish territory "with fear and trembling:—for in sober sadness, the moment a traveller crosses the frontier he may look upon all he has as publick [sic] property" (LL, 1:225–26). After the respite of his stay in Madrid, he took to the road again to face the threat of banditti. "You cannot imagine with what fear and trembling one travels at the present day in Spain," he wrote in his journal, also adding that "the thoughts of the traveler are always melancholy." At night, in an inn-kitchen, explains Longfellow, the thoughts of all travelers are focused on the robberies they narrowly avoided and the ones they may face the next day.[33]

But whereas this was the cruel reality that his travel writings recorded daily, in *Outre-Mer* he treated the problem of travel insecurity so jocosely that one really doubts that the terror Longfellow is referring to was a genuine social problem. Arriving in Seville, for example, he regrets not having been robbed, for he "had bought a watch large enough for the clock of a village church, for the express purpose of having it violently torn . . . by a fierce-whiskered highwayman" (OM, 1:117). Moreover, he relates that on several occasions he escaped a holdup by the skin of his teeth, and exclaims, "If I print this in a book, I am undone. What! Travel in Spain and not be robbed!" (OM, 1:117). In so facetiously manifesting his disappointment, Longfellow was perhaps criticizing stereotypes representing Spain as a locus of violence and terror and at the same time laughing at the masculinist discourse of some travel books where the male narrator kept a stiff upper lip against all travel odds. Moreover, in presenting coach robberies as something comic and remote, nearly as though he was describing an episode of *Don Quixote*, Longfellow seemed to underscore their fictional, romance-like quality. The cheerful, comic tone—reminiscent of Irving's lighthearted mood in *The Alhambra*—that *Outre-Mer* sometimes achieves undoubtedly iterates the escapist dimension of the book.

The comicity Longfellow deploys may iterate the scapist dimension of the book, but it also accentuates the degree to which he is working intertextually, playing his account off against stereotypes and discourses embedded in other accounts of travel, oral or literary—or fictional accounts of Spain. Longfellow's desultory representation of that country, as we have seen, did not furnish readers with much of the geographical, agricultural, or historical information present in Enlightenment travel writing. *Outre-Mer* lacks chapters on the history of the principal Spanish cities, the revenue produced by the main crops, or the relations between Spain and other countries. Reflecting the romantic turn in travel literature, Longfellow's book epitomizes Spanishness not through this previous fact-gathering discourse, but through picturesqueness. Longfellow relied strongly on character sketches with which he could construct the identity of Spain along the lines of gender, class, and ethnicity, even though otherness never was for him as strong a preoccupation as it was for Irving. Interestingly enough, one of the moments that best exemplifies this search for picturesque subjects is his voyeuristic positioning at the balcony of his room with the cycle of the day as a temporal frame. Just as Irving in "The Balcony" gazes at the motley crowd in the Vivarrambla of Granada, so in "A Tailor's Drawer" Longfellow describes the different types of people walking by the Puerta del Sol in Madrid. He sketches, among others, a young woman, a beau, a monk, and a water carrier, but his most peculiar character sketches are those of people from the provinces. Making use of the dominant gaze that Mary Louise Pratt sees as typical of colonial subjects, Longfellow observes and represents the diversity of subjects in the center of the empire and not in the fringes. Unlike Irving, who, as we saw in the previous chapter, deconstructed the political structure of Spain by situating its center in Granada, Longfellow enjoys being at the contemporary geopolitical center of the nation.

While in general one can agree with Thomas Pauly's observation that most of Longfellow's character types tend to highlight national traits rather than illustrating universal values, in several examples the opposite seems to be the case.[34] The common trait of at least two longer character sketches is the romantic exaltation of the solitary roving man. The first is a *sopista*, or young errant student living off the soup or charity of others, who seems literally lifted from a Golden Age picaresque novel (OM, 2:106–11). The second is a *contrabandista* or smuggler he runs into on the way to Granada:

> He was an athletic man, and rode a spirited horse of the Arab breed. A black bearskin jacket covered his broad shoulders, and around his waist was wound the crimson *faja*, so universally worn by the Spanish peasantry. His velvet breeches reached below his knee, just meeting a pair of leather gaiters of elegant workmanship. A gay silken handkerchief was tied round his head, and over this he wore the little round Andalusian hat, decked out with a profusion of tassels of silk and bugles of silver. The steed he mounted was dressed no less gaily than his rider. There was a silver star upon his forehead, and a bright-colored woollen

tassel between his ears; a blanket striped with blue and red covered his saddle and even the Moorish stirrups were ornamented with brass studs. (OM, 2:123–24)

This description, with its details of fabrics and colors, highlights the exoticism and diversity of the character. The solitary rider thus stands by itself almost as an icon of Andalusia, but by appearing against the snowy background of the Sierra Nevada his stature gains significance as a universal symbol of male romantic freedom. By representing a milieu populated by smugglers and other male derelicts, Longfellow became also instrumental in the overall gendering of Spanish travel writing. With Longfellow too the antebellum male armchair traveler could fancy himself traveling safely yet adventurously across dangerous ground at home.

Longfellow's conclusion, reached after the observation and inscription of many picturesque characters throughout his Spanish journey, is that sadness, melancholy, and passion form the national character. But unlike Ticknor and Irving, Longfellow does not study at length the relationship that may exist between the geography and history of Spain and the psychology of its inhabitants. Instead, in a sweeping statement on Spanish character he affirms that "its prominent traits are a generous pride of birth, a superstitious devotion to the dogmas of the Church, and an innate dignity, which exhibits itself even in the common and every-day employments of life" (OM, 1:206). All of these national traits he also found most visible in the ancient poetry of Spain, which, echoing romantic notions of folklore, he regarded as the record of the true soul of a country.

Out of all of these traits, however, nineteenth-century American travel writing diligently resorted to the deployment of religion for its textual construction of Spain. Longfellow was not altogether unaware of that attraction. Accordingly, along with its representation of the national traits of France, Spain, and Italy, another important characteristic of *Outre-Mer* is its religious theme. Longfellow's exploration of Roman Catholicism offered, on the one hand, a dose of romance to his readership, and also, on the other hand, a spiritual framework for the tour of his pilgrim-narrator. If the romance of character appealed to his readers, the same was possibly true of the romance of Roman Catholicism. The Protestant bias of the nineteenth-century American traveler in Spain that we saw in previous chapters is apparent above all in the letters Longfellow sent home. "They have as little pure religion as can be found upon the face of the earth," he wrote to his father on 16 July 1827 in connection with the religious services he had seen in Madrid (LL, 1:235). For

the Unitarian Longfellow the pomp and ceremonies of Roman Catholicism in Spain constituted an exotic and sometimes bizarre set
of customs. In particular, he found the passage of the Host to be
one of the most imposing rituals, even more so during the solemn
Corpus Christi procession when the paraphernalia of church banners, martial music, and kneeling onlookers powerfully ratified the
presence and sway of the church in Spain. Likewise, he detested
the association of Church and state publicized in two annual ceremonies in which, emulating Jesus Christ, the Queen and the King
respectively fed and washed some indigents in the royal palace.

Although, or perhaps because, Longfellow found certain Roman
Catholic rituals very peculiar, he chose not to include them in
Outre-Mer, where his religious criticisms struck a milder key. Once
again, the constructedness of the published travel text was making
itself manifest. Cecil Williams believes that Longfellow was "particularly ambivalent about the Catholic religion he encountered
everywhere; he obviously admired the devotion it evoked and the
respect for art it included, but he was skeptical of the morality of
some of its practices."[35] Instances of superstition and bigotry, of
course, are not absent from *Outre-Mer*. He depicted the bigotry in
a chapter of the French section ("The Baptism of Fire") describing
the martyrdom of a Huguenot under Henry II. Moreover, he mentioned the superstition recalling the belief some people in Spain
have in the existence of a portrait of the Saviour impressed on a
piece of linen.

By and large, however, what seemed to have attracted him more
powerfully was the mysterious and mystical aspect of Roman Catholicism. Religion, for Longfellow, constituted more a matter of
the heart than of the intellect; sentiment prevailed over understanding. This explains his elaborated account in "Jacqueline" of
a girl receiving the extreme unction at her deathbed, and also his
description of a group of youngsters reciting their catechism in
"The Village of Pardillo," where Longfellow's pilgrim leaves the
church convinced that children should not be bothered with meta-
physical subtleties. Other spiritual moments that captivated him
were the Andalusian devotion of the Virgin, and especially the stillness caused by their evening prayer:

> There is something beautiful in thus measuring the march of time . . .
> The close of the day,—the shadows of evening,—the calm of twilight,—
> inspire a feeling of tranquility; and though I may differ from the Catho-
> lic in regard to the object of his supplication, yet it seems to me a
> beautiful and appropriate solemnity, that, at the close of each daily
> epoch of life . . . the voice of a whole people, and of the whole world,

should go up to Heaven in praise, and supplication, and thankfulness. (OM, 1:121–22)

If *Outre-Mer* failed to provide a plain touristic discourse, Longfellow made it an opportunity for conveying a more spiritual type of message. It was one to which his audiences could sentimentally relate, and which should enable them to establish a mutual understanding with people of other cultures and religions sharing the same basic feelings. Unlike all the other travelers in Spain, Longfellow treated Roman Catholicism as one more form of religious expression rather than a sign of fundamental Spanish difference from American Protestantism. This, in a sense, was a foreshadowing of the stance upon which he was to found his subsequent poetical career. Longfellow became famous for a memorable versification and a mythmaking talent that popularized such figures as Miles Standish, Evangeline, or Hiawatha, but even more important for readers was his conception of poetry as a clear, simple, and heartfelt medium of communication between the poet and his audience.

The journey he had started in Maine as an educational grand tour seems at a certain point to have turned into a religious trip, as if the would-be scholar had realized that Europe was not only a cultural source but also a spiritual one. Consequently, his representation of Spain is mediated by the strong religious and moral undercurrent visible from the subtitle of the book ("A Pilgrimage Beyond the Sea") to the titles given to many chapters ("The Pilgrim of Outre-Mer," "The Baptism of Fire," "The Devotional Poetry of Spain," "The Pilgrim's Breviary"). In the light of this turn, then, his representation of Spain occupies a significant central portion in the narrator's pilgrimage. Longfellow's pilgrim (or *peregrinus*) is, in the double sense of the word, a foreigner writing his short (*brevis*) travel sketches and at the same time a religious quester carrying his *breviarium* wherever his pilgrimage takes him. If at times *Outre-Mer* reads like a breviary, it also evinces certain echoes of the Puritan personal narrative. Like Irving's Geoffrey Crayon, the pilgrimage of Longfellow's narrator also ends in the Alhambra, but in contrast, the visit is much less secular. As George William Curtis observed in a review of Longfellow's *Tales of a Wayside Inn* (1863) where he also compared *Outre-Mer* with *The Sketch Book*, "The moral and emotional elements are quite wanting in Irving; they are characteristic of Longfellow."[36]

The moral and emotional elements that characterize Longfellow's prose come in full force in his account of his journey to Granada and at the end of the book. At first, the episode of Granada seems a trip to the land of romance where the gothic setting of the

Alhambra mysteriously affects its beholder. However, only when the traveler's feelings begin to awaken progressively does their spiritual significance begin to emerge. Alone in his chamber, "sleepless,—spell-bound by the genius of the place—entranced by the beauty of the star-lit night," Longfellow asks: "Is this reality and not a dream? Am I indeed in Granada? Am I, indeed, within the walls of that earthly paradise of the Moorish kings?" The epiphany that he experiences on seeing the Moorish palace illuminated by the moonlight, like a surrealistic landscape, allows him to understand his mortality and his goals in life in a clearer way. It also makes him experience the same "buoyance of spirits" and "elasticity of frame" that Irving mentions in *The Alhambra*, being thus elevated to an Emersonian transparent state: "How my spirit is stirred within me! How my heart is lifted up! How my thoughts are rapt away in the visions of other days!" (OM, 2:126). Longfellow also muses, as the Enlightenment travelers did, over the passing of time and the falling of civilizations. But in this case there is a sort of teleological undercurrent, an epiphanic insight into what the traveler is to be and achieve, that no American travel book on Spain before *Outre-Mer* had expressed with so clear religious connotations:

> I may not know the purpose of my being—the end for which an all-wise Providence created me as I am, and placed me where I am; but I do know—for in such things faith is knowledge—that my being has a purpose in the omniscience of my Creator, and that all my actions tend to the completion, to the full accomplishment of that purpose. Is this fatality? No. I feel that I am free, though an infinite and invisible power overrules me. Man proposes, and God disposes. (OM, 2:128)

Longfellow expands these thoughts in the colophon to the book, which emphasizes once again the moral side of writing in general. After indicating that he has at last completed his European sketchbook, the pilgrim narrator adds:

> And as I write, the melancholy thought intrudes upon me—To what end is all this toil? Of what avail these midnight vigils? Dost thou covet fame? Vain dreamer! A few brief days, and what will the busy world know of thee? Alas, this little book is but a bubble on the stream; and although it may catch the sunshine for a moment, yet it will soon float down the swift-rushing current and be seen no more! (OM, 2:252)

No doubt one may suspect that there is a little bit of false pretension in young Longfellow's grandiloquence. His closing words are a rhetorical act performed by someone who indeed expects to be seen by the busy world. But no doubt, too, the religious rhetoric he is employing, though decidedly conventional, evinces the serious and stately tone of the moral literature cultivated in his times.

This moral tone appears as a convention, as a rhetorical bridge of didacticism connecting the travel writings of the Enlightenment with those of the romantic period. Regarded from this point of view, Longfellow also shares with Irving and Caleb Cushing the ballast of Enlightenment teachings. In his account of his romantic visit to Granada, however, Longfellow destabilizes the fixed meaning that the prior tradition of travel writing had assigned to the topic. The traveler, instead of apprehending and inscribing the foreign nation with reason, now does it with the spirit and the imagination. Yet, since this imaginative and spiritual strain in the romantic travel representation of Spain cannot ensure stable meanings, the reader begins to play a more important participant role. Longfellow says that having seen the Moorish palace he lacks words to describe its architecture, ornaments, and colors. "Vague recollections fill my mind,—images dazzling but undefined, like the memory of a gorgeous dream," says Longfellow. "They crowd my brain confusedly, but they will not stay; they change and mingle, like the tremulous sunshine on the wave, till imagination itself is dazzled—bewildered—overpowered!" (OM, 2:130). The role of the reader, then, is to fill in the gaps, the interstices that Longfellow's representation leaves to be filled out.

V

Longfellow never returned to Spain, but he always kept alive his reminiscences of the country as a locus of spirituality. This is especially evinced in "Castles in Spain" (1877), a poem written when he was seventy where he again summarized the journey from north to south he had made fifty years earlier.[37] The sentimental tone of *Outre-Mer* is still there, and so is the catalogue of things Spanish ranging from peasants toiling in the countryside to gaudily dressed muleteers, and from old Castilian towns to whitewashed coastal cities. Granada continues to be idealized. It still is the quester's goal, "The artist and the poet's theme, / The young man's vision, the old man's dream." The representation of Spain Longfellow made in this poem, however, displays a much deeper historical consciousness than what one could find in *Outre-Mer*, and not only quantitatively but qualitatively. Using one of Irving's favorite moments of the romance of Granada—the last sigh of the moor on seeing what he is abandoning before his banishment—Longfellow looks back to the past he is leaving behind and concludes that it is frail and ruinous like the castles he saw in Spain.

7

The American Couple Abroad: Gender and Class Empowerment in the Spanish Travel Writings of Caleb and Caroline Cushing

THE POLITICAL, ETHNOGRAPHIC, AND SENTIMENTAL NARRATION OF Spain circulated by Irving and his contemporaries fostered a notable cultural work that attains an even broader scope if considered alongside two other American books on peninsular travel published in the same decade: Caroline Cushing's *Letters, Descriptive of Public Monuments, Scenery, and Manners in France and Spain* (1832) and Caleb Cushing's *Reminiscences of Spain; the Country, Its People, History, and Amusements* (1833). For the first time these texts provided antebellum readers with a unique and stimulating opportunity to scrutinize two travelers—husband and wife—narrating through disparate literary genres—the letter and the romantic sketchbook—the journey they made together across Spain in 1829 and 1830.[1] Their significance to the overall view of Spain in the antebellum United States, however, lies not so much in their imaginative construction of the country as a locus of history and romance—a rhetorical convention they share with other travel writers—but rather in their use of the travel text as a vehicle for class and gender empowerment. Caleb Cushing's sketchbook displayed the amount of cultural capital that an aspiring politician and member of the New England elite could cash in while in Spain to reinforce his class position, whereas Caroline Cushing's letters destabilized the fixed masculine reading of the peninsular trek and stressed that young American women could also partake of the same collective experience that young men like Ticknor, Mackenzie, and Longfellow had lived through. Class and gender, then, permeate the Spanish narratives of these two New Englanders, and concomitantly contribute to building up the nationalistic rhetoric of antebellum travel writing.

This chapter focuses on the Cushings' representation of Spain not with the goal of comparing their travel records in search of in-consistencies, but rather with the intention of examining the differ-ence that genre and, above all, class and gender make in their construction of Spain in the antebellum United States. Apart from culture and pleasure, William Stowe remarks, the travel ritual of-fered "an exhilarating sense of freedom and power" to Americans abroad.[2] It is precisely in these two words, I think, that one finds the key to enter the texts produced by the Cushings. Caleb Cushing textualized Spain as a huge backdrop, a stage fit for historical remi-niscences and episodes that enabled the male writer to claim cul-tural power and authority as a member of a solid class. Conversely, Caroline Cushing, though sharing some of her husband's ideas on class and gender, envisioned traveling to and writing about Spain rather as an open gate to freedom, a liberation from the apparent domestic narrowness of New England.

There are several reasons, indeed, why Caroline Cushing stands out in the early nineteenth-century American representation of Spain. Traveling to and writing on Spain allowed her, on the one hand, to empower her class status of New England bourgeois housewife, but on the other hand it also permitted her to plant the seeds of an enduring tradition of foreign travel writing later fol-lowed—as Mary Schriber has recently demonstrated in *Writing Home: American Women Abroad, 1830–1920*—by numerous women. Leo Hamalian has observed that the term "abroad" be-came not a only geographical destination but also an abstract idea that emancipated and empowered women travelers. Similarly, Nina Baym has argued that for women like Caroline Cushing tour-ism was a deeply liberating experience. They did not care about being dubbed travelers or tourists; they simply wanted to go abroad and see what other people had seen, so they engaged in a cultural practice that gave them power.[3] From her domestic environment Cushing embarked on such a public activity as writing a travel book, and in so doing she indirectly became one of the first American women to challenge the dominance of men in a field, European travel writing, that antebellum American culture too often consid-ered marginal in the hands of women.[4] Finally, as far as Spanish travel writing is concerned, she became also a sort of pioneer au-thor. Women, let alone American women, have seldom been fa-vored as participants in the representation of Spain, even though their contribution to the travel writing on that country should un-doubtedly deserve more attention.[5] With her letters, Caroline Cushing began an unacknowledged yet long tradition of American women's writing on Spain that is still waiting to reclaim its proper space in literary history.

I

Neither Caleb Cushing nor Caroline Elizabeth Wilde, however, are remembered today for their travel writings on Spain. Whereas the former has found a niche in political or literary histories as congressman, attorney-general of the United States, and American Minister to Spain from 1874 to 1877, the latter is scarcely mentioned anywhere. The scion of a well-to-do family of Salisbury, Massachusetts, Caleb Cushing clearly epitomizes the northeastern intelligentsia that, as we saw in the introduction, traveled in Europe and acquired a cultural capital that later on yielded excellent benefits. He graduated from Harvard in 1817, studied law, and became a tutor there in 1819, the same year that Ticknor had arrived from Europe to teach Modern Languages. Having embarked on what was to become a long legal, political, and belletristic career, by the time he and his wife returned from Europe he had already published two books, *History of the Town of Newburyport* (1826) and *The Practical Principles of Political Economy* (1826).[6] It was, however, with the twenty-five essays and sketches on historical, literary, and social themes collected in the two volumes of *Reminiscences of Spain* that he made his literal entry into the world of creative writing.

Any aspiring litterateur eager to imitate Washington Irving's Crayonesque style in the 1820s and 1830s had to immerse himself into a hodgepodge of styles, personas, and moods. This Caleb Cushing scrupulously did in his Spanish account, which under the generic framework of the sketchbook still maintains the structure of a travel narrative. Apart from the thematic design provided by historical tales and poems, learned and moral essays, and romantic dream visions, the reader no doubt perceives the linearity of a physical and chronological progression. Cushing begins with "The Pyrenees, a Frontier Sketch" and ends with "Bellegarde, a Halt on the Col de Pertus," two border crossings. Moreover, between these poles he intersperses travel sketches that inform on miscellaneous aspects of the country. Finally, Cushing keeps to a minimum references in the text to his wife, whose book he cites, so as to give the fictional impression that he is traveling alone (RS, 2:287). The adoption of a Crayonesque persona strongly demanded that the male traveler maintain the fiction of an exclusive tour abroad full of thrilling episodes, and even though Cushing never becomes as humorous nor as playful a narrator as Irving's Crayon, he nevertheless employs this rhetorical strategy to assert and empower his authorial alter ego abroad.

Caroline Wilde, the daughter of Judge Samuel Sumner Wilde of Newburyport, of the supreme judicial court of Massachusetts, also was, like her future husband, another archetypal offspring of the northeastern elite. Raised and educated under the ideological precepts of republican womanhood, she married Caleb Cushing in November 1824 and duly assumed her position in the New England class system. As William J. Comley observed with a patriarchal bias, she was not only "an accomplished lady of literary and political tastes" but also a wife "who contributed not a little to her husband's career."[7] She should be regarded, however, as a woman who, instead of patterning her life along the social expectations of the Victorian "angel in the house" model, took advantage of her role as helpmate to become an independently minded writer and traveler. At a time when Europe had not yet been invaded by the commonplace figure of the "innocent" American tourist abroad nor by the likes of Daisy Miller, Caroline Cushing took part in the first wave of foreign women travelers who visited Spain, and became the author of one of the few women's travel books published in the United States in the 1830s.[8] Her participation in these two important cultural practices empowered her not only as a representative of her class but, above all, of her gender.

Caroline Cushing was no professional writer, and if she took the pen it was for one the reasons that Mary Suzanne Schriber adduces in her analysis of the emergence of women's travel writing. That is, Cushing wished to tell in writing an important experience just as contemporary travelers do with videos and photographs.[9] The twenty-seven letters that she wrote exclusively about Spain—a total of 344 pages—comprise the second volume of her European travel narrative, and it is thanks to her epistolarity that today we can reconstruct the itinerary she followed with her husband. These were letters addressed to a clear, visible familial audience but also to an implied readership of friends and neighbors.[10] Like her husband, Cushing on certain occasions presents herself in the text as if she was traveling solo, and thus also claims authority for the woman traveler in Spain both as a woman and as a member of a privileged class. All in all, her representation of Spain surpasses in insight, detail, and freshness the detached and tiresome academic approach that her husband provided in his sketchbook à la Irving. Her skill at using some of the conventions of gothic romance, her poignant re-creation of the dangers of travel, and her vivid description of some of the dreary inns in which they sojourned complement and offer a counterimage to the learned essays, literary translations, and evocations of historical figures present in *Reminiscences of Spain*.

The voyage to Europe that Caleb and Caroline Cushing undertook in 1829 became part of the cultural ritual embraced by many members of their class, but it was also propelled by significant personal motives. As Sister Michael Catherine Hodgson points out, because of "ill-health, and a political disappointment—he had lost the election to Congress in 1828" the young lawyer and politician set his eyes on Europe as a temporary escape.[11] The Cushings sailed to Holland with the intention of following the classic Continental Grand Tour, but soon changed the itinerary they had initially planned. Some of the Americans they met in Paris that September—Alexander H. Everett, Washington Irving, Peter Irving, and others—had just spent some time in Spain and were spellbound. They persuaded the young couple to abandon their idea of visiting Italy, and instead compelled them to go to Spain, furnishing them with letters of introduction and also assuring them that the danger of robbery was not very serious and there existed communication between all parts of the Peninsula. Claude Fuess, Cushing's biographer, states that, given the connections between Spain and America, Caleb Cushing did not hesitate to consider it the best course of action and thus they proceeded southwards.[12] The lure of Spain became thus an affair of the heart as much as an affair of the mind.

The Cushings followed the conventional southbound itinerary that Irving and other travelers had pursued before. They entered Spain through Irun on 3 November, traveled across the Basque Country towards Old Castile, and arrived at Burgos five days later. The first impressions of Spain they inscribed in their texts already set the tone for their disparate approaches to the country, approaches that become truly manifest throughout their travel narratives. While Caroline Cushing's letters tend toward a rather realistic point of view, her husband's sketches romanticize the land and fill it with historical and literary associations. Where Irving would probably find picturesqueness she cannot find but dirt and indolence. The arrival scene, which Mary Louise Pratt has demonstrated to be a crucial rhetorical trope in ethnographic as well as in travel writing, offers a good instance of the disparity between the spouses' accounts.[13] The crossing of the Pyrenees loses its liminal mystique in Caroline Cushing's first letter from Spain, where instead of finding a primeval landscape of edenic characters, she represents a scenario of wretchedness and poverty. Conversely, Caleb Cushing uses such a textual opportunity to comment on geopolitical influences and dynastic relations between France and Spain. Whether it was wretchedness or history, Spain nonetheless remained in the eyes of both travelers—and their readers—as an exotic locale to be explored.

The Cushings reached Madrid on 13 November and remained there until the new year. As it was customary for genteel travelers, during their stay in the capital they often met with their own compatriots as well as with local patricians. Fuess remarks that they "found several delightful friends in Madrid, among them being [Cornelius] Van Ness, the newly appointed American Minister, of whom they saw a good deal in a social way,—although Caleb Cushing compared him quite unfavorably with Alexander H. Everett."[14] The social effervescence they met in the capital, being less ebullient than in previous years, allowed them to devote time to educational and touristic pursuits. Moreover, it did not make them immune to the city's daily life. Eager to know the state of the country, Caleb Cushing spent a great deal of time collecting information on political and legislative issues. He also observed life in Madrid during the Christmas festivities and turned it into the subject of his essay "Christmas in Madrid." Likewise, Caroline Cushing lingered in the churches and museums of the capital, attended bullfights, and witnessed the festivities of the royal wedding between Ferdinand VII and Maria Cristina of Naples that took place that December.

The Cushings left for Toledo in early January, and from there they moved on toward the famed region of Andalusia. The trek across the Sierra Morena, the natural barrier between central and southern Spain, became not only a dangerous section of their itinerary but also one especially charged with powerful liminal significance in Caroline Cushing's book. "We passed the boundary stone, which divides La Mancha from Andalusia, and exchanged the wide extended and monotonous plains . . . for the wild romantic grandeur of Andalusia," she records in Letter XV, adding that "the difference in the landscape [was] more sudden and striking than in the weather, which became mild and delightful almost as soon as we entered Andalusia" (LD, 2:181–82). Once in this textualized romantic milieu, both travelers reached Cordova on 11 January, and three days later arrived at Seville.

Andalusia was no doubt the region that held more historical and poetical associations for the young couple. From Seville they traveled to Cádiz, and after a brief visit to the city proceeded toward Gibraltar. They reentered Spain a few days later, through San Roque, where Caroline Cushing rejoiced in their return: "There a supper was served in the Spanish style; and so long had I been habituated to the mode of cooking in Spain, and to the simple manners of the people, that I experienced no small degree of satisfaction on finding myself among them once more, and hearing the melodious accents of the Castilian tongue" (LD, 2:265). Finally, they continued on muleback across the mountains of Málaga and the coastal towns of Estepona, Marbella, and Fuengirola, an itinerary which finally led to Granada. The city and its beautiful setting lived up to the travelers' expectations, but not so much its famous palace.[15] "I could scarcely persuade myself," affirms Caroline Cushing, "that the dingy red towers, so entirely destitute, not only of beauty and elegance, but even of ordinary taste in their design, could possibly belong to that wondrous palace, whose interior is the delight of every beholder" (LD, 2:295). In contrast to her forthright approach, her husband was to inscribe Granada, as we shall see later, as a setting of one of his romantic dream visions in *Reminiscences of Spain*.

After visiting Granada, the young couple traveled toward Murcia, a city which they left on March 5 in order to follow the northbound coastal route to France. The moment of their departure from Spain in late March 1830 becomes for Caleb Cushing as drenched with symbolic significance as their crossing into Andalusia had been for his wife three months before. Cushing, after affirming that "romantic as may be the land, still more romantic is the people of Spain," produces a liminal outpouring akin to Mordecai M. Noah's words on seeing Spain for the last time. As the coach climbs the mountain pass that separates France from Catalonia, he harks back to the different historical periods of Spain and wonders where the grandeur of its empire lies. The answer comes by way of a list of recommendations. Only by doing away with religious bigotry, recognizing the independent American states fully, and repealing restrictions on commerce will Spain enable future travelers to see it "restored to equal prosperity, if not equal power, with that which she could boast of when she was the rival of England, the terror of France, and the mistress of Italy" (RS, 2:300). The once mighty Spain was left behind for ever shrouded in the self-complacent decadence of its imperial glories.

II

The Cushings, like many of the other antebellum Americans who traveled to the Old World, set to the task of narrating their travel experiences as soon as they returned to their native Massachusetts. They both wanted to participate in the textualization of foreign lands and peoples that travelers were undertaking those years, and they did so under clear conventions and constraints of genre, gender, and class. It is no coincidence, for example, that instead of writing realistically about his travel experiences Caleb Cushing chose the sketchbook form—by then a fashionable literary genre among male writers—to evoke his reminiscences. The "conceptual, rather than representational, rendering of experience" that Thomas Pauly defines as the major characteristic of the literary sketch became the best medium of expression for writers who, like Caleb Cushing, felt caught between the learned, commonsensical educational background and the emerging romantic aesthetics of early nineteenth-century America.[16] The literary travel sketch had already begun to be accepted, partly because of Irving's successful *Sketch Book of Geoffrey Crayon*, and partly because it was being culturally sanctioned by the New England literary elite, but this acceptance had not been easy. As Lawrence Buell notes, in the early decades of the nineteenth century critics did not know what to make of travel accounts that combined facts and fiction. They were puzzled by the new mode of writing and wavered between praise and criticism.[17] The reception of *Reminiscences of Spain* then evidences the ambivalent position between the didactic and the pleasurable—that is, the factual and the fictional—to which Caleb Cushing had to respond.

His representation of Spain, however, reveals a protracted and carefully thought process of composition beyond the mere choice of a conventional genre. Apart from exchanging ideas with Irving in Paris, Caleb Cushing also sought and found in Boston support for his sketchbook project in the staff of the *North American Review*. His links to that periodical dated back to his student years at Harvard, where Edward Everett—brother of Alexander H. Everett and one of his former tutors—had encouraged him to write for them. Cushing contributed two essays on Christopher Columbus and Americo Vespucci to that periodical, which he later was to retrieve for his sketchbook. *Reminiscences of Spain* was finally published in Boston by Carter, Hendee and Allen & Ticknor, but sold poorly because, as Fuess observes, "it appeared within a few weeks after Washington Irving's Alhambra."[18] The long shadow of Cushing's master had inevitably clouded the success of his first venture into creative writing.

Admittedly, the indebtedness of *Reminiscences from Spain* to Irving's influential sketchbook became one of the issues that immediately drew more attention from the critics. In the pages of the *North American Review*, on the one hand, Alexander Hill Everett commended Cushing for having adopted an Irvingesque "sort of miscellany, made up of historical and geographical sketches, moral essays, tales and poems," yet considered it "rather a dangerous experiment . . . for a young author to bring himself into direct comparison with a justly popular model."[19] The anonymous reviewer of the *American Monthly Review*, on the other hand, held a more disparaging opinion:

> This book is not marked by the airiness and grace of Mr. Irving's Alhambra. It has little of the poetical playfulness—the inimitable tact—the exquisitely chosen expression—that run through those fascinating volumes. There are not shown the sense of beauty—the just proportion—the delicate shading—the finished art-concealing art—which throw such a charm over the page of Geoffrey Crayon. On the contrary Mr. Cushing's style is too formal, and generally moves with stately buskined tread. There is not variety enough to suit the various subjects that pass in review before him. . . . We rise from Mr. Irving's Alhambra with a sense of luxurious enjoyment . . . but we rise from this with a sober consciousness that we have been reading the earnest language of a thoughtful and accomplished mind upon the fortunes of a people, whose character is made up of the loftiest elements of our nature; whose past character is full of glory, whose present is sunk in degradation, and whose future is overspread with thick darkness, unrelieved save here and there by an uncertain glimmer of hope.[20]

In opposing Irving's airiness, grace, playfulness, inimitable tact, sense of beauty, and just proportion to Cushing's "earnest language" and "sober consciousness," the reviewer highlights the formality of the latter, but he unjustly criticizes *Reminiscences of Spain* for not being varied enough when in fact it did touch upon multiple aspects of Spanish history and culture.

Caleb Cushing's representation of Spain was not as well received as it was expected because it departed from the conventional didacticism of Enlightenment travel writing. If the *American Monthly Review* was not too prone to praise Cushing's sketchbook, less predisposed to do so was the *American Monthly Magazine*. Its anonymous reviewer accused Cushing of writing a much too popular book to attract the reader, thus neglecting usefulness. The reviewer's initial comments are certainly worth quoting because they verbalize not only the educational view of travel writing prevalent throughout the Enlightenment, but also the cyclical conception of history still strongly valued in the early nineteenth-century United States:

> There are so many causes which combine to render Spain an object of interest in the eyes of all men,—the great moral lesson which may be deduced from her former glory, and present degradation,—degradation so manifest, that it would almost lead us to believe that, to kingdoms as to mortals, there is a regular succession of stages, from youth, to manhood, decrepitude, and death.—The mighty benefits conferred by her, in bygone centuries, upon the cause of civilization,—the gigantic states which are struggling into existence, from beneath her iron yoke of anarchy and ignorance,—all contributing to keep alive an eager anxiety concerning the present condition and future prospects, no less than the past history of fallen Spain,—that we hailed the appearance of Mr. Cushing's book with the most sanguine anticipations.[21]

However, after this preamble, the reviewer begins his scathing criticism. He first affirms that the title has a "diffuse and somewhat pompous" title which hides "a series of tales, gracefully indeed, and entertainingly written, but affording no food to the mind," and also believes that "the moralizing strain of reflections into which he frequently falls, is generally correct, though distinguished by no particular depth or originality of thought." He then finds that in general Cushing gives false information about the agriculture of Spain, little information about monuments, and nothing about crime. Finally, he concludes: "We fear that Mr. Cushing is of a temperament too poetical to make an accurate observer; we think we can see traces, throughout his book, of an excitable imagination constantly prevailing over his better judgement!"[22] If these criticisms evince that for some arbiters of taste the construction of abroad in antebellum America still depended on didactic discourses, they also show nevertheless that writers were more and more clearly shifting towards imaginative and impressionistic forms of expression. The romantic construction of foreign milieus was already founded on a solid block that critics from now on would find hard to remove.

The accusation of formality and extreme seriousness charged against Cushing in the 1830s has been repeated in our century. Claude M. Fuess, for example, finds that the essays in the book have a "heavy" style and are "serious to the verge of severity, and there is in his pages no note either of playfulness or satire. The book is readable but not entertaining."[23] Similarly, Stanley Williams has written that Cushing was "more learned than Irving, even if inferior in style," and that his two volumes are "for their purpose somewhat too orderly, perhaps even pedantic." Still, Williams admits that "Cushing's knowledge of Spain represents a distinct advance" in American travel writing on that country, as his translations and his familiarity with foreign and local authors alike presented him "to American readers with something like the authority of the scholar and poet."[24] Cushing may have written a weighty book, indeed, but out of the American travel writers discussed in this study he definitely stands as one who makes a very conscious display of intertextuality. He quotes directly from the Spanish, translates ancient poems and legends, and cites romantic authors like Schiller, Lockhart, Scott, and Byron, who also wrote about Spain. In short, he seems to be firing a battery of cultural power cannons throughout the book to display his academic dominance and thus compete with Irving for the centrality of an erudite textualization of things Spanish.

The process of composition and reception of Caleb Cushing's Spanish book demonstrates significantly the critical and sociocultural constraints imposed upon a genre, travel writing, whose formal expectations became even stiffer whenever the writer was a woman. In her study of travel writing and colonialism, Sara Mills remarks that while men were supposed to deal with the public spheres of law, government, and institutions, women travel writers were expected to write about the private spheres of morals and manners notwithstanding their engagement in such public activities as traveling and writing. And the best way to talk about those emotions and manners, Mills adds, was through loose, unstructured genres which were considered to be the most suited for women: autobiography, letters, and journals.[25] Autobiography, at least for the female writer coming from a Protestant background, has traditionally been one way of displaying the self in order to attain self-introspection. The same is true of the journal form, a genre whose fragmentation and discontinuous movement, as Mary Suzanne Schriber suggests, parallel "the rhythm of women's domestic lives and travel."[26] However, whereas these genres have enjoyed a certain degree of elasticity, letter-writing has been historically subject to stronger generic restrictions.

Letter writing has arguably been the site of long and determined literary gender struggles. Elizabeth Goldsmith, for example, has analyzed the critical stereotype that arose in late seventeenth-century France which assigned such characteristics as emotion, natural-

REMINISCENCES

OF

SPAIN,

THE COUNTRY, ITS PEOPLE, HISTORY,

AND MONUMENTS.

BY CALEB CUSHING.

·España, venerable de presencia,
Llena de glorias y grandezas tantas.
LOPE DE VEGA.

IN TWO VOLUMES.

VOL. I.

BOSTON:
CARTER, HENDEE AND CO.
AND
ALLEN AND TICKNOR.

1833.

Title page from the first volume of *Reminiscences of Spain* (1832), by Caleb Cushing. Courtesy of Biblioteca, Universitat Pompeu Fabra (Barcelona).

ness, authenticity, spontaneity, and charm—traits considered the natural sphere of women—to feminine epistolary writing. Instead of praising this type of literary production, critics in fact denied women's letters their literariness and thus basically reduced their avenues of publication.[27] Caroline Cushing's letters, revealing wide interests, a good talent of observation, social commentary, and intellect, go beyond this critical stereotype. Unlike her husband, she worked literally on her own without the support of any journal in her determination to go public and make available to a wider audience the private correspondence she had sent from Europe. She began to retrieve the travel journal and letters she had sent to her father with a view to publish them as a collection of letters, but she died during the process of edition. Had it not been for the New England filiopietism of her husband and family, who managed to publish her papers privately in Newburyport, her collection of letters might have never been printed.

No doubt one of the major obstacles nineteenth-century women travel writers like Caroline Cushing had to face resided in the publication of their texts. No doubt, too, another equally important constraint they had to endure was their poor marketing and reception. Mary Suzanne Schriber has noted, for example, that "books by 'ladies' were typed as the work of the 'young' and the 'impressionable.' Reviewers of women travel accounts both before and after the Civil War judged performance in the genre by reference to gender."[28] Similarly, Sara Mills has cogently remarked that the male critics' biases and prejudices more often than not presented women's travel texts as either too factual, too false, or too unfeminine.[29] In the light of these comments, it is hardly surprising that Caroline Cushing's letters remained ignored in the intellectual circles of New England, and that the statements written about them in some cases evince a blatant gender bias.

Writing from the pages of the *North American Review*, Alexander Hill Everett stated that they contained "an unpretending but very well written and interesting account of the scenes that fell under the observation of the travellers" and offered "a most favorable impression of the intellectual and moral qualities of the author," but he dismissed them by saying that they could "hardly, with propriety, be made the subject of detailed criticism." Everett, instead of commenting on the texts, betrayed the gender bias of the New England male highbrows and focused on personal aspects of the writer: "The community, as well as her family and friends, have much cause to regret the premature termination of the earthly career of this accomplished lady, who, as is sufficiently evident from these volumes, was equally well fitted to shine in the higher spheres of letters, and to grace the private walks of social and domestic life."[30]

Posterior discussions of Caroline Cushing's letters also follow a slightly disparaging view. Apart from James S. Loring, for whom the letters "convey a highly decided conception of her intellectual and moral powers," other comments on them are brief and rather condescending. Stanley Williams, for example, considers them to be "matter-of-fact" and "too unadorned, too impersonal, too unenlivened by anecdote," while Claude M. Fuess highlights the writer's qualities as entertainer, for even though she was "without her husband's profound knowledge, [she] had in her letters rather more grace of style and ease of manner." Besides, Fuess adds that Caroline Cushing "liked scenery, music, pictures, plays, and frivolity" and "possessed, moreover, a keen eye for the picturesque and a gift of accurate description which made her adventures seem very real."[31] The conventional male propensity to label women's writing as graceful, easy, and natural surfaces once again in these comments, and denies the writer's gender the very power it was struggling to achieve through the textualization of a foreign experience.

III

The representation of Spain in the antebellum United States was, as previous chapters have manifested, majoritarily carried out by male travelers who gave vent to their American nationalism and individualism abroad. Unlike the American woman traveler, for whom the very act of traveling indeed represented a form of domestic liberation, the male traveler took for granted the freedom of leaving his nation and as a result also felt at ease to choose among a wide variety of genres, personas, moods, and conventions available to him. If the traveler belonged to the leading cultural aristocracy, he was most likely inclined to display the geographical, literary, and historical knowledge that distinguished him as an agent of his class. Moreover, if he was a new Englander, as Caleb Cushing was, he was likely to express the usual biases toward Spain that were part and parcel of his cultural tradition. *Reminiscences of Spain* provides a good example of how many of these formal and ideological elements of travel writing, including history and romance, coalesce in a single text. Cushing employed, on the one hand, conventions like the romantic dream vision and gothic romance to decry the dark state of Spain, but he also appealed, on the other hand, to the northern values of its historical figures—particularly Queen Isabella—to instil a glint of hope into his textualization of the foreign nation. In addition, he passed judgment on things abroad and concurrently commented on such domestic affairs as the social position of women. In short, while he was feeding antebellum audiences with romantic glimpses of Spain he was also reasserting the views on gender, class, and race held by the political and cultural elite to which he belonged.

To begin with, the most visible formal convention of Caleb Cushing's account, which he shares with Irving and Longfellow, is the use of genre. Cushing's romantic sketchbook attempts to present before the reader a dispersed, rather impressionistic image of Spain. It is endowed with a dreamy aura, whose epiphanic quality is nowhere as visible as in the section entitled "Granada, a Retrospect of the Fortunes of Spain." Cushing's dream vision, triggered by the contemplation of the Court of Lions at the palace of the Alhambra, conducts him through diverse episodes in the history of the city:

> As occasionally happens when the mind is filled with a single engrossing subject, my sleeping thoughts lingered around the scenes where I rested, and conjured up before me a thousand confused images of events, half real and half imaginary, associated with the diverse fortunes of the Alhambra, containing too much of fact to be treated wholly as a dream, and too much of fiction to admit of being ascribed to the exclusive agency of the memory. . . . I could not deny that imagination and recollection had united their magic influence, to raise before my mind's eye a sort of moving phantasmagoria of the real fortunes of Granada. (RS, 1:21)

Like Irving and Longfellow in the Moorish palace, the ethereal atmosphere of that milieu wraps him up in a transcendental moment of "moving phantasmagoria" where present and past, fact and fiction, history and romance, coalesce before the traveler's "mind's eye," which foreshadows the Emersonian transparent eyeball. The chasm between "too much of fact" and "too much of fiction" that so much animates and creates tension in the American representation of Spain makes itself manifest again in these magic surroundings, and by mixing objective and subjective discourses places the traveler's text as a genre between history and romance.

Spain, like the texts that purported to represent it, also contained "too much of fact to be treated wholly as a dream" and consequently travelers could not always turn their back on the country's harsh realities as easily as they would like to. Moral reflections, no

matter how abstract or difficult to realize, became a stock response.
Having regained consciousness after his dream vision, Cushing
tells us he abandoned the Alhambra, "descended the street of the
Gomeles, and paced the Bivarrambla in pensive meditation," won-
dering what was left from the glorious past. The answer is blunt
and rather commonplace, full of conventional ideas on which we
have already focused earlier in discussing other travel writers.
There is nothing left

> but a country, a nation, a people, which affords a standing monument
> of the public degradation and private misery, to which vicious political
> institutions can reduce a country the richest in its natural resources
> among the states of Europe, a nation once the most powerful in all the
> elements of political greatness, and a people surpassed by none, even
> in the present day, in genious, courage, and every moral capability. (RS,
> 1:45–46)

Cushing's discourse, which reproduces the standard views of the
New England male intelligentsia, conveys not only the allegorical
lesson the traveler learns and transmits on contemplating a fallen
empire but also the conventional political complaint uttered by the
American republican on seeing Spain under a despotic regime. He
nevertheless concludes his meditation on the history of Granada
with a strong appeal for change and a clear note of hope: "Enough.
I saw beneath my feet the same fervent soil, above me the same
auspicious heavens, around me the same manly forms, which Granada possessed of yore—the body of greatness remained here with
her still; but she wanted the glorious and ethereal soul of greatness,
the unquenchable spirit without which the rest is naught,—for she
wanted FREEDOM" (RS, 1:47). The travel writer summons the
dormant essence of the country—referred to with appelations like
"the glorious and ethereal soul" and "the unquenchable spirit"—
and addresses it as the last glimpse of hope to overcome the current
sociopolitical circumstances. His words suggest that the genius loci
is still alive, an idea that Longfellow also expresses with similar
terms in *Outre-Mer* by saying that the honor of Castile does not lie
buried with the ashes of El Cid. Cushing's sketch on Granada,
then, textualizes the image of the traveler as a champion of freedom abroad, as a sort of learned philosopher whose analyses of
things Spanish bespeak cultural power. It is the cultural power
that, as a member of his class, he partly achieved abroad in the act
of traveling and at home in the act of writing and publishing a travel
book.

The causes that brought Spain to the disastrous situation denounced by many travelers were diverse and sometimes difficult to discern. Cushing nevertheless employs the usual American nationalistic bias against Spanish despotism and Roman Catholicism to render a sinister representation of the country highlighted with conventions of gothic romance. These conventions, though noticeable in various sketches of the book, appear particularly stressed in such tales as "Francisco de Toledo, The King Killer," which focuses on the nobleman who assassinated the Inca leader Tupac Amaru, and "Garci Pérez, a Tale of the Holy Office," set in seventeenth-century Spain. It is especially in the latter, however, that Cushing deploys more settings and characters typical of gothic fiction in order to exaggerate the already negative image of the Spanish Inquisition. The tale unravels the mysterious murders of Gil Cano, a Valencian surgeon, and Father Arteaga, a court confessor, at the hands of Don Diego de Orotava, a revengeful father whose daughter seemingly was ravished by Philip II before his accession to the throne. A secret member of the Holy Office, Don Diego pursues vengeance all his life until he finally reaches the king's chambers. There he gives himself away, chooses not to commit regicide, and escapes unharmed, leaving the King astonished and full of remorse in his palace. Cushing, with this tale of mysterious assassinations and courtly intrigues, resorted to and thus revived many Spanish stereotypes present in the Elizabethan revenge tragedies. Consequently, he gave antebellum American audiences a very sinister image of the Holy Office in keeping with the prejudices of his class and age.

The historical discourse embedded in early nineteenth-century American travel writing on Spain adopts, generally speaking, a tone that often wavers between condescending pity for and downright anger at the political plight of the country. In both cases, no matter what he chooses, the travel writer's voice always asserts his authority. The long citation from Cushing's sketch on Granada already demonstrated these ambivalent positions. But apart from merely speculating on the internal problems of Spain, Cushing demonstrates that the right spirit to find political solutions does exist within the country if one cares to peruse its gallery of virtuous men and women. Cushing's overall choice of historical characters is indeed a catalogue of models of republican virtue: Abderahman, Fernan González, Isabel of Castile, and Don Alonso Pérez de Guzmán stand all as eminent figures who lived for their compatriots' well-being. Their virtue, however, is yoked to the ethos of the ruling class, which becomes nearly more important than their national spirit.

If class is an important matter for a travel writer like Cushing, so is race, since at a closer inspection his ideological agenda becomes immediately evident. Many of the historic or nearly legendary characters that *Reminiscences of Spain* inscribes are almost all of northern stock. The sketch entitled "March of Conquest" clearly states, for instance, that because the Spaniards are descendants of the Franks and the Goths they are a northern race. Granted, the Arabs may have left more and better monuments, but the features and values of the people from the North are visible in today's Spaniards. Thus sooner or later the country can regenerate itself aided by these northern values that readers surely connected with those of American democracy and republicanism. Instead of focusing on a feminized Muslim world, as Irving did, Cushing emphasizes the bold and enterprising Germanic affiliation of Spain and its paramount role in the Western cultural tradition. Like Ticknor and many other members of the New England gentility, Cushing regarded Spain as a country of genius and enterprise until superstition and bigotry corrupted its spirit; it had carried its civilizing mission, and now was already superseded, as millennialist ideologues would put it, by the beacon light of the new imperialist civilization, the United States.

The foundation of the Spanish empire was, as the gallery of characters in *Reminiscences of Spain* might suggest, a long, cumulative process sharpened by the republican values of male citizens. But paradoxical as it may seem, among all of these famous men Cushing takes good care to highlight the presence of a woman: Isabel of Castile. She stands not only as the galvanizing figure of a long nation-building process but as the true propeller of imperial energies. Apart from devoting a full sketch to the Spanish queen, he praises her in several passages of his narrative and demonstrates on the whole a fascination that no doubt prefigures that of Prescott in *Ferdinand and Isabella* (1837). Cushing once again deploys his cultural authority by providing readers with facts about the Catholic monarch. Yet, before focusing on her public importance, he first describes her along clearly gendered parameters. Cushing portrays her as

the lovely and the loved, the model of queens, of wives, and of mothers,—the unaffected reality of all that her false-hearted namesake of England, Elizabeth, affected to be, but was not,—a woman, namely, with all a woman's sensibilities, and yet a great and high-souled princess,—that Isabel, whose reign is the golden age of prosperity and glory in the annals of fallen Spain. (RS, 1:236)

In representing Queen Isabella under such terms, Cushing constructs her as an emblem of republican motherhood fit to be imitated by mothers, daughters, and wives. But most importantly, by equating the queen with the country she almost matriarchally ruled, Cushing indirectly suggests that Spain can be textualized as a bold yet feminine entity.

The representation of Queen Isabella became in fact a useful cultural commodity because in this historical figure travel writing found the proper ground to blend the discourses of history and romance. The queen's accession to the throne of Castile, her matrimony with Ferdinand of Aragon, her role in the rise of modern Spain, and her promotion of oceanic exploration literally transport her to the realm of fiction. Notice how Cushing portrays, for example, the young princess at court, where she had to endure the opposition of her rival, Juana la Beltraneja:

> Isabel . . . possessed a native dignity and purity of character, fortified and refined by the seeming mischances of her lot, which, however, had but taught her the 'sweet uses' of adversity; and she passed through the fiery ordeal of a dissolute court unscathed, or rather with her genuine nobility of soul yet more elevated by a shrinking repulsion for the foul atmosphere she had been compelled to breathe. (RS, 1:245)

Here the romantic discourse he conveys is not that of gothic romance but rather one charged with the diction of sentimental prose. The implications of his historical portrait nevertheless appear to be at odds with the patriarchal tenets of antebellum American culture, for here is the case of a woman who, tired of the "foul atmosphere" of her fifteenth-century Castilian court, steps out of her domestic sphere to rule the vastest empire in the world.

Yet, even though the representation of Queen Isabella may read like a feminist statement, other sketches in *Reminiscences of Spain* demonstrate that Cushing's notion of the separate spheres of gender did not differ at all from the standard ones in the period. If anything at all, they pose the paradox that while he was somehow empowering women abroad through the iconicity of Queen Isabella, he seemed to deny them gender empowerment at home. The essay entitled "Woman in Europe and America" expresses the author's views on womanhood and at the same time asserts the public hegemonic position of his gender in antebellum American culture.

Voicing the rhetoric of American exceptionalism and betraying a blatant class optimism, he begins with a long and jubilant praise for the present times, which he considers to be the best for men and women alike. However, his discourse asserts that, despite the present circumstances, woman still is to hold a subordinate position in society: "The appropriate sphere of woman is domestic life, and if she must labor, her labors are either in discharging the duties of family care, or in departments of industry as require skill only, not strength, and as completely exempt and preserve her from all exposure to the elements, and to the rudeness of the other sex" (RS, 2:252). Cushing's views on gender contain a nationalist undercurrent, for he was comparing the harsh situation of working women in Europe with that of their counterparts in the United States. However, his comparison is part of the stock response that, as Mary Suzanne Schriber points out, many male travelers articulated on seeing "other" women.[32] In addition to this politicized argument, Cushing also resorts to the traditional male statement that considers woman's domestic sphere as an entity that is naturalized rather than socially constructed:

> Still it is enough to consider, that nature has clearly indicated the endearing offices of social intercourse, the kindly duties of the domestic circle, as the nobler scene for the display of feminine excellence. Woman, when she comes forth into the bustle, and among the harassing cares, the heartless employments, the cruel passions, which occupy and agitate the world, loses her most exquisite grace, her most potent charm, because, in abandoning those situations in which her influence is unequalled and supreme, she places herself on a level with all that is ungenerous, selfish, ambitious, revengeful, and ceases to be the tender and lovely being, which nature designed for the solace of life (RS, 2:263–64).

The adjectivation and nominalization ("harassing cares" and "heartless employments" versus "most exquisite grace" and "most potent charm") that Cushing employs to strengthen the separate spheres speaks for itself here. The irony of these lines, however, lies in the fact that it was precisely his wife who left her New England domestic sphere to "come forth into the bustle," that is, to travel to the Old World. And even more ironic, I think, is the fact that he, along with other family members, ultimately was the person responsible for the publication of his wife's private papers, bringing them from the private sphere of her domestic circle to the bustling and heartless public sphere of the literary marketplace. With this act he was not only indirectly publicizing the moral superiority of

American women like his wife, but displaying once again the afflu-
ence of a class that could afford to travel to and write about the
land of Don Quixote, Sancho Panza, and Gil Blas.

IV

Clearly the polarization between the public and the private
spheres of woman that Caleb Cushing verbalizes in *Reminiscences
of Spain* is one of the issues that has remained at the center of feminist scholarship in recent decades. Nancy Cott has observed that
from the 1780s until the 1830s New England women were shaken
by important transformations that progressively circumscribed
them to the domain of their homes, which men in turn symbolically
transformed into repositories of familial and religious values from
where mothers, housewives, and daughters should be able to exert
their proper moral influence on the rest of the world.[33] In order to
further demarcate the sphere of women's influence, by the 1840s
there took place what Mary Ryan has termed a "gendering of geography" whereby several public spaces were naturalized as exclusively male and others as exclusively female.[34] Nineteenth-century
women, however, did not regard the outside-of-the-home world
and the domestic world as different territories separated by a
clearly defined boundary but rather as intercommunicated spheres
that complemented each other even at the cost of creating tensions. These were tensions, as Mary Kelley has shown, that particularly affected women writers. The public writings of what she terms
"the literary domestics" embedded many private issues pertaining
womanhood and displayed conflicting feelings between their cultural power as writers and their social powerlessness as housewives.[35] The progressive separation of spheres along lines of gender
became, to put it briefly, an issue of antebellum American culture
that also influenced the production and reception of travel writing.
   The inconsistencies between the stifled domesticity of a private
space and the open horizons of foreign travel become apparent particularly in the public careers of women travelers, whose anoma-
lous situation L. K. Worley has expressed in the following terms:

Since men were assumed to possess such characteristics as activity, energy, independence, and intellectual prowess to be used in public life
and the wide world, their travel and any writing based on these travels
were fully in harmony with society's expectations. The situation was
quite different from women for whom travel meant leaving the postu-

lated 'female' sphere, a sphere limited to the interior realm and domestic life. . . . A woman attempting to write an account of her travels would sense that her activities were diametrically opposed to those of the nineteenth-century ideal . . . for not only had she ventured out of the domestic circle into the wide world, but the very act of writing . . . might reveal an unwomanly preoccupation with the self.[36]

Whether or not their writing revealed a strong concern with the self, and regardless of the misgivings that cultural practices like travel and writing may have created, women travelers in general took advantage of European travel to broaden their domestic horizons and adopt, at least textually, the persona of the independent, free woman. This presumed independence, however, has been recently relativized by Mary Suzanne Schriber, who has noted that the cultural practice of traveling abroad paradoxically offered women freedom at the same time that it operated as a disciplinary agent by placing and reiterating before them the existence of a solid capitalistic marketplace and a home left behind.[37] This freedom, no matter how real or textually constructed it may be, became nevertheless highly empowering for women travel writers.

The journey to Spain stood as an especially apt cultural practice not only because it could enable women travelers to expand their imaginary horizons through literary associations of history and romance but because it signified access to a domain hitherto reserved to male travelers. Moreover, as Leonardo Buonomo observes apropos of Margaret Fuller's and Julia Ward Howe's writings on Italy, a trip to the South implied for women the literal crossing of a new frontier, "a territory to be explored" whose discovery brought about the experience of transgression.[38] Reluctant to adopt unfamiliar discourses, when women enter the southern playground of the male adventurer they often do so with their own tools of inscription. Karen Lawrence, for example, affirms that "in general, women writers of travel have tended to mistrust the rhetoric of mastery, conquest, and quest that has funded a good deal of male fictional and nonfictional travel."[39] However, although women hold their own views of otherness and adventurousness, sometimes they cannot avoid male discourses. Sara Mills, who has dissected this incongruity in her study of British women traveling during the late colonial period, observes that women were often compelled to adopt the plot structure of the adventure travel book. As there were no other forms available to them, they had to accept this model with uneasiness, following and concomitantly confronting the rhetoric of the adventure male hero and its "stiff upper lip" formula of colonial subjectivity.[40] Caroline Cushing's letters on Spain are no exception to this. They reveal the ambivalent feeling between the inchoate value of the historicist and nationalist discourses embedded in New England male literary culture, and her own perception of Spanish travel as personal self-discovery and freedom.

To be sure, Caroline Cushing's letters evince her mastery of the rhetorical conventions needed for a romantic construction of Spain, and likewise display issues of great concern for women. The gendering of her narration, as I shall demonstrate, is noticeable in several areas: her focus on domesticity, which encompasses material culture, family ethos, and women's work; her emphasis on the dangers of travel; her comments on physical vulnerability; her refusal to express womanly disgust; her rejection of the dry rhetoric of male history; and, finally, her use of disclaimers to assert her authorial value. There are several aspects, however, in which her letters also verbalize some of the major discourses of men's travel writing. "Once having traveled," Mary Suzanne Schriber remarks, "women wrote for the same reason as many American men; that is, they wrote to promote the superiority and the manifest destiny of American political and spiritual values, for which the travel book was a fit form."[41] Cushing knew the discursive potential of historical and political issues, and, accordingly, in some letters she follows the same type of criticisms on the social, political, and religious state of Spain that male travel writers like her husband were disseminating those decades. Her class and national values, noticeable in passages where she describes churches or ruins of historic buildings, remain untouched throughout the narrative, and contribute to the nationalistic agenda of nineteenth-century American travel writing abroad. While she could not altogether cast off the baggage of the social background that she shared with her husband, her representation of Spain still demonstrates in an ostensible manner the difference that gender makes in travel writing.

One of the most important elements that genders Cushing's narrative is her focus on domestic issues. Nineteenth-century women travel writers, whether embracing or rejecting it, often capitalized on the discourse of domesticity. Caroline Cushing follows this convention and fully incorporates to the representation of Spain this discursive formation that had been already adumbrated in previous chapters. The Enlightenment travel writers, for example, also payed attention to domestic material culture, yet as part of their objective economic scrutiny of otherness. Similarly, romantic travelers like Mackenzie, Irving, and Longfellow also tried to appeal to their audiences by way of domestic and sentimental discourses.

However, the fact that Cushing is a woman traveler and that throughout her letters she remains more aware than her male counterparts of little domestic details—ranging from the food cooked with rancid oil at an inn near Vitoria to the straw mattings at the inn in Burgos—means that domestic awareness acquires new gendered connotations in and adds a new element to the male-dominated representation of Spain. The Cushings spent part of their sojourn in Madrid in private lodgings, which gave Caroline the opportunity to describe the furniture, decoration, and even the distribution of families in the local houses. Furthermore, she wrote about meal times, the scarcity of coffee, butter, and tea. Finally, she also revealed her interest in the manner of cooking as well as in the cleanliness of the kitchen (LD, 2:49–53). No doubt, Cushing's domestic awareness stemmed from a socially constructed type of antebellum American womanhood that expected her to write about these domestic subjects. But no doubt, too, it arose from her class interests and concerns, which made her lay an additional stress on material things and welfare.

Yet, whereas many of the examples that Caroline Cushing cites reveal her careful scrutiny of domesticity in reference to popular mores and architectural interiors, in other instances she represents the domestic sphere at its most drenched semiotic level. That is, domesticity is shown to be not only a matter of material culture but one that sheds light on the moral fiber of the foreign country as well. Letter XIV, which describes the happy family of José, at the village of Tembleque, in the Quixotic region of La Mancha, supports this semiotic reading. Cushing clearly represents the mule-teer and his family as an emblem of perfect bliss almost drawn from the plates of Currier & Ives:

> Here we found every thing in the cleanest and neatest order . . . and the family, consisting of Jose, his wife, and several remarkably pretty children, paid every attention to our comfort. . . . I could not but be interested in the picture of domestic happiness exhibited beneath this lowly roof. The return of the husband and father, after a short absence, was greeted with quiet satisfaction by the wife, but with more noisy joy by the group of little urchins, who came out to meet him almost as soon as he entered the village, and welcomed him home by demonstrations of pleasure not to be mistaken; and when he was quietly seated by his own fireside, they gathered around his chair, while his youngest child, a beautiful little rosy-cheeked girl, two years old, climbed upon his knee, and would scarcely be persuaded to leave him even for bed. The perfect obedience of these children to their parents, too, shewed that they had been properly brought up. (LD, 2:171)

Even though Cushing's class biases surface in her condescending view of the whole scene, foregrounded by phrases like "lowly roof" and "little urchins," she nevertheless dwells on it to represent the faultlessness of family values. Here she is offering readers a slice of what we might call "Republican parenthood," and in so doing she symbolically converts the scene into an iconic repository of middle-class values.

The Victorian cult of domesticity and the idolization of the "Home, Sweet Home" motto started, as Nancy Cott points out, in the 1820s and 1830s. It was a discourse that, impinging on religious and patriarchal rhetoric of women's difference from men, re-iterated the domestic vocation of women and the isolated quality of their pure, cozy environment as well as its stabilizing function. Whether they focused on motherhood, history, or child rearing, all kinds of books collaborated in the spreading of this rhetoric.[42] Caroline Cushing's letters, as these examples demonstrate, were not immune to this prevalent discourse, and in capitalizing on the notion of domesticity they also became powerful textual agents of it. Her letters paradoxically reinforce the cult of the home through a medium—the letter from abroad—whose deictic function is precisely to remark the traveler's absence from there.

It was abroad, however, where the separate spheres and the antebellum discourses of domesticity seemed to reveal their inconsistencies and weaknesses to the women traveler. Like her husband, Cushing observed and compared the state of European women with that of American women, but unlike him, she came to different conclusions. Her gender-based comments, which become particularly noticeable in the volume devoted to France, were to affect her perception of Spanish woman as well. Cushing relates in her French letters that on one occasion the chief manager of the diligence who took them to Tolouse was a woman who also worked as driver along the way and wore none of the clothes that "mark the traveller; but the same gown, apron, and cap, that she would probably have worn in superintending the domestic affairs of her family" (LD, 1:216–17). The boundary between the public and the domestic spheres of work and home, usually identified by means of different garments, appears conspicuously erased in the example she adduces, which is used to uphold the privileged superiority of American womanhood. "It is indeed no unusual sight in France," she continues, "to see women assume the coarse and masculine air and manner of the other sex; nor is it strange it should be so, when we see them engaged in all the laborious employments, that, in our favored country, are performed by men alone" (LD 1:217).

The nationalistic subtext asserts its superiority over the feminist text in this passage.

Cushing, however, subsequently redresses her argument by expressing her assurance that all women are capable of performing all kinds of work. The fact that European women of diverse social classes take part in many different types of agricultural and mercantile businesses "is certainly an argument in favor of their intellectual properties, and is one great proof, among others, that the female sex is not naturally incapacitated for exertions of the kind in question, when habit and the usages of society lead them to follow such pursuits" (LD, 1:342). Unlike the male travelers, Caroline Cushing did not see Spanish women as passive subjects to be merely inscribed and idealized as emblems of Spanish beauty. On the contrary, even though throughout her journey across the country she often complained about the general indolence of the Spaniards, she nevertheless approved of the presence of women digging and hoeing outdoors, or going about their daily businesses on the streets of cities like Madrid. She was witnessing, in other words, that the public sphere of men was constantly appropriated by women of all social classes.

Cushing's comments on the dangers of travel constitute another rhetorical convention where the gendering of her narrative surfaces. In the early nineteenth century, the first and most important step for the potential woman travel writer circumscribed to the home was to step out into the world, for once the female traveler was away from home she could gather enough materials to textualize her experience of unfamiliar scenes. The rhetorical manipulation of foreign experiences meets a powerful ally in the conventional discourse of romance, which in Caroline Cushing's letters emerges in her focus on the traveler's perils and misadventures arising from roads and modes of transportation alike. Take, for instance, this passage from Letter I, which describes the ascent of a mountain pass in the province of Guipuzcoa:

> The road wound up the abrupt side of the mountain, not around it; and as our vehicle passed and repassed the very edge of the precipice, on both sides, in turning the sharp angles made by the winding of the road, I involuntarily drew back in terror, at sight of the terrible depths before me,—observing, also, that no barrier separated us from them, except small stone pillars, two or three feet in height, and with such long intervals from stone to stone, that the animals might easily have plunged over the side of the mountains, between the pillars, had they, from sudden fright . . . been so disposed. (LD, 2:14)

These lines echo what Percy Adams calls "the coach motif," which we already mentioned in discussing the Enlightenment travelers' jeremiads on the bad peninsular roads. Furthermore, they also foreground what Mary Suzanne Schriber has termed "the vehicle convention."[43] The perils of the tortuous and unsafe road, accentuated by means of appropriate diction like "the very edge of the precipice," "drew back in terror," and "terrible depths," no doubt convey the idea of Spain as the land of danger and adventure where travelers are at the mercy of reckless drivers and debilitated or ungovernable mule teams.

Yet, apart from italicizing danger, these lines also underscore the womanliness of the female traveler, who was socially constructed to experience fright and, therefore, request protection. The salience that certain precarious modes of transportation achieve in women's travel writing raises then a topic of great significance for gender issues: female vulnerability. All foreigners traveling in early nineteenth-century Spain, regardless of their sex or age, were liable to be robbed or suffer an accident. However, as James Buzard has convincingly demonstrated, the traveler's vulnerability became a gendered issue in nineteenth-century touristic discourse as the accession of women to the Continental Grand Tour began to signify a threat to a traditionally male activity. Hence, Buzard observes, the presence in nineteenth-century travel writing of a masculine discourse that constantly demanded protection for women travelers.[44] Mary Suzanne Schriber, who has also dissected this penchant of nineteenth-century male discourse to talk about female vulnerability, nevertheless argues that whereas men's texts insisted on protecting the female body, women's texts made an issue of traveling solo and taking care of themselves.[45] If women were to assert the achievement of freedom abroad, then they had to unmask the fallacies behind the discourses that meant to keep them at home. Caroline Cushing often seems to textualize her Spanish experiences with that goal in mind.

Even though Cushing's real vulnerability becomes indeed noticeable in several instances of her narrative, the traveler's presumed defenselessness in Spain is one of the conventions of travel writing that her letters implicitly strive to undermine. For instance, as early as in Letter III, which signals the presence of highway bandits on the road to Madrid, Cushing fashions herself as a calm, self-possessed traveler who laconically discards the danger of robbery that other travelers romanticized so much and so often. "It is universally acknowledged, in regard to robbers in Spain," she affirms, "that they are seldom known to injure travellers in their person,

Caroline Elizabeth Wilde Cushing. Engraving from the frontispiece to the first volume of her *Letters Descriptive of Public Monuments, Scenery, and Manners in France and Spain* (1833). Courtesy of The Free Library of Philadelphia.

unless resistance be offered, or some cause of hostility prompt to revenge" (LD, 2:45). The apparently detached attitude and carefree tone that she inscribes in the text may be either a rhetorical strategy to minimize a real threat or a moment of gender empowerment, but in any case it significantly does not obliterate the uneasiness she felt at particular situations in several parts of her journey.

The presence of rough, wild-looking Spanish men along with the absence of women appears as one of the travel scenarios which often make Caroline Cushing shudder with fear. Bonnie Frederick and Virginia Hyde, who have affirmed that the most important dangers women inscribe in their journals are sexual dangers, argue that rape is implicit in many women's travel narratives.[46] This is true of Letter XIX, which recounts Cushing's overnight stay at Ventorrillo de las Torres Locas. She employs the conventions of gothic romance to relate her experience. Outside it is rainy and windy, the local inn is forlorn and dreary, and her room is very spartan, but most importantly she seems to harbor fears of being raped or perhaps of being assailed, since there are no women at the venta. If we compare this scenario with Ticknor's romanticizing of his outdoor life in the company of smugglers, or with Longfellow's humorous regret for not having been robbed on the Spanish by-ways, then the gendering of travel makes itself manifest. The travel-er's vulnerability emerges as a serious element in the early American representation of Spain, yet not as an opportunity to dis-play prowess or heroism, as the masculine narratives do, but as a menacing scenario for the woman traveler.

The vulnerability of the woman traveler increases even more when the otherness of Spanish men is doubled on account of racial difference. Nineteenth-century American travel writing, as we have seen in previous chapters, rhetorically played with the racial construction of Spanishness as something placed halfway between the East and the West. Despite their garlic-smelling breath, oil-based diet, and dark-skinned complexion, the Spaniards were nev-ertheless regarded and represented as Europeans rather than as Africans. The same was not true, however, of other forms of differ-ence, and particularly of nomadic people like the gypsies. Letter XXVI narrates the fears that Cushing experienced as they met a party of this ethnic group. "I was unable to pass them without a shudder, so malignant and full of evil was the expression of their swarthy features, and keen, penetrating black eyes," she notes, bi-ased by the xenophobic comments of a local guide. "The men, par-ticularly, were an exact personification of all my preconceived ideas of a murderous Spaniard. . . . I could easily imagine them capable of any and every crime" (LD, 2:336). Cushing mistrusts the gypsies because they stand before her as an unpredictable threat which she carefully represents with an adjectivation of gothic fiction: "malig-nant and full of evil," "penetrating black eyes," and "murderous Spaniard." Her anxiety stems both from her being observed by men and from her close encounter with what she regards as a frighten-ing form of otherness.

Yet, there are other episodes in which Cushing's epistolary text resists this presumed female vulnerability and tries to debunk it. The narrative at times represents her as someone who prefers to travel solo, ahead of her traveling companions, and does not make qualms about mixing with Spaniards of all social conditions. Even though, as mentioned before, she sometimes writes as if she was traveling alone, on other occasions she even laughs at the panic felt by some of her male traveling companions, particularly a Briton called Mr. Nicholas. Furthermore, Cushing manages to abandon the role of spectator by putting herself in the middle of things, interacting with the Spaniards she describes and even reproducing their language. She soon adopted the courteous *Vaya usted con Dios* to greet other travelers on the road. Many words italicized in Spanish—*venta, cochero, borricas, miqueletes, mantilla, brasero, malhechores, sereno, arriero, huerta*—contribute to giving the text an exotic flavor. The nocturnal episode at the Venta de Valdecaba, near Toledo, described in Letter XII, offers a good example of this debunking of female vulnerability. At first Cushing represents the place as dreary and uninviting, but later on she writes about it as if her imagination had transported her into a locus of fiction. The evening becomes more animated as someone asks permission to play the guitar she carries, and finally the people sing and dance. By mixing with these merry Spaniards she adopts a position of transculturality that other travelers in her time did their best to avoid, and in so doing she valorizes the realism of her narrative and refuses to voice the disgust that women travelers were expected to express at certain situations. In short, the male-constructed myth of the rough and dangerous peninsular trip is shown here to be gendered and ridiculed as well. Placed alongside the contemporary American male narratives of Spanish travel, Cushing's account demonstrated that women could also travel in rugged Spain, and reap the same pleasures than men did.

The American woman traveling in Spain could, if she wanted to, experience and textualize pleasure, but in order to do that she also had to become free from the gendered constraints that socially constructed and expected her to inscribe disgust in her foreign narration. One of the forms of displeasure most common in women's travel accounts has to do, as Mary Suzanne Schriber remarks, with the condition of "other" women, but there are obviously more.[47] We have already seen the gendering of Cushing's letters in her comments on foreign women as well as in her descriptions of the dangers of travel, which proclaimed her womanliness through the utterance of terror. There are other instances, however, in which Cushing's refusal to express repugnance at things Spanish genders her narrative even more, making it clearly different from the average American male travel account. One such case is the common complaint—a rhetorical convention in itself—against the frequent habit of Spanish men to smoke cigarettes in public. In Letter XIV, Cushing once again debunks the notion of female vulnerability, for instead of expressing her disgust at being choked by smoke and her fear at being surrounded by "other" men, she explains that "[she] learned to be enveloped in tobacco smoke without minding it in the least, and to take considerable pleasure in watching the ready manufacture of those little cigars, which [she] saw afford so much happiness to all around [her]" (LD, 2:178). The enveloping that this scene suggests can without a doubt be stretched a little bit to stand symbolically for the cultural immersion in Spanish mores that she sought everywhere in her letters.

Equally significant is her refusal to express disgust at the quintessential Spanish feast, the bullfight, so often denigrated by the male American traveler. "You may perhaps be surprised . . . that a lady could experience any thing but disgust in witnessing a species of amusement so barbarous and unnatural," she wrote to her father after describing the Spanish feast. Her reaction, however, falls apparently far from what antebellum readers might expect to be the standard one by a lady of her class. Cushing herself seems to be surprised at her own unwomanly response:

> Such was my own opinion respecting it after reading similar accounts; but strange as it may appear, there was a fascination about the whole scene, which did away in a considerable degree, [with] the painful and revolting feelings, which arise at the view of suffering even if it be the suffering of a brute. . . . I would be far from intimating, however, that I really enjoyed the spectacle, or that I did not turn away from it at times with a sickening sense of its barbarity. But such feelings were much less frequent and much less strong than I imagined they would be. (LD, 2:129)

Even though the American men who wrote on Spain were equally fascinated by the struggle between man and animal on the arena, or by the display of human dexterity alongside brute force, on many occasions the rhetorical discourse they deployed revolved more around moral reprobation than physical disgust. Bullfighting was constructed as an unenlightened cultural practice that, leaving its picturesque aspects aside, was extremely atrocious, overtly cruel, and above all conducive to violent reactions among the populace. Still, it was a sport that men could endure. Caroline Cushing, far from denying the barbaric quality of the spectacle, acknowledges it, yet concurrently suggesting that the female viewer also has the right to exhibit the same callousness that the men present in the bullring can manifest.

The enjoyment of Spanish travel, of course, did not reside in the woman traveler's capacity to endure bad roads, smoky diligences, and bloody spectacles. The pleasures of foreign travel could also be heightened if she carried a carpetbag full of historical readings, reminiscences, and facts. History was an extremely important area of nineteenth-century women's writing from which Caroline Cushing and other women travelers could draw discursive elements to comment on things Spanish. Nina Baym has demonstrated that history writing—and also, one might add, travel writing—was one of the areas taken over by women because it blended the "public" importance of history with allusions to "private" women's issues. Moreover, history writing was part of republican motherhood, as it instilled national values in children and created national identity by placing the United States in world history.[48] The rhetoric of historical facts deployed by the learned male traveler does not constitute, however, the type of historical consciousness that Caroline Cushing's letters manifest.

Throughout her letters Cushing presents herself as a writer cognizant of Spanish history, but she does not burden her letters with historic dates, famous battles, or sketches of renowned characters; it rather seems as though she had willingly handed over the drab rhetoric of facts to her husband. In so doing she asserts that it is not her objective to attain the cultural power that her husband's sketchbook strove to achieve with its textualization of the past, but rather to relate her experience of the present. She expresses this goal very clearly in the opening letter of the book, which operates as a disclaimer before her father and other implied readers of the text. "I shall endeavor to give you a faithful account of every thing singular and striking, which engages my attention," she affirms before starting her tour in France. But immediately after she adds: "You will not, of course, expect from me grave or learned dissertations. My only aim will be to enable you, by simple description, to see in fancy those things, that actually come within my own observation" (LD, 1:1–2). The use of such disclaimers by women may be attributed to disparate rhetorical strategies.[49] Yet, whether Cushing was displaying her insecurity in a male-dominated genre or assuaging the gender expectations of antebellum readers, she reiterated her eyewitness experience and opened little textual gaps to give her opinions on Spanish affairs.

Undoubtedly, Cushing's representation of Spain was inflected by the gender issues hitherto discussed. Ideologically speaking, however, her letters do not constitute *strictu sensu* a major departure from the overall male view observed in previous chapters of this study. On the contrary, her comments embed class and national prejudices close to those expressed in the men's texts, thus allow-ing her to empower herself both as an American and a member of the leading class.[50] The ideological background of Cushing's observation of contemporary Spanish affairs becomes particularly patent in the visits she made to several churches in Madrid and elsewhere, during which she gathered impressions that she was to use subsequently to condemn institutionalized Roman Catholicism even more strongly than her husband. Letter VII, for example, relates her visit to the church of San Andrés in Madrid, where she cannot understand why "any persons, possessed of common intelligence" worship the gaudy, tasteless images there, and affirms that any Protestant would try to suppress them immediately (LD, 2: 85). Likewise, on visiting the magnificent cathedral of Seville, in Letter XVII, she comments that

> although the first view of these treasures excites a feeling of admiration at their splendor; yet the contemplation of them cannot but awaken sensations of melancholy, when [I] contrast such hordes of useless wealth, with the pitiable state of the numberless beggars, who fill the streets of Seville, and crowd around the doors of this very church, uttering their oft repeated, and as oft disregarded, petition for the means of obtaining necessary food to keep them from starvation. (LD, 2:212)

The iconoclast discourse of New England Protestantism surely finds in these examples enough evidence to attack Roman Catholic liturgy. Moreover, her letters evince that another target of her anger is the huge gap between the poverty of the common parishioners and the richness of the institution.

Cushing's criticisms reach an even harsher tone when she leaves the Church aside and instead compares the state of the Crown with that of the common Spanish citizens. This is true, for example, of Letter X, which relates her visit to the church of Atocha in Madrid. This passage is certainly interesting because gender and class issues clearly blend themselves in it with the nationalistic agenda of the American traveler abroad. On leaving the building Cushing notices the presence of a woman begging for alms, and she rhetorically employs her as an icon of poverty that is immediately contrasted with the royal pageant that had taken place in the capital those days. With ironic tone, careful diction, and balanced syntactic structures Cushing represses her exasperation, and affirms:

> It is melancholy indeed to reflect upon the thousands of wretched beings in Madrid, who are absolutely dying with hunger and cold; while the money, lavished upon the jewels alone of the new Queen, is computed at two millions of dollars. How many suffering creatures a small

portion of these superfluous gems might have saved from starvation and despair! But such are the blessings of an absolute monarchy. The life, often, of the subject is considered but a trifle, when put in competition with the luxurious wants of the sovereign; and while he is surrounded with all that wealth and power can furnish him, his miserable people are too often reduced to the terrible alternative of expiring with famine, or of seeking a subsistence, purchased at the price of crime, and of never ending dishonor. And this is far from being an overwrought picture. It is one which was often, very often, the subject of my own contemplations in Spain, and to which I could not shut my eyes. (LD, 2:114–15)

In alluding to the "overwrought picture" and appealing to her true spectatorship before a scene "to which [she] could not shut [her] eyes," Cushing introduces a disclaimer to assert the authority of her gaze. In contrast, the middle- or upper-middle class male American traveler abroad seldom had to justify his inscription of the foreign experience by way of such rhetorical statements. Cushing, however, insists on the truthfulness of her account, and it is perhaps for this reason that she closes off this passage touching upon the nationalistic discourse that American travel writing fed its domestic readerships: "In our fortunate country, where so many paths to an easy competency are always open to the active and industrious, no man need starve, except by choice. But in Spain it is entirely the reverse" (LD, 2:115).[51] The source of authority for the woman travel writer in the antebellum United States, as these lines reveal, thus originates not only in gender and class but also in national identity.

Caroline Cushing found in churches and cathedrals a pretext to deploy the rhetoric of American nationalism, but she also drew materials for political discourse from the symbolic inscription of some dilapidated historical buildings of Spain. The romantic fascination for ruins became indeed a powerful rhetorical convention of travel writing that the male traveler skilfully employed to collapse in single scenes historical and national interests with imaginative pursuits. Caroline Cushing also adopted this standard male discourse on ruins in her letters, since its verbalization, according to Nina Baym, signified that the woman traveler was able "to have the right emotions and responses to the right sights, thus partaking in educated society." Baym also points out that the historical epiphanies that women tourists experienced before the ruins of the Old World constituted an indisputable proof of their cultural participation in male discourses. More often than not these women triggered historical memories and reminiscences through deceptive standard processes of association that ultimately anchored the epiphanic moment to the "here-and-now" the author was experiencing.[52] A compelling example of this epiphanic moment can be found in Cushing's visit to the Alcázar of Toledo, where she begins her excursus by summoning the past:

> I know of few objects, that more involuntarily awaken in the mind a train of serious and mournful reflections, than the sight of a vast and beautiful ruin. How sad the recollections of all the toil and treasure, which have been spent in its completion; of the scenes of pomp and grandeur, to which its majestic walls have been witness, while they echoed to the mirthful dance, the joyous footsteps, and merry voices of successive generations of happy beings, who have gone down one after another to the dark oblivion of the grave! And how does the imagination love to clothe these deserted and venerable monuments of ancient greatness in all their former splendor and glory; to people them with those long forgotten forms, now sunk in the sleep of ages, until the visions of by-gone days seem distinctly visible to our view!

Clearly the language she uses, whether conventional or not, sets the tone for the mood of her reflections: serious and mournful before a beautiful ruin and a venerable monument. Making use of this diction, Cushing reminds readers that they are in the realm of lichen, ivy, and worn-out stones, the very setting of Hawthornean romance. Her ruminations, however, continue with an even more melancholic subtext that slowly introduces history into the aesthetic category of the sublime:

> But alas! we have only to cast our eyes around upon the desolate courts and ruined walls, to remember how distant were those days from ours, when we see that even the hard and flinty rock has yielded to the destroying hand of time. And then, how naturally follow those reflections, which are calculated to repress every feeling of pride and worldly glory, by reminding us, that in a few fleeting years, at most, we too shall have ceased to be; that future generations will stand amid the ruins of our present greatness, to reflect upon the short duration of human pride and human grandeur, when all, who are now the inhabitants of this earth, shall have passed away, and have given place to others, who in their turn must also die and be forgotten. Thoughts like these peculiarly belong to the contemplation of such an object as the ruined but still beautiful Alcazar of Toledo. (LD, 2:155–56)

Cushing gradually moves her argument down to finally mark the transcendence of time and end with a moral reading of the topic of ruins—the classical *ubi sunt* theme—laden with the rhetoric of sentimentalism. The contrast between Spain's glorious past and its grim present thus becomes another one of the themes in American travel writing on Spain that Cushing co-opts and develops as adroitly as the male travel writers did, that is, embedding the ideology of empire in the contemplation of ruins.[53] Yet, far from blatantly manifesting the postcolonial, jingoistic imperialism of other nineteenth-century male travel accounts, her letters rather aim at a didactic Christian transcendentalism that values self-reflection, humility, and submission. The American woman traveling in Spain was accepting, in short, the ideological agenda of her male counterparts with certain misgivings that once more asserted the gendered nature of her travel narrative.

V

The Cushings produced a representation of Spain that, taken as a whole textual construct, deploys and enacts the empowerment of the upper-class American couple abroad. It is, however, when we approach their narratives separately that their true significance in antebellum American culture becomes more palpable, for whereas Caleb Cushing stands as a romantic sketcher following Irving, Caroline Cushing emerges as the initiator of a new branch of Spanish travel writing. The politically charged and gendered ruminations present in her letters allowed her to partake in the unfolding American construction of Spain in the antebellum United States. She adjusted her discourse to the ideological principles of contemporary travelers like her own husband yet exposing the impact of gender on the textualizing of Spain and asserting its relevance at a time when that category had not become a full marketable commodity in travel writing. Unlike Caleb Cushing, for whom the value of Spanish travel resided in the display of the cultural capital and authority pertaining to his class, she envisioned the wide horizons of Castile and the Moorish monuments of Andalusia as landmarks of freedom, and therefore made Spain available to the female imagination at home in a way it was not available in the male representations.

Being the first woman to have published—though posthumously—a full-fledged narrative of Spanish travel in the antebellum United States, her letters on Spain thus provide a starting point to study what we might call a tradition of American women's writing on Spain that continued throughout the century with serious contributions like Octavia Walton LeVert's *Souvenirs of Travel*

(1857), Kate Field's *Ten Days in Spain* (1875), Susan Hale's *A Family Flight through Spain* (1883), and Miriam Cole Harris's *A Corner of Spain* (1898). In short, her letters proved to many an American that Spain did not solely lie within the walls of Granada and the Moorish palace that Irving had popularized; there was more to Spain. From gloomy inns to sunny plains and from stately religious or aristocratic celebrations to lively gatherings in humble taverns, this country held out to the woman traveler the same thrills, challenges, and even dangers of discovery that it held out to the men. Cushing proved that the American woman, too, could abandon her domestic environment to travel to Spain, see the land and the people for herself, and write as much as she wanted about them to audiences back home.

Conclusion

THE PREVIOUS CHAPTERS HAVE DELINEATED THE CONTOURS OF A discourse about Spain that, disseminated by travel writings, emerged and developed in the United States between the Revolutionary War and the first three decades of the nineteenth century. In the period from the late 1820s to the mid-1830s the realistic and politicized view of Spain fostered by late Enlightenment and pre-romantic travelers like Noah, Ticknor, and Mackenzie gave way to the impressionistic representation of romantic writers like Longfellow, Irving, and the Cushings. While the former presented Spain as a disagreeable reminder of what once had been a powerful nation, and thus used the didactic implications of such a view to enlighten domestic audiences, the latter used a rhetoric of sentiment to construct it as a romantic retreat where the traveler and his readers could escape the constraints of what Irving termed "the bustle and business of the dusty world."

The first existing travel accounts on Spain written by Americans date from the Revolutionary period and evince a rational, common-sensical approach to the representation of that country. Fictional and nonfictional books imported from Europe had already introduced popular notions of Spain and the Spaniards in the United States during the colonial period. However, the travel correspondence, journals, and notebooks of Adams, Monroe, and Jay are far from popular in their approach. They contain serious observations on climate, crops, architecture, living conditions, and government, among other subjects. Moreover, using an encyclopedic discourse that capitalized upon factuality and objectivity, their chief aim was to present an accurate view of the state of Spain under Charles IV to a small circle of readers back home. These writers became the first American political and cultural scouts inaugurating a tradition of travel writing on Spain that, due to lack of diffusion, posterior travelers had to initiate once again.

During the first two decades of the nineteenth century, Noah, Ticknor, and Mackenzie, the indirect successors of the eighteenth-century diplomatic travelers, produced a much more didactic, dogmatic, and homilectic representation of Spain than their predecessors. It was didactic because by means of a fact-gathering, encyclopedic type of travel book it attempted not only to inform republican readers but to educate them. It was dogmatic and homilectic because, charged as it was with Protestant and republican values, it decried the Roman Catholicism and royal despotism that they regarded as the principal causes of degradation in Spain under Ferdinand VII. To convey these messages in a pleasurable manner, these travelers combined them with the entertainment of their own travels. Their aim often remained untouched: to edify the audiences within the values of American republicanism. However, through their appreciation of the barren ruggedness of the peninsular landscape and their symbolic description of certain characters and places they also displayed the first stirrings of what we might call a pre-romantic representation of Spain. In short, wavering between the rhetoric of historical fact and that of adventurous romance, they were late representatives of the eighteenth-century mindset at a time when the influence of romantic picturesque tourism was beginning to be felt in the United States.

The travel books that Irving, Longfellow, and to a certain extent the Cushings published in the early 1830s rejected the kind of rational approach to Spain of Noah and Ticknor as well as the political involvement and physical graphicism of Mackenzie in favor of a more subjective, prettified, and nostalgic romanticism. These travelers retrenched from the problems of the present and thus for them romance itself was a way of evading from direct political involvement with the here-and-now in favor of a distanced aesthetic spectatorship. The romantic conception of Spain they offered to their audiences, then, entailed a retreat from contemporary affairs and political commentary that had to do more with the reactionary *Weltanschauung* of Chateaubriand, Wordsworth, and Scott than with the revolutionary stance of Gautier and Hugo. They did not represent Spain as an arena of struggle between despotism and constitutionalism, nor as a historical lesson on the fall of powerful empires. Spain became a grandiose past accesible through an ethnographic primitivistic present for Irving, a spiritual domain for Longfellow, a cultural quarry for Caleb Cushing, and a way out from the domestic sphere for Caroline Cushing. Through this shift from a perception based for the most part on politics to one based on pseudo-ethnography, spirituality, and class or gender empowerment, American audiences were enabled to cease seeing Spain as an eerie and ugly country and began to see it as a kinder, gentler milieu. Romantic travel writing thus turned

Spain, a geographically remote destination by early nineteenth-century travel standards, into an almost otherworldy nation in the reader's imagination.

The turn to romanticism in American travel writing on Spain is noticeable at the formal level through the metamorphosis from the didactic type of Enlightenment travel book to the more desultory and introspective romantic sketchbook. The Enlightenment travel book offered readers a peep into otherness, but on many occasions this was done to demonstrate that this otherness was precisely the society they would not like to replicate in the United States. On the contrary, the romantic travel book, rather than spoonfeeding information to its readers with a sweet coating of travel incidents, offered audiences that which their own country did not offer them and thus they would like to have. No doubt the imagination of many a domestic reader soared to fourteenth- and fifteenth-century Spain on reading Caleb Cushing's translations of Spanish medieval romances. No doubt, too, many a reader wished himself in the paradisiacal enclosure of the Alhambra or under the sunny skies of Madrid, rather than in a society where, according to Irving, everything seemed to be "commonplace."

The romantic representation of Spain in American travel writing does not constitute, however, a phenomenon that began ex nihilo. The stylistic shift that brought out sketchbooks like Irving's *The Alhambra*, Longfellow's *Outre-Mer*, and Cushing's *Reminiscences of Spain* was part of a continuum rather than a split in the early representation of this country in the United States. The early nineteenth-century travelers who visited Spain carried a cultural baggage full of literary knowledge from previous readings that permitted them to make historical and poetical associations on the way. They had read or were familiar with Cervantes's *Don Quixote* as well as Lesage's *Gil Blas*. Moreover, they also had some knowledge of foreign travelers who had written on Spain. Even so, the example of Irving's *Sketch Book* remains paramount in the development of a new form of romantic representation, especially given Irving's influence on other writers. We may affirm that, as American writers influenced by or following Irving, these travelers "invented a tradition of Spain"—to borrow a term from Eric Hobsbawm and Terence Ranger—that was to last until the twentieth century.[1] Not only did they represent Spain but also defined what they wanted it to stand for, and thus from those decades onwards subsequent Americans looked at compatriots like Irving as much as to other foreign voices.

Irving's influence notwithstanding, the romantic travel book on

Spain also deploys formal, ideological, and aesthetic conventions from the earlier travel-writing tradition that cannot be overlooked. Irving, Longfellow, and the Cushings had been raised under Common Sense principles and did not completely reject their Enlightenment baggage. Irving carried over into *The Alhambra* the historical scholarship he had applied to *Life and Voyages of Christopher Columbus* and *Chronicle of the Conquest of Granada*. Longfellow, too, testified to his reliance upon the preceding fact-gathering discourse by including scholarly essays on Spanish literature in *Outre-Mer*. Caleb Cushing turned *Reminiscences of Spain* into a repository of cultural power by way of his learned essays and his historical sketches, thus showing that even in the wider context of romantic travel writing the discourse of facts often became stronger than that of adventurousness. Finally, Caroline Cushing's travel narrative, though formally not a sketchbook, revealed that the old discourse of epistolarity proved still useful for the romantic inscription of Spain by offering snippets of an enchanting land to female readers who until then had imaginatively flown abroad on the wings of men's travel narratives.

Even though women must have comprised part of the readership that the male travel writers targeted, the early American travel books on Spain were visibly gendered, often addressing an implied masculine audience, and constructing Spain as a male domain where, due to the rough topography, impoverished economy, and unstable political situation, only male travelers should venture to travel. The spartan inns, unpassable roads, and bad food stand as an invitation to avoid Spain in the travel writings of the first American diplomats. In the travel accounts written after the Peninsular War, on the other hand, it is the political violence and the lawlessness of the roads that convert the trip into a male experience. Caroline Cushing's exceptional case serves to debunk this masculinist conception of the Spanish tour, and it also demonstrates through its uniqueness that in the first decades of the nineteenth century women did not enjoy the opportunity to travel to Spain, let alone textualize it. They could travel only imaginatively to the land of history and romance after perusing the pages of the men's accounts. The previous chapters have nevertheless stressed the reception of these texts to show the existence of an eager market for books on Spain that created what Terry Caesar terms—echoing Benedict Anderson's words—"an imagined community" of readers.[2] Women constituted an important segment of this imagined reading community interested in Spain, and with the publication of Caroline Cushing's letters they also became a traveling and writing community that moderated the purely manful representations of things Spanish by adding their own viewpoints to it.

By and large, the masculine gendering of the peninsular trek seems to originate in two different cultural perspectives on European travel and travel writing current in the Victorian United States. It may be interpreted, on the one hand, as a phenomenon coeval with and partly attributable to the masculinization of the Grand Tour that, according to James Buzard, was caused by the influence of the Byronic model and its anti-touristic conventions, which allowed men to imagine themselves free of family and social ties in Europe. The masculinization of travel, on the other hand, has different overtones for William Stowe, who affirms that for many writers European travel was a way of reasserting their maleness in a society that regarded writers as effeminate.[3] Whatever may have been the rhetorical strategies that these male travel writers adopted to textualize their Spanish adventures, very often they clearly set the foundations for a narration of Spain that paid homage to physical prowess and daring adventurousness, and thus drew the attention of male and female readers alike. If the former perhaps read into this narration the potential realization of their masculine fantasies of freedom and dominance, the latter probably regarded it as a dreamy getaway in which they were convinced that sooner or later they would be roving as well.

This masculine image of Spain in American travel writing was nevertheless transformed in some parts of the romantic sketchbooks of Irving, Longfellow, and Cushing into a prettified, sometimes even feminized representation of the country. It is not, though, part of the overall "feminization of American culture" that Ann Douglass has studied,[4] but a sort of gradual polishing of the sharp edges in the image of Spain that the first travelers had produced. No doubt Irving romanticized the male trek across the peninsular mountains as he approached Granada. No doubt, too, Longfellow toyed with the constant threat of robbery on the Spanish roads. But the feminization of Spain in their Spanish travel books is visible and clearly sets them apart from the former writers. Irving, for example, endowed the ornamented interiors of the Alhambra with powerful domestic and feminine qualities that equally offered him protection and seduction. Similarly, by representing Queen Isabella as a virtuous wife and symbolic matriarch of modern Spain, Caleb Cushing equated her femininity with the country she ruled over. The feminized occurrences present in early American travel writing on Spain were a pretext to enhance the seductive aura of a place that, as the rhetorical conventions of these texts worked hard to suggest, inevitably attracted antebellum American travelers and readers alike.

The gendering of Spanish travel must not be solely relegated, however, to the masculinizing and feminizing antics of the male travel writers. *Between History and Romance* has also stressed the fundamental role that Caroline Cushing's epistolary narrative plays if we are to assess early nineteenth-century American travel writing on Spain *in toto*. The only female travel writer to have constructed an account of Spain during that early period, her posthumous letters deconstruct the myth of the rough peninsular crossing only fit for male travelers. Her focus on domestic concerns, the gendered nature of her travel writing, and her partial co-optation of classist and nationalistic discourses present in male travel accounts testify to the social construction of women's travel writing in antebellum American culture. In her text Spain ceases to be a male preserve since she clearly demonstrates that nineteenth-century women could also travel to the land of history and romance and write about it with doses of commonsensical domestic sagacity that tempered the evasive strain too often present in men's travel writing.

Irving and Longfellow surely are the writers who best epitomize this evasive strain in the romantic representation of Spain. Their accounts illustrate the romantic traveler's search for blissful spots or moments untouched by the political and social upheavals of their age. By and large, they adopted a more cheerful and humorous tone that contributed to softening the American view of Spain produced earlier. Noah, Ticknor, and Mackenzie employed a grave, somber discourse that too often focused on the ugly and the politically turbulent, and consequently lacked moments of light humor. Noah could not avoid his hatred of Spain throughout his trip; Ticknor was always coldly analyzing aspects of Spanish society; and Mackenzie took his revolutionary criticisms too seriously. If they tried to amuse, it was usually in connection with their aim of enlightening the reader. Caleb Cushing, despite having produced an Irvingesque sketchbook, never struck a humorous tone either; he was formal and grave. On the contrary, Irving, Longfellow, and even Caroline Cushing offered a more humorous side of Spain. The former two did so by means of the comic personas of Crayon and the pilgrim-narrator respectively, whereas the latter accomplished her goal by ridiculing certain male travelers' attitudes. In short, by providing a lighthearted narration of Spain they were reiterating the escapist dimension of their romantic travel accounts.

To break away from the political reading of Spain imposed by previous travelers, the romantic travel writers relied strongly on romance to highlight an otherwordly image of Spain. Noah, Ticknor, and Mackenzie did not allow their narratives to slip over into the realm of imagination in an excessive manner. They employed romance only to leaven the dry encyclopedic discourse of their travel writings and thus produce a representation of Spain palatable to their audiences. In their texts romance did not signify the departure from a world they were deeply anchored in, but the display of an agreeable discourse of adventurousness. Likewise, Caroline Cushing rhetorically played with her condition of woman traveling in an environment textually constructed for and by men to display the romance of domestic freedom as experienced by the woman traveler. That is not true, however, of Irving, Longfellow, and Caleb Cushing, for whom generic romance offered the escapism they sought. The romance encapsulated in their texts worked as an ambiguous force that endowed travel writing and the site and people it represented with supernatural or otherwordly qualities.

For these writers of romantic sketchbooks romance was then a means to avoid the pressures of history, not to confront it. Conversely, for travelers like Noah, Ticknor, and Mackenzie it was not easy to escape history, for during their Spanish travels they were constantly reminded of postwar destruction, political strife, royal repression, and religious bigotry. Mackenzie, for example, adopts the persona of the young Byronic traveler abroad who commits himself politically to the country he is representing. Spanish history for them was not an irrelevant recollection of past events but an unfolding process whereby the present was seen as a direct consequence of past historical episodes. This historicized approach to current events was precisely what Irving, Longfellow, and Cushing rejected by focusing on Spanish history in the sense of the Spain of the past. Irving's forays into Christian and Moslem medieval history, Longfellow's analyses of the devotional poetry of medieval Spain, and Caleb Cushing's learned profiles of historical figures manifested that history had become an aspect of an escapist mode.

Yet, these romantic travel writers did not stop there. Instead, they pushed their Spanish sojourn to the limit, so that in the transparency and weightlessness they experienced in the Alhambra one may perceive their attempt to transcend history itself to position themselves in a timeless sphere. This rhetorical strategy echoing Emersonian self-reliance was only possible, of course, if the American traveler was a white, male, well-off Anglo-Saxon Protestant; if the travel writer was a woman, then the traveler's discourse had to be modified to some degree. Caroline Cushing, fulfilling some of these characteristics and adopting new ones into the early American discourse on Spain, implicitly questioned the exclusivity of these transcendental episodes abroad with her representation of Spain. But while her letters suggested that women travelers could accompany their husbands and witness the contrasts of Spanish society, they also revealed that Spain triggered epiphanic moments for the female travelers as well as the male.

With this implicit and optimistic self-reliance, Caroline Cushing and her contemporaries fundamentally bespeak an ideological agenda that exhibits the interrelationship between travel, class empowerment, and national expansionism at a time—the late 1820s and the 1830s—in which travel writing was closely connected with the construction of a strong national identity for the new republic. All literary genres collaborated in the rise of nationalism, including the travel book, and all foreign countries, including Spain, helped to define by contrast the character of the young United States. However, the ideological agenda of early nineteenth-century American travel writing on Spain ultimately shows the paradoxical futility of these travelers' attempt to transcend history through the textualization of apparently naive sojourns. No matter how much these romantic authors sought to give a different impression, traveling to and writing about Spain was inevitably a political act in itself.

Even so, the cultural work of these travel narratives had an even greater impact. It is clear, as the previous chapters have demonstrated, that travel for travel's sake was seldom the norm; what brought these travelers to Spain was a specific purpose—even though they seldom reveal it plainly—from which they reaped a profit. Moreover, throughout their Spanish tour these travelers became agents of discourses that contributed to the rising tide of nationalism in American letters. While tourists like the Cushings proclaimed their Americanism openly, others like Irving and Longfellow chose their private travel writings rather than their romantic sketchbooks to do so. They decoupled Spain in part from an English-dominated political drama, and thus they tried to depoliticize their foreign narration and their project in general. Yet, whether voicing their own ambitions or acting as agents of contemporary discourses, these travelers left an indelible imprint in antebellum American culture, for if their travel books on Spain, on the one hand, seemingly contributed to the isolationism of antebellum American letters with their nationalist stance, on the other hand they were also instrumental in setting the foundations of a more cosmopolitan culture in pre- and post–Civil War America. The teaching of Spanish in the United States received substantial impetus through the efforts of Ticknor and Longfellow. Both academics not only tried to configure their expertise on Spain and the Spaniards to their profesional niche; they also tried to expand it and popularize it; Ticknor with his *History of Spanish Literature* and Longfellow with his essays. The same is true of the field of history, where works like Irving's *Life and Voyages of Christopher Columbus*, and Prescott's *Ferdinand and Isabella* incorporated American historiography on an equal footing with Continental historians and engaged American authors in a transcontinental dialogue. In short, American literature had finally opened a conspicuous niche in the Western representation of Romantic Spain.

The appeal of Romantic Spain in the United States, however, outlasted the early decades of the century that created it, since it prevailed throughout all the postbellum period and grew well into the twentieth century. The rhetorical, thematic, and descriptive conventions of the earlier travel accounts were modified, for instance, to effectively cater to the new reading tastes. Thus, whereas some of the new books full of photographs and illustrations perhaps took away part of the romantic aura surrounding previous accounts, other narratives continued to boost it by appealing to less-explored parts of the country or to unconventional means of transportation. Titles like William Parker Bodfish's *Through Spain on Donkey-Back* (1893), Fanny Bullock Workman's *Sketches Awheel in Modern Iberia* (1897), Archer M. Huntington's *A Note-Book in Northern Spain* (1898), and Miriam Coles Harris's *A Corner of Spain* (1898) reveal this new trend in the late nineteenth-century representation of Spain in the United States.

Long after the Civil War, and in spite of the visible changes that travel writing and American representations of otherness suffered, some authors still textualized their Spanish experiences in terms that transport the reader back to the 1830s. General George W. Cullum's arrival into the region of Andalusia in *Spain: The Orient and the Occident* (1889), for example, reads like many excerpts from earlier travelogues. Cullum describes his train crossing of the defile of Despeñaperros with the diction of adventurous romance employed by those who traveled by diligence. Moreover, he continues to describe Andalusia as a powerfully liminal region: "Here, as by magic, everything is changed; vegetation, customs, architecture, and even the climate. . . . The very name of this land of the aloe, orange, and olive, is musical and suggestive of pastoral delights."[5] The same is true of Charles F. Sessions, president of the Ohio Historical and Archeological Society, whose narrative *In Western Levant* (1890) inscribes the beggars at the mosque in Cordova with words that seem literally lifted from Irving's writings: "outcast sons of nobles," "tattered and unsandaled courtiers," and "kings turned paupers."[6] Even though Spain was no longer under its earlier absolutism, it had developed a railroad network that was increasingly arriving everywhere, and its population was gradually reaping the benefits of economic progress, some texts refused to verbalize its complex changes and rather preferred to remain anchored in the simplicity of frozen images.

The popularity of this romantic representation of Spain before and after the Civil War was also strongly propelled by the Alhambraistic cult that progressively followed the publication of Irving's *The Alhambra*. "The Alhambra is all that, in the eyes of travelers, gives prominence over a dozen Spanish towns," wrote the Californian traveler John Franklin Swift in 1868, adding that "Washington Irving has done more to raise the Alhambra to a high place among the ancient Moorish palaces of Spain than did its architects and painters."[7] True, the gusto for Moorish Spain owed as much to Irving's canonization as to the vogue of orientalist motifs in the Romantic and Victorian periods, but the importance of *Chronicle of the Conquest of Granada* and *The Alhambra* in the consolidation of a commodified idea of Spain in the United States was crucial. The tradition of writings on Granada before Irving, as we have seen, was rich and ranged from Dryden to Chateaubriand, but after Irving, American travelers and writers continued to pay homage to Boabdil's palace and to regard it as an important European landmark. The publishing market itself, which experienced an unprecedented growth in the decades following the Civil War, became very aware of that attraction, and thus it is not surprising to see how publishers capitalized on the romantic connotations of a name like Granada to increase sales of such titles as Samuel Irenaeus Prime's *The Alhambra and the Kremlin* (1873) and James Henry Chapin's *From Japan to Granada* (1889).

If the late nineteenth-century American traveler often continued to envision Spain as nearly the same picturesque and paradisiacal escape it had been for Irving and his contemporaries, the same is also true of writers in our century. In the 1930s those who witnessed or fought in the Spanish Civil War (1936–1939) often regarded that conflagration as a romantic cause. It seemed to resuscitate at the same time Mackenzie's subversive revolutionary overtones and Irving's romantic utterances of almost a century before. Similarly, more than two decades ago, Chicano writer Nash Candelaria used the locale of Granada as a significant cultural landmark in his novel *Memories of the Alhambra* (1977), which poignantly expresses the frantic search for his Spanish origins of the New Mexican protagonist, José Rafa. In this novel Spain at last is for an American fictional traveler as much a classic ground as England was for Irving's Crayon. In the 1990s, the globalization of media events has given further publicity to the cult of Romantic Spain in general and the Alhambra in particular. Take, for example, the media coverage of the 1992 Olympic Games in Barcelona, which on many occasions resorted to stereotyped commonplaces of Spanish local color to assuage the cultural expectations of the American public. Or President Clinton's 1997 official trip to Spain, which scheduled a much-publicized, late afternoon visit to the Alhambra to see one of the most dramatic sunsets in the world set against the backdrop of the Sierra Nevada. The epiphanic moment textualized by the early nineteenth-century traveler and only read by a few is carefully staged here and disseminated to millions. The armchair travelers of today must have been as stirred by these pseudoromantic, broadcast spells as their fireside predecessors were on reading the American romantic accounts of the early nineteenth century.

Without a doubt, a good summary of this enduring attitude toward the textual construction of Romantic Spain between the discourses of history and romance can be found, by way of conclusion, in the opening lines of James Michener's Spanish travel book, *Iberia. Spanish Travels and Reflections*:

> I have long believed that any man interested in either the mystic or the romantic aspects of life must sooner or later define his attitude concerning Spain. For just as this forbidding peninsula physically juts into the Atlantic and stands isolated, so philosophically the concept of Spain intrudes into the imagination, creating effects and raising questions unlike those evoked by other nations.[8]

Michener wrote these sentences in 1968, a significant date for romantic revivalisms. Still, the fact that today many year abroad programs in Spain offered by American universities continue to employ the rhetoric of Romantic Spain evidences in part that the representation of Spain produced by the writers studied in *Between History and Romance* persistently refuses to yield the floor to the modern country of today. Spain, the mecca of today's sun-seeking, northern European tourists, would surely not be able to recognize itself in the travel books produced by the restless travelers of the early nineteenth-century United States.

Notes

Chapter 1. Introduction: Spain, Travel, and Textuality in the Early Nineteenth-Century United States

1. For a comprehensive view of foreign travelers in nineteenth-century Spain, see Jaime del Burgo, *La aventura histórica de los viajeros extranjeros del siglo XIX y la España desconocida de Cenac-Moncaut* (Pamplona: Ed. Gómez, 1963); Alfonso de Figueroa y Melgar, *Viajeros románticos por España* (Madrid: E.P. Sagrado Corazón, 1971); Alejandro Sánchez, "Els somniadors del romanticisme," *L'Avenç* 51 (1981): 66–73; David Mitchell, *Travellers in Spain. An Illustrated Anthology* (London: Cassell, 1990); Helena Fernandez Herr, *Les origines de l'Espagne romantique: les recits de voyage: 1755–1823* (Paris: Didier, 1974); Margaret A. Rees, *French Authors on Spain, 1800–1850: A Checklist* (London: Grant & Cutler, 1977); Jean Rene Aymes, *L'Espagne romantique: temoignages de voyageurs français* (Paris: A.M. Metailie, 1983); María del Mar Serrano, "Viajes y viajeros por la España del siglo XIX" *Geo Crítica* 98 (Sept. 1993): 6–58; José Fernández Sánchez, *Viajeros rusos por la España del siglo XIX* (Madrid: El Museo Universal, 1975); Estuardo Núñez, *España vista por viajeros hispanoamericanos* (Madrid: Ediciones Cultura Hispánica, Instituto de Cooperación Iberoamericana, 1985); Arcadio Pardo, *La visión del arte español en los viajeros franceses del siglo XIX* (Valladolid: Secretariado de Publicaciones de la Universidad de Valladolid, 1985); Julio César Santoyo, *Viajeros ingleses del siglo XIX* (Vitoria: Obra cultural de la Caja de Ahorros Municipal de la Ciudad de Vitoria, 1978).

2. Throughout the text of this study I invariably use the terms "America" and "American" alongside that of "United States" even though the latter is the term that appears in the title of the book. I do so because the term "American" still enjoys widespread currency in critical studies despite having been contested for being a reductionist name that excludes other voices from the same continent. Indeed, today many Spanish readers may in the first place think of an "American" as someone coming from South America, but the context of this study makes it quite clear which country in the American continent the book is referring to. Thus, I am totally aware of how slippery and fraught the above-mentioned terms are and have always been. In the past the situation was no less clear: the travelers mentioned in this study regarded themselves as Americans and often boasted about it, while the Spaniards often referred to them as *ingleses* on account of the language they spoke rather than the nation or continent they came from.

3. Severn Teackle Wallis, *Glimpses of Spain: or, Notes of an Unfinished Tour in 1847* (New York: Harper & Brothers, 1849), vi.

4. Henry David Thoreau, *Walden*, ed. J. Lyndon Shanley (Princeton: Princeton University Press, 1971), 94–95, vol. 1 of *The Writings of Henry David Thoreau*.

5. "Introduction: History, Culture, and Text," in *The New Cultural History*,

ed. Lynn Hunt (Berkeley and Los Angeles: University of California Press, 1989), 17. In *Keywords* (New York: Oxford University Press, 1976), 222–25, Raymond Williams has surveyed the different usages of the term "representative," pointing out the existence of a political nuance alongside the artistic significance. By representation of Spain, then, I refer to both an artistic and a political enterprise.

6. For a listing of travelers see Harold S. Smith, *American Travelers Abroad: A Bibliography of Accounts Published Before 1900* (Carbondale: Southern Illinois University Press, 1969), 164.

7. Iris L. Whitman, *Longfellow and Spain* (New York: Instituto de las Españas, 1927), 26.

8. Throughout this study I have taken into account the two concepts of nation that Eric Hobsbawm propounds in *Nations and Nationalism Since 1780* (New York: Cambridge University Press, 1991), 18–22. One, originating in linguistic unity, builds the idea of nation on cultural identity; the other, arising from state sovereignty, on political identity. The early American travelers in Spain remained, by and large, aware of the multiculturalism and linguistic differences between diverse peninsular regions, though mainly for picturesque purposes. They never challenged the dominant reading of Spain as a monolithic political unit, perhaps because that view would have epistemologically countered the process of consolidation of their own republic. As a people whose national motto celebrates their being as the unification of differences, they preferred to interpret Spain in the same manner.

9. Smith, *American Travelers Abroad,* iii.

10. Sara Mills, *Discourses of Difference. An Analysis of Women's Travel Writing and Colonialism* (London and New York: Routledge, 1991), 38.

11. William Stowe, *Going Abroad: European Travel in Nineteenth-Century American Culture* (Princeton: Princeton University Press, 1994), 55.

12. Everett was Minister to Spain from 1825 until 1829. In June of 1829 he was replaced by Cornelius Van Ness, who held that position until December 1836 and apparently did not take as much interest as his predecessor in publicizing Spain in the United States.

13. Edward Said, *Orientalism* (New York: Vintage, 1978), 3.

14. For a historical account of the origins of Hispanism in the United States see Miguel Romera-Navarro, *El hispanismo en Norte-América* (Madrid: Renacimiento, 1917). More chronologically restricted, yet equally relevant, is Mar Vilar's *La prensa en los orígenes de la enseñanza del español en los Estados Unidos (1823–33)* (Murcia: Universidad de Murcia, 1996).

15. Many entries from February, March, and early April show that he spent the evening chatting with Alexander Slidell Mackenzie (JIV, 68–77).

16. Claude M. Fuess, *The Life of Caleb Cushing*, 2 vols. (1923; Hamden, Conn.: Archon, 1965), 1:114.

17. Van Wyck Brooks, *The World of Washington Irving* (New York: Dutton, 1944), 251.

18. See his letter (18 December 1830) to John Murray III (LII, 571).

19. *The Life and Letters of Washington Irving*, ed. Pierre M. Irving, 4 vols. (New York: Putnam, 1862–64), 4:312.

20. In the same letter from New York (24 February 1836), Irving acknowledged that Mackenzie's second travel book, *The American in England*, was not as good as he expected, but nevertheless he pressed Murray to give Mackenzie a second opportunity, which he did not do.

21. Stanley T. Williams, *The Spanish Background of American Literature*, 2

vols. (New Haven: Yale University Press, 1955), 2:158. For more facts on the Irving-Longfellow relationship, see Stanley T. Williams, *The Life of Washington Irving*, 2 vols. (New York: Oxford University Press, 1935), 1:476–77.

22. Mackenzie had in mind some fictional work of Spanish theme, but Longfellow dissuaded him: "When you enter the realm of fiction, I want you to march in with a more lofty step" (LL, 2:233). This and other excerpts from Longfellow's letters, which come mostly from the Longfellow Trust Collection, are henceforth reprinted by permission of the Belknap Press of Harvard University Press.

23. Two good overviews of the turbulent Spanish history of that period are Raymond Carr, *Spain 1808–1939*, 2nd ed. (1966; New York: Oxford University Press, 1982), and Miguel Artola, *La burguesía revolucionaria* (1978; Madrid: Alianza Ed., 1992).

24. Carr nevertheless tries to downplay the type of repression taking place those years—the very repression represented by some of the travelers here examined—by suggesting it was more the work of local authorities than of the monarch: "In the confusions of the thirties the ominous decade appeared almost desirable as an era of social peace and optimistic expansion. A king who travelled across his kingdom in a single carriage without an escort could not be said to have ruled by brute force." *Spain 1808–1939*, 2nd ed., 147.

25. Enoch C. Wines, *Two Years and a Half in the Navy*. 2 vols. (Philadelphia: Carey & Lea, 1832), 1:221.

26. Théophile Gautier, *Tra los Montes* (Paris, 1843), reprinted as *Voyage en Espagne* (1845); Richard Ford, *A Handbook for Travelers in Spain* (London, 1845) and *Gatherings from Spain* (London, 1846); George Borrow, *The Bible in Spain* (London, 1842). Three engaging books that have examined the romantic representation of Spain are Francisco Calvo Serraller's *La imagen romántica de España* (Madrid: Alianza, 1995), María de los Santos García Felguera's *Imagen romántica de España* (Madrid: Ministerio de Cultura. Dirección General de Bellas Artes, 1981), and Leon François Hoffman's *Romantique Espagne: L'image de l'Espagne en France entre 1800 et 1850* (Paris: P.U.F., 1961).

27. For the "discovery" of Spain in eighteenth-century British travel writing, see Charles L. Batten's *Pleasurable Instruction. Form and Convention in Eighteenth-Century Travel Literature* (Berkeley and Los Angeles: University of California Press, 1978), 92–93. For particular information on individual travelers, see Geoffrey W. Ribbans's *Catalunya i València vistes pels viatges anglesos del segle XVIIIè* (Barcelona: Ed. Barcino, 1955), and Ana Clara Guerrero's *Viajeros británicos en la España del siglo XVIII* (Madrid: Aguilar, 1990). The late eighteenth-century British gusto for landscape description, which played so conspicuous a role in the early picturesque representation of Spain, was nevertheless superseded after the Napoleonic Wars by the breathtaking romanticism of the French accounts. In fact, France rather than Britain can be said to have prompted the fad for "Romantic Spain" that spread across Europe in the first half of the nineteenth century.

28. This quote by Octavia Walton LeVert comes from her *Souvenirs of Travel*, 2 vols. (New York: Goetzel, 1857), 1:319. In *Byron and Byronism in America* (1907; New York: Gordian Press, 1963), 19–35, William Ellery Leonard explains that by the 1820s *Childe Harold* and *Don Juan* were cited everywhere. However, some of the travelers who went to Spain did not let themselves be dazzled by this Byronic fad. Joseph Hart, for example, wrote that "Byron, whose works I managed to carry with the rest, also wrote about Spain in my own time, and was therefore somewhat modern. He is not to be relied for any thing substantial. . . . His poetic

license, however, has passed quite current for truth with many English writers upon Spanish morals, who quote him with profound deference." Hart, *The Romance of Yachting*, 2 vols. (New York: Harper, 1848), 1:69.

29. James Buzard, *The Beaten Track* (New York: Oxford University Press, 1993), 121–22, 130.

30. Dennis Porter, *Haunted Journeys. Desire and Transgression in European Travel Writing* (Princeton: Princeton University Press, 1990), 9. I am particularly following his theoretically based introduction, 3–21.

31. Jeffrey Rubin-Dorsky, *Adrift in the Old World. The Psychological Pilgrimage of Washington Irving* (Chicago: University of Chicago Press, 1988), xiii–xix, 1–31.

32. For another insightful theoretical articulation of the concept of belatedness in travel writing see the introduction ("The Predicaments of Belatedness") in Ali Behdad's *Belated Travelers* (Durham, N.C.: Duke University Press, 1994), 1–17. This author argues that the nineteenth-century authors who visited the Orient in the late colonial period "could not help but experience a sense of displacement in time and place, an experience that produced either a sense of disorientation and loss or an obsessive urge to discover an 'authentic' Other" (13). Behdad's study also proposes a contemporary reexamination of colonial belatedness in order to see remnants of the past in today's discourses, a reexamination that no doubt would be equally striking if one were to dissect current American discourses on Hispanism.

33. Christopher Mulvey, *Anglo-American Landscapes* (New York: Cambridge University Press, 1983), 16.

34. Harriet Trowbridge Allen, *Travels in Europe and the East: During the Years 1858–59 and 1863–64* (New Haven: Tuttle, Moorehouse & Taylor, 1879), 462–63.

35. [Sarah Rogers Haight], *Over the Ocean, or Glimpses in Many Lands. By a Lady of New York* (New York: Paine & Burgess, 1846), 289.

36. Carl Bode has remarked that for many nineteenth-century American readers travel books were the source of pleasure their Calvinistic society denied them. *The Anatomy of American Popular Fiction 1840–61* (Berkeley and Los Angeles: University of California Press, 1959), 222–23.

37. Mary Louise Pratt, *Imperial Eyes. Travel Writing and Transculturation* (New York and London: Routledge, 1992), 4.

38. Ibid., 7–8.

39. Mills, *Discourses of Difference*, 18–20.

40. According to Willard Thorp, during that period "the United States lived very much to itself. Contacts with Europe were slighter than at any time before or since. Transportation by steamship was initiated in the thirties, but it was irregular and unreliable. Communication by cable had not yet been attempted. Consular and diplomatic exchanges were few. . . . For three decades, Washington and New York and even Boston moved westward across the globe—farther from Europe, nearer the Rocky Mountains." See "Pilgrims' Return," in *Literary History of the United States*, rev. ed. in one vol., ed. Robert E. Spiller et al. (New York: Macmillan, 1953), 219.

41. Nina Baym, *American Women Writers and the Work of History* (New Brunswick, N.J.: Rutgers University Press, 1995), 132.

42. Allison Lockwood in *Passionate Pilgrims* (Rutherford, N.J.: Fairleigh Dickinson University Press, 1981), 196–207, has shown that for many early American travelers their trip to Britain was a return home to the mother country, but their attitude changed when negative British accounts of the United States began to be

published. Terry Caesar, on the other hand, argues for a constant search of a stable home in American travel writing. At first it was England, but progressively the mere fact of traveling and the exploration of "abroad" helped Americans to define and imagine themselves as a "home" or nation. See his *Forgiving the Boundaries: Home as Abroad in American Travel Writing* (Athens: University of Georgia Press, 1995), 43–45.

43. Washington Irving, "The Author," in *Bracebridge Hall*, ed. Herbert F. Smith (Boston: Twayne, 1977), 4.

44. Indeed, as Karen Lawrence has remarked, the search for the new itself constitutes a major convention in the literature of travel. See her *Penelope Voyages: Women and Travel in the British Literary Imagination* (Ithaca: Cornell University Press, 1994), 19.

45. Marie Suzanne Schriber, in *Telling Travels: Selected Writings by Nineteenth-Century American Women Abroad* (DeKalb: Northern Illinois University Press, 1995), xxiii, refers to the elasticity of the genre, which she defines as "something of a literary carpetbag into which travelers pack all that they need for their travels and all that they collect along the way." Similarly, William Stowe argues in *Going Abroad*, 243, that travel writing was not a problematic narrative form at all; on the contrary, it "served as a meeting place for various narrative voices, literary styles, levels of speech, and kinds of subjects, combining disparate modes of discourse without necessarily generating any tension among them or forging them into a 'higher unity.' " Michael Kowalewski has also highlighted this "androgynous" quality of travel writing, which allows the mixture of "a sense of freedom with social awareness, an itch to escape with a candid respect for unfamiliar landscapes and cultures." See his "Introduction: The Modern Literature of Travel," in *Temperamental Journeys. Essays on the Modern Literature of Travel*, ed. Michael Kowalewski (Athens: University of Georgia Press, 1992), 8.

46. Paul Fussell has argued for the connection between the presence of romance in travel writing and the marketability of the genre: "A travel book, at its purest, is addressed to those who do not plan to follow the traveler at all, but who require the exotic or comic anomalies, wonders, and scandals of the literary form *romance* which their own time and place cannot entirely supply." See his *Abroad: British Literary Traveling Between the Wars* (New York: Oxford University Press, 1980), 203.

47. William Charvat, *Literary Publishing in America: 1790–50* (Philadelphia: University of Pennsylvania Press, 1959), 74. More recently, Terry Caesar has also stressed the social prestige of nineteenth-century American travel writing on the grounds of its usefulness for national self-representation. Caesar, *Forgiving the Boundaries*, 61.

48. Charvat, *Literary Publishing in America*, 76. In *The Popular Book* (Berkeley and Los Angeles: University of California Press, 1963), 29, James Hart also mentions the popularity achieved by *The Chronicle of the Conquest of Granada* in the United States.

49. William Charvat, *The Profession of Authorship in America, 1800–70*, ed. Matthew J. Bruccoli (1968; New York: Columbia University Press, 1992), 50.

50. Cited in Thomas Low Nichols, *Forty Years of American Life*, 2 vols. (1864; rpt. New York and London: Johnson Reprint Corporation, 1969), 1:343.

51. In a letter (2 January 1840) from Harvard to George W. Greene, Longfellow complained that "most publishers will not look at a book, and are working off the obligations they had on hand" (LL, 2:201).

52. This citation is from "Cortes and the Conquest of Mexico," a review origi-

nally published in the *Southern Quarterly Review* VI (July 1844): 163–227. I cite from the reprint in *Views and Reviews in American Literature, History, and Fiction, First Series*, ed. C. Hugh Holman (1845; Cambridge: Harvard University Press, 1962), 178–79. Simms never visited Spain, but his attraction for that country found expression in his unsuccessful romances, *Pelayo: A Story of the Goth* (1839) and *Count Julian; or, The Last Days of the Goth* (1845).

53. Nathaniel Hawthorne, *The House of the Seven Gables* (Columbus: Ohio State University Press, 1962), 1. William Spengemann goes even a step further from the mixture of facts and fiction and defines romantic American travel literature not as "an analysis of experiences undergone prior to the writing," but as that which "enacts and records a series of imagined experiences." See his *The Adventurous Muse. The Poetics of American Fiction, 1789–1900* (New Haven: Yale University Press, 1977), 66.

54. Sarah Josepha Hale, "The Romance of Traveling," in *Traits of American Life* (Philadelphia: Carey & Hart, 1835), 187–208.

55. *The Marble Faun: or, The Romance of Monte Beni* (Columbus: Ohio State University Press, 1968), 3.

56. Quoted in *American Romanticism: A Shape for Fiction*, ed. Stanley Bank (New York: Putnam's, 1969), 120.

57. Twentieth-century American travelers, Thomas F. McGann observed in 1963, have also felt this ambivalent attraction toward Spain, mixing romantic elements with those of repulsion such as "dismay at the dirtily cassocked and unshaven priests," "alarm over the apparent political incapacity of the Spaniards," and "mistrust of non-businessmen who carry no clock in their brains, keep no appointments on time—and are not thereby in the least disturbed." *Portrait of Spain. British and American Accounts of Spain in the Nineteenth and Twentieth Centuries*, ed. Thomas F. McGann (New York: Knopf, 1963), ix.

58. Here I follow some studies that have paid attention to the connection between anthropology and travel writing: James Boon's *Other Tribes, Other Scribes* (New York: Cambridge University Press, 1982); Christopher Herbert's *Culture and Anomie: Ethnographic Imagination in the Nineteenth Century* (Chicago: University of Chicago Press, 1991); *Writing Culture: The Poetics and Politics of Ethnography*, eds. James Clifford and George E. Marcus (Berkeley and Los Angeles: University of California Press, 1986)—especially the essays by Clifford, Pratt, and Crapanzano; and James Clifford's *The Predicament of Culture* (Cambridge: Harvard University Press, 1988).

59. Quoted in McGann, *Portrait of Spain*, 92.

60. Valerie Wheeler, "Travelers' Tales: Observations on the Travel Book and Ethnography," *Anthropological Quarterly* 59 (1986): 52.

61. James M. Buckley, *Travels in Three Continents* (New York: Hunt and Eaton, 1895), 66.

62. Vincent Crapanzano, "Hermes' Dilemma: The Masking of Subversion in Ethnographic Description," in *Writing Culture*, eds. Clifford and Marcus, 51–53.

63. James Buzard, *The Beaten Track*, 8–10, 156. William Stowe has also focused on the connections between travel and textual practices: "The traveling class was a reading class, and travel was seen as a preeminently literary activity. Itineraries were drawn up with the monuments of literary history in mind, and the pleasure of travel derived in part from the way it reminded the traveler of past literary pleasures." Stowe, *Going Abroad*, 13.

64. Caesar, *Forgiving the Boundaries*, 36–37.

CHAPTER 2. FIRST IMPRESSIONS: WRITING FROM AND ABOUT SPAIN IN THE COLONIAL AND EARLY NATIONAL PERIODS

1. [Alexander H. Everett], "The Peninsula," *Annual Register* 5 (1829–30): 414.

2. "The Spaniards; Their Character and Customs," *Southern Literary Messenger* V (August 1839): 519.

3. Frederick S. Stimson, *Orígenes del hispanismo norteamericano* (Mexico: Ed. De Andrea, 1961), 69. This is the Spanish translation of his doctoral dissertation "Spanish Themes in Early American Literature in Novels, Drama, and Verse, 1770–1830" (University of Michigan, 1952). Stanley T. Williams's argument for a progressive widening of American perceptions of Spain is found in the chapters "Spanish Culture in the Seventeenth-Century Colonies" and "Widening Consciousness of Spanish Culture in Eighteenth-Century America," in his *The Spanish Background of American Literature*, 2 vols. (New Haven: Yale University Press, 1955), 1:3–47. These works by Stimson and Williams are the best resources for information on Spanish-American cultural relations during the colonial and early national periods.

4. Percy G. Adams, *Travel Literature and the Evolution of the Novel* (Lexington: University Press of Kentucky, 1983), 242.

5. Homi Bhabha, "The Other Question," *Screen* 24 (December 1983): 18–19.

6. Severn Teackle Wallis, *Glimpses of Spain; or, Notes of an Unfinished Tour in 1847* (New York: Harper & Brothers, 1849), 365. The portrait that Wallis provides was a prevalent one, indeed, for several years later James J. Pettigrew was to complain about the same: "The conception we still retain of the Spaniard, notwithstanding the many excellent productions for which the world is indebted to our countrymen, would represent him enveloped in a huge cloak, shaded by a still huger sombrero, and rejoicing in a half-drawn stiletto, his country devastated by the Inquisition, and the abode of ignorance, idleness, and prejudice. Such I have not found it." *Notes on Spain and the Spaniards, in the Summer of 1859. By a Carolinian* (Charleston, S.C.: Evans & Cogswell, 1861), iii.

7. Judith Adler, "Origins of Sightseeing," *Annals of Tourism Research* 16 (1989): 8.

8. Edith F. Helman, "Early Interest in Spanish in New England (1815–1835)," *Hispania* XXIX (1946): 342.

9. Maria Concepción Zardoya, "España en la poesía americana," Ph.D. diss. (University of Illinois at Urbana-Champaign, 1952), 1–3.

10. In this dialogue Britain tries to obtain assurance from its European neighbors that they will not aid the American revolutionists. Spain refuses to grant that because in the past Britain helped Holland's uprising against Spain. Benjamin Franklin, *Representative Selections*, rev. ed., introduction, bibliography, and notes by Chester E. Jorgenson and Frank Luther Mott (1936; New York: Hill & Wang, 1962), 394–97.

11. Zardoya, "España en la poesía americana," 14.

12. Philip Freneau, *The Poems of Philip Freneau, Poet of the American Revolution*, 3 vols., ed. Fred Lewis Pattee (1902–7; rpt. New York: Russell & Russell, 1963), 1:66.

13. María Luisa Colón, "Impresos en español publicados en Filadelfia durante los años 1800 a 1835," M.A. Thesis (Catholic University of America, Washington, D.C., 1951), 5.

14. Williams, *The Spanish Background of American Literature*, 1:9, 45.

15. Harry Bernstein, "Las primeras relaciones intelectuales entre New England y el mundo hispánico (1700–1815)," *Revista Hispánica Moderna* V (1939): 1–17. Some of the information produced in this essay appears further expanded in *Origins of Inter-America:: Interest, 1700–1812* (Philadelphia: University of Pennsylvania Press, 1945). The 1835 catalog of the Library Company of Philadelphia is undoubtedly a good index of the circulation of authors and titles devoted to Spain. A century after its foundation by Benjamin Franklin, this institution could already boast the most influential authors of Enlightenment travel writing on Spain: Jean François Bourgoing, Henry Swinburne, Philip Thicknesse, Sir John Carr, Alexandre de Laborde, William Dalrymple, and Friedrich Augustus Fischer, among many others. See *A Catalog of the Books Belonging to the Library Company of Philadelphia*. 2 vols. (Philadelphia: C. Sherman & Co., 1835).

16. Adams, *Travel Literature and the Evolution of the Novel*, 244–45.

17. Charles Brockden Brown, *Wieland and Memoirs of Carwin*, ed. Sydney J. Krause and S. W. Reid (Kent, Ohio: Kent State University Press, 1988), 67.

18. Frederick Stimson, *Orígenes del hispanismo norteamericano*, 19–25, 41–55. Some of the romances with Spanish themes cited by Stimson are *Adventures of Alonzo* (1775), *Fortune's Football: or, the Adventures of Mercutio* (1797), *Ramon; the Rover of Cuba* (1824), *Laffite, or the Baratarian Chief* (1825), and *Francis Berrian, or the Mexican Patriot* (1826). Stimson adds that writers often used the exoticism of Spanish elements regardless of their source. That is, to them anything from Spain, Mexico or any South American nation was simply "Spanish." In drama the vogue of Spain for exotic scenery or romantic plots also ran high, evinced by plays like Mercy Otis Warren's *The Ladies of Castile* (1790), James Gates Percival's *Zamor, a Tragedy* (1815), or James Nelson Barker's *How to Try a Lover* (1817).

19. Williams, *The Spanish Background of American Literature*, 1:18–20.

20. Francis B. Crowninshield, *The Story of George Crowninshield's Yacht Cleopatra's Barge on a Voyage of Pleasure to the Western Islands and the Mediterranean 1816–1817* (Boston: privately printed, 1913), 97–98.

21. John Quincy Adams, *Diary of John Quincy Adams*, ed. Robert J. Taylor and Marc Friedlaender, 2 vols. (Cambridge: The Belknap Press of Harvard University Press, 1981), 1:25.

22. Crowninshield, *The Story of George Crowninshield's Yacht Cleopatra's Barge*, 136. By the time Crowninshield visited Spain, two major Spanish works criticizing the Holy Office were already available to any well-informed American traveller. One was Antonio Puigblanch's *La Inquisición sin máscara* (1812), which was translated and published in London under the title *The Inquisition Unmasked* (1816). The other work was Juan Antonio Llorente's *Memoria histórica sobre cual ha sido la opinión nacional de España acerca del tribunal de la Inquisición* (1812), available in French translation. The American interest in the Holy office never stopped, and culminated in Henry Charles Lea's scholarship, which produced *History of the Inquisition of Spain* (1906) and *The Inquisition in the Spanish Dependencies* (1908).

23. Zardoya, "España en la poesía americana," 1; Williams, *The Spanish Background of American Literature*, 1:15.

24. Williams, *The Spanish Background of American Literature*, 1:31. Apart from books, Cervantes's works also became frequently present, either through excerpts or critical assessments, in many periodicals. One of them commenced an essay on "Don Quixote" with the following cultural remark: "It seems a problem

in literature, that a nation the gravest and most seriously disposed by its natural temper, and the gloomy despotism of its government and religion, should have produced the most lively work that ever was written. It abounds in original humour and exquisite satire. It displays the most copious invention, the most whimsical incidents, and the keenest remarks on the follies of its contemporaries. There is no book in whatever language that so eminently possesses the power of exciting laughter." *Literary Magazine, and American Register* VIII (1 November, 1807): 174.

25. Merrill F. Heiser, "Cervantes in the United States," *Hispanic Review* XV (1947): 409–35.

26. A valuable examination of Robertson's influence in America can be found in Frederick Stimson's *Orígenes del hispanismo norteamericano*, 73–79. In addition to Joel Barlow and Philip Freneau, several other American poets have paid attention to the figure of Columbus. Zardoya, in her study, cites James Russell Lowell ("To Columbus"), Walt Whitman ("Prayer of Columbus"), Howard H. Caldwell ("Columbus"), Henry Howard Brownell ("The Tomb of Columbus"), Joaquin Miller ("Columbus"), Will Carleton ("Three Scenes in the Life of Columbus"), Edgar Lee Masters (*The New World*), and John Gould Fletcher ("To Columbus"). For the Columbian influence in other spheres of American culture see Claudia L. Bushman's *America Discovers Columbus: How an Italian Explorer Became an American Hero* (Hanover, N.H.: University Press of New England, 1992).

27. Stimson, *Orígenes del hispanismo norteamericano*, 59–60. In *Reminiscences of Spain*, Caleb Cushing begins his essay on Columbus with two paragraphs in which he says that Americans ought to thank Columbus for having added the New World to the civilized world (RS, 1:259). Similarly, Joseph Hart describes his stops at the Columbian sights as some of the most thrilling moments in his Spanish journey. He visited Columbus's house, touched his letters, read from some of the very same books the admiral owned, and finally stood before his tomb in Seville's cathedral. "No man, except an American," he concludes, "can appreciate the feelings of an American, surrounded as I was by all that remains of the first knowledge of our continent by civilized man." Hart, *The Romance of Yachting*, 2 vols. (New York: Harper, 1848), 1:62. In contrast with this veneration of Columbian artifacts, two decades later readers found the nonchalant attitude that Mark Twain expressed in *Innocents Abroad*, where some American tourists in Genoa manifest indifference at the Italian guide's overexcitement at showing them a parchment written by Columbus himself. No doubt, Twain was poking fun at the absurdity of certain guides' views. But no doubt, too, he was also indirectly laughing at a firmly established convention of European travel, that is, the visit to Columbian sites and the near worship of Columbian objects. Mark Twain, *Innocents Abroad* and *Roughing It* (New York: Library of America, 1984), 229–31.

28. Freneau, *The Poems of Philip Freneau*, 1:104.

29. Joel Barlow, *The Works of Joel Barlow*, ed. William K. Bottorff and Arthur L. Ford, 2 vols. (Gainesville, Fla.: Scholar's Facsimiles & Reprints, 1970), 2:121.

30. Ibid., 2:358.

31. Thomas Jefferson, *Writings*, ed. Merrill D. Peterson (New York: Library of America, 1984), 904. Two decades later an anonymous essayist who complained about the negative image of some Americans abroad wrote equally careful remarks: "Foreign travel should be the last, and therefore must be an important, part of the education of a gentleman. Though it does not strengthen the mind, it purifies it from the disease of prejudices, inhaled with the atmosphere of our native community; though it cannot create taste, it refines and directs it; and though

it may not confirm the moral principles, it certainly polishes the manners." However, as the essayist pointed out, "the vicious disposition is never changed by change of place; nor will he ever become profound, who is originally shallow." See "American Travellers," *Monthly Anthology, and Boston Review* III (December 1806): 628–29.

32. Royall Tyler, *The Contrast*, in *The Norton Anthology of American Literature*. 3rd. ed., ed. Nina Baym et al., 2 vols. (New York: Norton, 1989), 1:750.

33. A cogent overview of eighteenth-century American travelers in Europe is given in Foster Rhea Dulles, *Americans Abroad. Two Centuries of European Travel* (Ann Arbor: University of Michigan Press, 1964), 8–42.

34. Nathalia Wright, *American Novelists in Italy* (Philadelphia: University of Pennsylvania Press, 1965), 17–33.

35. The account of his mission, consisting of diplomatic papers in the main, can be found in *The Correspondence and Public Papers of John Jay, 1794–1826*, ed. Henry P. Johnston, 4 vols. (New York: Putnam's, 1890–93), 1:251–460, 2:1–307. Louis Littlepage and William Carmichael served with John Jay in this mission. When Jay left for Paris in 1802 the latter remained as *chargé of affaires* until 1790. He returned to Madrid in 1793, appointed by President Washington, but fell ill and died there in 1795. Samuel Gwynn Coe, "William Carmichael," *Dictionary of American Biography*, ed. Dumas Malone 11 vols. (New York: Scribner, 1964), 2:497–98.

36. They arrived at El Ferrol on 5 December 1779 aboard the French frigate *Sensible*. On 23 January 1780, they reached the French city of Bayonne. The unexpected sojourn is described in *Diary and Autobiography of John Adams*, ed. L. H. Butterfield, 4 vols. (Cambridge: The Belknap Press of Harvard University Press, 1961), 2:404–33, 4:190–238; *Diary of John Quincy Adams*, ed. J. Taylor and Marc Friedlaender, 2 vols. (Cambridge: The Belknap Press of Harvard University Press, 1981), 1:10–31; and letters 257 through 260 in *Familiar Letters of John Adams and His Wife Abigail Adams, during the Revolution*, ed. Charles Francis Adams (Boston: Houghton, 1876), 370–74.

37. Francis Landon Humphreys, *Life and Times of David Humphreys, Soldier, Statesman, Poet*, 2 vols. (New York: Putnam's, 1917), 2:85–89.

38. James Monroe, *The Autobiography of James Monroe*, ed. Stuart Gerry Brown (Syracuse, N.Y.: Syracuse University Press, 1959), 203–21.

39. Jarvis wanted to improve the local sheep breeds in Connecticut. Jefferson commended him for the success of his mission. See Mary Pepperrell Sparhawk Cutts, *The Life and Times of Hon. William Jarvis* (New York: Hurd & Houghton, 1869). It was believed that in the future sheepherding could be very beneficial to the United States, and this interest is reflected in a series of essays that, under the title "Account of the Sheep and Sheep-Walks of Spain," the *New York Magazine* published from August through October 1790. Their author was Peter Collinson, a naturalist from London who corresponded with Benjamin Franklin.

40. Thomas Atwood Digges, *Adventures of Alonzo* (1775; rpt. Upper Saddle River, N.J.: Literature House/Gregg Press, 1970), 23–24.

41. Richard Henry Lee, *Life of Arthur Lee, Ll.D.*, 2 vols. (Boston: Wells & Lilly, 1829), 1:72–76. On Lee's diplomatic mission, see Julio César Santoyo's *Arthur Lee: historia de una embajada secreta* (Vitoria: Obra Cultural de la Caja de Ahorros Municipal de la Ciudad de Vitoria, 1977).

42. Adams, *Diary and Autobiography of John Adams*, 2:426.

43. Three excellent sources of information on travel conditions are Lockwood, *Passionate Pilgrims: The American Traveler in Great Britain*, 32–40; Robert E.

Spiller, *The American in England during the First Half Century of Independence* (1926; rpt. Philadelphia: Porcupine Press, 1976), 3–32; Dulles, *Americans Abroad*, 26–27, 43.

44. George Coggeshall, *Thirty-Six Voyages to Various Parts of the World, Made Between the Years 1799 and 1841*, 3rd ed. (1851; New York: Putnam, 1858), 32.

45. Coggeshall, *Thirty-Six Voyages to Various Parts of the World*, 209–31.

46. Victor Marie Dupont, *Journey to France and Spain. 1801*, ed. Charles W. David (Ithaca: Cornell University Press, 1961), 66–87.

47. Spiller, *The American in England*, 18–19.

48. An excellent survey and analysis of the state of Spanish roads in that period can be found in vol. 1 of Santos Madrazo's *El sistema de transportes en España, 1750–1850*, 2 vols. (Madrid: Colegio de Ingenieros de Caminos, Canales y Puertos, Editorial Turner, 1984).

49. Jay, *The Correspondence and Public Papers*, 1:334.

50. Percy G. Adams, *Travel Literature and the Evolution of the Novel*, 213–19.

51. The best study on how these travelers saw the Spanish inns of that period still is Carrie E. Farnham's *American Travellers in Spain: the Spanish Inns, 1776–1867* (New York: Columbia University Press, 1921).

52. Jay, *The Correspondence and Public Papers*, 1:335.

53. Adams, *Diary of John Quincy Adams*, 1:25.

54. Adams, *Diary and Autobiography of John Adams*, 1:419.

CHAPTER 3. TOWARD ROMANTIC SPAIN: MORDECAI M. NOAH, GEORGE TICKNOR, AND THE ALLURE OF A FALLEN EMPIRE

1. The best documented biographies on Noah are Jonathan D. Sarna's *Jacksonian Jew: The Two Worlds of Mordecai Noah* (New York: Holmes & Meier, 1981) and Isaac Goldberg's *Major Noah: American-Jewish Pioneer* (Philadelphia: The Jewish Publication Society of America, 1938). Also interesting are: Simon Wolf's *Mordecai Manuel Noah, a Biographical Sketch*. (Philadelphia: The Levytype Company, 1897), reprinted in *Selected Addresses and Papers* (Cincinnati: Union of American Hebrew Congregations, 1926), 108–54; Abraham B. Makover's *Mordecai Manuel Noah, His Life and Work from the Jewish View Point* (New York: Bloch Publishing, 1917); Arthur Hertzberg's *The Jews in America* (New York: Simon and Schuster, 1989), 93–98; and H. W. Schoenberger's entry "Mordecai Manuel Noah" in *Dictionary of American Biography*, ed. Dumas Malone, 11 vols. (New York: Scribner, 1964), 7:534–35.

2. Noah summarized his dramatic career in a letter published in William Dunlap's *History of American Theatre* (1832), later reprinted in Evert A. and George L. Duyckinck, *Cyclopedia of American Literature*, 2 vols. (New York: Scribner, 1855), 2:74–76. Other short overviews of Noah's theatrical activities can be found in Jack A. Vaugh's *Early American Dramatists. From the Beginnings to 1900* (New York: Ungar, 1981), 59–63, and the *Oxford Companion to American Theatre*, ed. Gerald Bordman (New York: Oxford University Press, 1992), 509–10. Noah's major writings, dramatic and otherwise, have been recently anthologized by M. Shuldiner and D. J. Kleinfeld in *The Selected Writings of Mordecai Noah* (New York: Greenwood Press, 1999).

3. David B. Tyack, *George Ticknor and the Boston Brahmins* (Cambridge: Harvard University Press, 1967), 2. This is the most thorough study so far of Tick-

nor's career and relation with the Boston intelligentsia. Other good overviews of Ticknor are Orie W. Long's *Literary Pioneers. Early American Explorers of European Culture* (1935; rpt. New York: Russell & Russell, 1963), 3–62; Jeremiah D. M. Ford's entry "George Ticknor," in *Dictionary of American Biography*, 9: 525–528, and Stanley T. Williams's *The Spanish Background of American Literature*, 2 vols. (New Haven: Yale University Press, 1955), 2:46–77.

4. Duyckinck, *Cyclopedia of American Literature*, 2:74.

5. An excellent discussion of these critical and aesthetic principles is given in William Charvat's *The Origins of American Critical Thought 1810–1835* (1936; rpt. New York: Barnes, 1961), 7–59. Thomas R. Hart, Jr., in a compelling analysis of Ticknor's *History of Spanish Literature*, also calls attention to these precepts as Ticknor's New England bias. See his "George Ticknor's History of Spanish Literature: The New England Background," *PMLA* LXIX (March 1954): 76–88. Noah, though not associated to the Boston intellectual circles, was equally influenced by these critical principles.

6. Charles Batten, *Pleasurable Instruction. Form and Convention in Eighteenth-Century Travel Literature* (Berkeley and Los Angeles: University of California Press, 1978), 28.

7. Mary Louise Pratt, *Imperial Eyes. Travel Writing and Transculturation* (New York and London: Routledge, 1992), 58–85.

8. Williams, *The Spanish Background of American Literature*, 1:61.

9. Tyack, *George Ticknor and the Boston Brahmins*, 73, 79.

10. The same year that the first American edition was published in New York John Miller issued the British edition in London. Besides, in 1819 Kirk and Mercein also published in New York an abridged edition inlaid in large octavo sheets, entitled *Spain and the Barbary States, in the years 1813–14 and 15*. There is also another edition of the book, possibly pirated, using the same pagination of the original, and entitled *Noah's Travels*. It was probably published in New York in 1819 by C. S. Van Winkle. In 1906 an abridged translation in Hebrew was published in Warsaw. On the reception of Noah's book see Sarna, *Jacksonian Jew*, 32.

11. Upon his return to the United States Noah defended himself by publishing *Correspondence and Documents Relative to the Attempt to Negotiate for the Release of the American Captives at Algiers* (Washington City, 1816), which in fact became the genesis of his travel book. His political enemies, however, not satisfied with Noah's explanation, considered it instead a further attack against the administration. Both John Adams and John Quincy Adams looked at Noah's political ambitions with mistrust. When in 1820 Noah tried to obtain a new foreign appointment, the latter referred to him as "a Jew, who was once Consul at Tunis, recalled for indiscretions, who has published a Book of Travels against Mr. Madison and Mr. Monroe." Quoted in Goldberg, *Major Noah*, 147.

12. Ticknor's eighteen-volume journals deposited at the Dartmouth College Library, correspond to his first (1815–19) and second (1835–39) European journeys, the latter with his family. All in all, according to Allaback and Medlicott, these journals amount to 8,900 manuscript pages, which were made available in microfilm in five reels in 1974 by University Microfilms. The second half of volume 7 (reel 1) and the first half of volume 8 (reel 2) are the parts dealing with Spain in Ticknor's 1816–38 Journals. See *A Guide to the Microfilm Edition of the European Journals of George and Anna Ticknor*, ed. Steven Allaback and Alexander Medlicott Jr. (Hanover, N.H.: Dartmouth College Library, 1978). Before these microfilms could provide an uninterrupted reading of Ticknor's Spanish travels, students of Ticknor had to reconstruct his representation of Spain from a variety

of different sources to which, for the sake of clarity and accessability, I will still refer in my own citations.

13. His Spanish impressions can be found in *Life, Letters, and Journals of George Ticknor*, eds. George S. Hillard, Mrs. Anna Ticknor, and Anna Eliot Ticknor, 2 vols. (Boston: Osgood, 1876), 1:185–242. The British edition was published in London in 1876 by Sampson & Low. Citations in the text, however, come from a later edition with an introduction by Ferris Greenslet. Ticknor's observations on Spain not included in the 1876 volume were finally brought to light with the publication of *George Ticknor's Travels in Spain*, ed. George T. Northup, *University of Toronto Studies* 2 (1913).

14. George Ticknor, *History of Spanish Literature*, 3 vols. (New York: Harper and Brothers, 1849). Subsequent citations of this work in this study will be from a later facsimile edition (New York: Ungar, 1965). For information on circumstances pertinent to the preparation and reception of Ticknor's *History of Spanish Literature* see Franco Meregalli's "George Ticknor and Spain," in *Homenaje al profesor Antonio Vilanova*, 2 vols, eds. Adolfo Sotelo y Marta Cristina (Barcelona: Universitat de Barcelona, 1989), 2:413–26.

15. For similarities between Ticknor's lectures and his *History of Spanish Literature* see Thomas R. Hart, Jr., "George Ticknor's History of Spanish Literature: The New England Background," *PMLA* LXIX: 78–79.

16. "This journal was made up and sent home to my family in small parcels as I found opportunities." Allaback and Medlicott, *A Guide to the Microfilm Edition of the European Journals of George and Anna Ticknor*, 4.

17. Goldberg, *Major Noah*, 81, 88.

18. A good account of Ticknor's negotiations with the Harvard trustees can be found in Long, *Literary Pioneers*, 25–26.

19. Goldberg, *Major Noah*, 112–19.

20. Batten, *Pleasurable Instruction*, 76–77.

21. Goldberg, *Major Noah*, 24.

22. Mary Suzanne Schriber, "Edith Wharton and the Dog-Eared Travel Book," in *Wretched Exotic: Essays on Edith Wharton in Europe*, eds. Katherine Joslin and Alan Price (New York: Peter Lang, 1993), 152–53.

23. Stowe, *Going Abroad*, 55.

24. Ticknor, Preface to *History of Spanish Literature*, 1:v.

25. Quoted in Long, *Literary Pioneers*, 35.

26. David Levin, *History as Romantic Art: Bancroft, Prescott, Motley, and Parkman* (1959; rpt. New York: AMS Press, 1967), 106. Levin provides a detailed discussion of the representation and role of Roman Catholicism in the historical works of Ticknor's New England contemporaries in the chapter "Priestcraft and Catholicism," 93–125.

27. See the letter to his father, dated Madrid, 3 June 1818, where he provides more details regarding his strict course of studies in Spanish (TT, 37–39).

28. After his return from Europe Ticknor published an excellent analysis of bullfights and other Spanish amusements in "Amusements in Spain," *North American Review* XXI (July 1825): 59–78.

29. The royal monastery of San Lorenzo del Escorial, 30 miles northwest of Madrid, was founded by Philip II in 1563 to commemorate his victory over the French at St. Quentin in 1557. The works, started by Juan B. de Toledo and finished by Juan de Herrera, took twenty-one years. In addition to having been built as a royal pantheon and quiet residence, the monastery housed also an excellent library and art collection. The palace of La Granja de San Ildefonso, near Segovia,

had been built in the first half of the eighteenth century by Philip V in imitation of Versailles.

30. The royal fortress-palace of the Alhambra, whose construction begun in the mid-1200s, achieved the artistic proportions for which it is known today during the fourteenth century, through the auspices of the Nasrid rulers of Granada. The palace is famous for its pools, courtyards (the best known being the Court of the Myrtles and the Court of the Lions), lattice, and stalactite vaults. For a full architectural description of the palace as well as an account of its history, see Oleg Grabar's *The Alhambra* (Cambridge: Harvard University Press, 1978).

31. Charvat, *The Origins of American Critical Thought*, 9–13.

32. Batten, *Pleasurable Instruction*, 47–115.

33. Percy Adams, *Travellers and Travel Liars* (Berkeley: University of California Press, 1962), 97.

34. Spengemann, *The Adventurous Muse*, 45–47; Caesar, *Forgiving the Boundaries*, 96.

35. Caesar, *Forgiving the Boundaries*, 31.

36. *An Address Delivered before the General Society of Mechanics and Tradesmen of the City of New York* (New York: A. Mercein, 1822). Quoted in Goldberg's *Major Noah*, 27–28.

37. One of the main characteristics of the American literature produced in those years is, as Robert A. Ferguson observes, its capacity to foreshadow optimism and pessimism at the same time: "The American literature of the period thrives in the resonant space between the hope of blessing and the fear of curse. It defines itself in that crisis; this is where it holds its audiences. In so doing, early republican writings depend heavily upon the process of the Enlightenment. It is the struggle towards realization, not the celebration of knowledge, that creates meaning and interest." "What is Enlightenment? Some American Answers," in *The Cambridge History of American Literature, Vol. 1, 1590–1820*, ed. Sacvan Bercovitch (New York: Cambridge University Press, 1994), 387.

38. David Levin has analyzed in great detail the ideology of empire embedded in the nineteenth-century histories of Bancroft, Prescott, Motley, and Parkman. Many of his conclusions no doubt are also true of Noah and, even more, Ticknor. For concepts of historiography during the Enlightenment, including the idea of history as progress (or the opposite), see also Hayden White's *Metahistory. The Historical Imagination in Nineteenth-Century Europe* (Baltimore: The Johns Hopkins University Press, 1973), 45–80.

39. "Noah's Travels." *American Monthly Magazine and Critical Review* IV (1819): 343.

40. On theories of the Picturesque see Malcolm Andrews, *The Search for the Picturesque* (Aldershot: Scholar's Press, 1989) and Buzard, *The Beaten Track*, 187–215. Beth L. Lueck's *American Writers and the Picturesque Tour* (New York: Garland, 1997) has recently added new insights into the American travel writers' ideological use of this cultural practice for the self-discovery of their own land, particularly upstate New York and New England.

41. Meregalli, "George Ticknor and Spain," 419, 422–23.

CHAPTER 4. THE YOUNG AMERICAN ABROAD: ALEXANDER SLIDELL MACKENZIE AND THE CALL OF REVOLUTIONARY TRAVELING

1. Alexander Slidell was born in New York City in 1803 and died in Tarrytown, New York, in 1848. He adopted the surname Mackenzie in 1837 at the request of

a childless maternal uncle who wished to preserve the family name. For convenience, throughout this study I have referred to him by the surname Mackenzie, as this is the one under which his works are usually catalogued. However, Everett, Irving, and Longfellow usually called him [Lieutenant] Slidell. The main biographical sources I rely on are: Philip James McFarland's *Sea Dangers: The Affair of the Somers* (New York: Schocken, 1985); Charles O. Paulin's entry "Alexander Slidell Mackenzie," in *Dictionary of American Biography*, ed. Dumas Malone, 11 vols. (New York: Scribner, 1964), 6:90–91; Evert A. and George L. Duyckinck, *Cyclopedia of American Literature* (New York: Scribner, 1855), II:360–65; and Barbara Ryan's chapter "Alexander Slidell Mackenzie," in *American Travel Writers, 1776–1864*, eds. James J. Schramer and Donald Ross (Detroit: Gale, 1997), 224–30.

2. In addition to the book by McFarland already mentioned, information on the *Somers* affair can be found in *The Somers Mutiny Affair: A Book of Primary Source Materials*, ed. Harrison Hayford (Englewood Cliffs, N.J.: Prentice-Hall, 1959) and in Frederic Franklyn Van de Water's *The Captain Called It Mutiny* (New York: Washburn, 1954).

3. "I expected the event," Washington Irving wrote to a friend on 5 May 1827. "The diligence in which he started had been attacked on its way to Madrid, but the robbers were repulsed; I thought it probable they would make another attempt on it on its way back. The robbery took place about thirty leagues from Madrid. Eight robbers well mounted, and armed to the teeth attacked and drove off the guard consisting of four men. They then took all the money watches &c of the passengers; opened their trunks and helped themselves to whatever they fancied and then asking pardon of the passengers for the trouble they gave them, retired very slowly & tranquilly" (LII, 232).

4. [Alexander Slidell Mackenzie], *The American in England. By the Author of A Year in Spain*, 2 vols. (New York: Harper & Brothers, 1835), 1:xiv.

5. McFarland, *Sea Dangers,* 21.

6. *North American Review* XXX (January 1830): 237.

7. The second edition was published in 1830 in New York by Carvill, whereas the latest edition appeared in 1857. Several excerpts from Mackenzie's book were also reprinted in local periodicals, which attests to the household popularity of *A Year in Spain*. Take, for instance, "Scenes in Campillo," *Southern Literary Messenger* II (August 1830): 540–41; "The Poor Officer—Traveling Sketch," *Rural Repository* XVII (10 October 1840): 64; and "A Spanish Bull-Fight," *New-England Family Magazine* I (June 1845): 197–204.

8. Ben Harris McClary, "Washington Irving's British Edition of Slidell's *A Year in Spain*," *Bulletin of the New York Public Library* 73 (June 1969): 369. For Irving's own comments on his editing of Mackenzie's book see LII, 571, 576.

9. Quoted in Duyckinck, *Cyclopedia of American Literature*, 2:361.

10. "A Year in Spain," *Quarterly Review* 44 (February 1831): 319–42. This review was heavily revised by John G. Lockhart, editor of that journal. Here I am quoting from the reprint in Washington Irving's *Miscellaneous Writings. 1803–1859*, ed. Wayne R. Kime, 2 vols. (Boston: Twayne, 1981), 2:30–31.

11. "A Year in Spain. By a Young American," *Literary Gazette* (26 February 1831): 132.

12. "A Year in Spain," *Fraser's Magazine* III (May 1831): 437.

13. Mackenzie had apparently been trying for some time to publish what subsequently became book 3 of the Harper's edition of *A Year in Spain*. Irving, in a letter to Pierre Munro Irving (London, 6 February 1832), suggests that Mackenzie publish his account of Granada with the same house that was undertaking his own *Alhambra*, which he was preparing by then (LII, 689–91).

14. "A Year in Spain," *Southern Literary Messenger* 2 (August 1836): 593.

15. "A Year in Spain—By A Young American," *New Yorker* I (6 August 1836): 317; "A Year in Spain. By a Young American," *Knickerbocker* VIII (September 1836): 366–68. The notice printed by the *Maine Monthly Magazine* (September 1836): 143, took the opportunity to criticize the American public's neglect of its own authors by saying that "the book was originally published in 1829, and after lying a long time neglected upon the bookseller's shelf, it was by chance commended by one of the foreign quarterlies."

16. "A Year in Spain. By a Young American, third edition," *American Monthly Magazine*, n.s. 2 (August 1836): 204.

17. *Ett år i Spanien, af En ung Amerikanare. Öf versättning från engelskan, i tva volymer* (Stockholm: L.J. Hjerta, 1836).

18. Thomas Paine, "The Crisis, No. 1," in *The Norton Anthology of American Literature*, 3rd. ed., 2 vols., ed. Nina Baym et al. (New York: Norton, 1989), 1:629.

19. Terry Caesar, *Forgiving the Boundaries: Home as Abroad in American Travel Writing* (Athens: University of Georgia Press, 1995), 15.

20. James Buzard, *The Beaten Track: European Tourism, Literature, and the Ways to "Culture"* (New York: Oxford University Press, 1993), 114–30.

21. "A Year in Spain. By a Young American," *Southern Review* 8 (November 1831): 154.

22. In his "Advice to Authors. By the Late Mr. Robert Slender" (1788), Philip Freneau already wrote against such a slavish convention: "When you write a book for the public, have nothing to do with *Epistles Dedicatory*. They were first invented by slaves, and have been continued by fools and sycophants. I would not give a farthing more for a book or account of its being patronized by all the noblemen or crowned heads in Christendom. If it does not possess intrinsic merit enough to protect itself and force its way through the world, their supposed protection will be of no avail: besides, by this ridiculous practice you degrade the dignity authorial, the honour of authorship, which ought to be uppermost in your thoughts." Quoted in Robert Spiller's *The American Literary Revolution* (New York: New York University Press, 1967), 9.

23. In *Spain Revisited*, however, with Ferdinand safely dead, he retracted himself from his attacks against the monarch: "I became acquainted with many facts relating to Ferdinand, the late king, which place his character in an entirely different light. . . . I had described him in my previous work as a stupid, slothful, and ignorant, but rather good-natured individual. But I now found that he had much natural cleverness, had read extensively, and was well acquainted with the laws of his country and with history generally" (SR, 1:249).

24. Frederick Douglass, *Narrative of the Life of Frederick Douglass, an American Slave*, in *Autobiographies*, ed. Houston Baker, Jr. (New York: Library of America, 1994), 18.

25. Richard H. Brodhead, "Sparing the Rod: Discipline and Fiction in Antebellum America," in *The New American Studies*, ed. Philip Fisher (Berkeley: University of California Press, 1991), 141–70.

26. Michel Foucault, *Discipline and Punish*, trans. Alan Sheridan (New York: Vintage, 1979), 48–49. Witnessing an execution no doubt shed light on power relations, but it also allowed travelers to see the ethos of the populace. This is what the anonymous author of the article "A Spanish Execution" remarked in 1834: "I had an opportunity, while at Barcelona, of being present at an execution, the first I had seen in Spain. The man had been condemned to the galleys for some previous offence, and had murdered one of his fellow convicts; and, although this is not an

agreeable spectacle, yet, as in every country, public spectacles, whether agreeable or the reverse, exhibit some peculiarities either of character or of manners, I resolved to be present." *New York Mirror* XII (30 August, 1834): 66. Further descriptions of Spanish executions could also be found in the anonymous *Scenes in Spain* (1837).

27. Buzard, *The Beaten Track*, 186.

28. Duyckinck, *Cyclopedia of American Literature*, 2:362.

Chapter 5. Between Oriental Past and Ethnographic Present: Washington Irving and the Romancing of Tattered Spaniards

1. Stanley T. Williams, *The Spanish Background of American Literature*, 2 vols. (New Haven: Yale University Press, 1955), 2:38.

2. *Legends of the Conquest of Spain*, which were part of *The Crayon Miscellany*, comprised "The Legend of Don Roderick," "The Legend of the Subjugation of Spain," and "The Legend of Count Julian and his Family." Some of these legends were republished posthumously in *Spanish Papers and Other Miscellanies* (1866), which included "Don Juan: A Spectral Research," "Legend of the Engulphed Convent," "The Adelantado of the Seven Cities," and "The Abencerrage."

3. Jeffrey Rubin-Dorsky, *Adrift in the Old World. The Psychological Pilgrimage of Washington Irving* (Chicago: University of Chicago Press, 1988), 233; William L. Hedges, *Washington Irving: An American Study, 1802–1832* (Baltimore: Johns Hopkins University Press, 1965), 239.

4. In particular, Suzan Jamil Fakahani cites *The World Displayed* (Philadelphia, 1795–96). See her Ph.D. dissertation "Irving's *The Alhambra*: Background, Sources, and Motifs" (Florida State University, 1988), 15–16.

5. For convenience, instead of using the 1832 Geoffrey Crayon edition, I have preferred to use the author's revised edition of 1851. However, the passages cited from it follow either completely or very closely those in the original edition.

6. For the major historical and literary sources Irving used in writing *The Alhambra* see Stanley T. Williams, *Life of Washington Irving*, 2 vols. (New York: Oxford University Press, 1935), 2:314–315, and Fakahani, "Irving's *The Alhambra*, 31–86.

7. Everett told Jared Sparks: "The people here are greatly pleased with him, but, not knowing much of American literature (or, indeed, any other), have confounded him with Cooper, and he generally goes under the title of the American Walter Scott." Cited in Herbert B. Adams, *The Life and Writings of Jared Sparks*, 2 vols. (Boston: Houghton, 1893), 1:285.

8. A good account of Irving's acquaintances in Madrid can be found in Claude G. Bowers, *The Spanish Adventures of Washington Irving* (Boston: Houghton, 1940), 22–48. Also relevant for information on Irving's Spanish sojourns is Philip McFarland's chapter "Don Washington Irving in Spain," in his *Sojourners* (New York: Atheneum, 1979), 301–85.

9. Rubin-Dorsky, *Adrift in the Old World*, 231.

10. James Buzard, *The Beaten Track. European Tourism, Literature, and the Ways to "Culture."* (New York: Oxford University Press, 1993), 110.

11. William Cullen Bryant, *Letters of a Traveller. Second Series* (New York: Appleton, 1859), 20.

12. Irving offered a good account of his trip from Granada to Málaga in his letter to Mme. Antoinette Bolviller, dated Málaga, 2 April 1828 (LII, 292–296).

13. For an account of this excursion see the appendix "A Visit to Palos" in Irving's *Voyages and Discoveries of the Companions of Columbus*, ed. James W. Tuttleton (Boston: Twayne, 1986), 348–62.

14. Terry Caesar, *Forgiving the Boundaries. Home as Abroad in American Travel Writing* (Athens: University of Georgia Press, 1995), 7.

15. For circumstances of publication of *The Alhambra* see *Washington Irving and the House of Murray: Geoffrey Crayon Charms the British, 1817–1856*, ed. Ben Harris McClary (Knoxville: University of Tennessee Press, 1969), 155–67.

16. A full list of reviews of the book, both in the United States and Europe, has been culled by Haskell Springer in *Washington Irving: A Reference Guide* (Boston: G.K. Hall, 1976), 30–33. Stanley T. Williams provides additional facts on the reception of the book in his *Life of Washington Irving*, 2:316–19. Finally, the fortunes of Irving's output in Spain can be traced in Juan José Lanero and Secundino Villoria, *Literatura en traducción. Versiones españolas de autores americanos del siglo XIX* (León: Secretariado de Publicaciones de la Universidad de León, 1996), 39–65.

17. "The Alhambra and A Chronicle of the Conquest of Granada," *Eclectic Review* 103 (July 1832): 1–8; "Washington Irving's *Alhambra*," *Westminster Review* 17 (July 1832): 132–45.

18. "The Alhambra," *New England Magazine* 3 (July 1832): 81.

19. "The Alhambra: A Series of Tales and Sketches of the Moors and Spaniards," *American Monthly Review* 2 (September 1832): 177–89. I quote from the reprint in *Critical Essays on Washington Irving*, ed. Ralph M. Aderman (Boston: G.K. Hall & Co., 1990), 102.

20. [Alexander H. Everett], "Irving's *Alhambra*," *North American Review* XXXV (October 1832): 270, 277.

21. "Washington Irving's *Alhambra*," *Westminster Review* 17 (July 1832): 135.

22. [Theodore S. Fay], "The Alhambra," *New York Mirror* 9 (23 June 1832): 401–3. I quote from the reprint in Ralph Aderman, *Critical Essays on Washington Irving* (Boston: G.K. Hall, 1990), 95.

23. "The Alhambra," *Monthly Review*, n.s. 2 (June 1832): 222.

24. An excellent collation of the principal editions of *The Alhambra* can be consulted in the "Textual Commentary" of the Twayne standard edition (A, 280–34).

25. Dispossessed of his palace of the Alhambra, Boabdil (nicknamed *El Chico*), the last king of Granada, came to represent the alienated hero for Irving. Goaded by his mother, the sultana Aixa, Boabdil spent his years in Granada fighting with his father and his uncle, and also being deceived by the politic Ferdinand of Aragon. Once exiled to his estate in the Alpujarras, his counselor, the vizier Aben Comixa, betrayed him. Boabdil left Spain in 1493 with his family and some of his followers, and died in 1527 fighting for his relative, the caliph of Fez.

26. Fakahani, "Irving's *The Alhambra*," 3. Opinions on the unity and form of Irving's text continued throughout the century. As late as 1892, a review of the luxuriously illustrated Darro edition of *The Alhambra* stated the following: "It is historical, but it is not a history; it is a personal record of wandering, yet no one would call it a book of travel; it deals with the remains of antiquity, but it does not belong to the literature of antiquarianism; and though we have few more charming collections of romantic legends, there would be something eccentric in a de-

scription of it as a work of fiction. And yet the charms of history, of travel, of antiquarianism, and of fiction, are all there; but they are present in a fine amalgam, fused together by the action of imagination, and cast in a new mould of beauty." See "Washington Irving's *Alhambra*," *Spectator* 69 (9 July 1892): 66–67.

27. Buzard, *The Beaten Track*, 167.

28. Caesar, *Forgiving the Boundaries*, 54.

29. This letter, which dates from 2 November 1857, is quoted in Samuel Austin Allibone, *A Critical Dictionary of English Literature and British and American Authors*, 2 vols. (1858–71; rpt. Philadelphia: Lippincott, 1891), 1:943.

30. Dean MacCannell, *The Tourist* (New York: Schocken, 1989), 136.

31. Percy Adams, *Travellers and Travel Liars* (Berkeley and Los Angeles: University of California Press, 1962), 197–98.

32. James Boon, *Other Tribes, Other Scribes* (New York: Cambridge University Press, 1982), 5.

33. Clifford Geertz mistrusts cognitive anthropology and the notion of a measurable culture. As he contends in *The Interpretation of Cultures* (New York: Basic Books, 1973), 10, the ethnographer's cultural analysis ought to deal with "a multiplicity of complex conceptual structures, many of them superimposed upon or knotted into one another, which are at once strange, irregular, and inexplicit, and which he must contrive somehow first to grasp and then to render." The novelty of such a view, however, has been contested by Christopher Herbert in *Culture and Anomie. Ethnographic Imagination in the Nineteenth Century* (Chicago: University of Chicago Press, 1991), 17–20. Herbert dissects the emergence of anthropological ideas of culture from the nineteenth century to the present, and affirms that the discipline has suffered contradictions from its very inception. The example of Geertz's reliance on the study of meaning helps Herbert to show that to a certain extent contemporary anthropology is not far from the positivism of nineteenth-century social theory and the romantic rhetoric of wholeness deployed by the early ethnographers.

34. Mary L. Pratt, *Imperial Eyes. Travel Writing and Transculturation* (New York and London: Routledge, 1992), 60–61.

35. Irving's interest in Spanish literature is particularly evident in his "Notebook: Spanish Literature, 1826," where Irving entered summaries and transcriptions of literary critics and historians like Bouterwek, Schelegel, and Argüelles (JIV, 340–74).

36. Pratt, *Imperial Eyes*, 6.

37. The complete text of this poem in Spanish appears reprinted in Washington Irving, *Miscellaneous Writings 1:1803–1859*, ed. Wayne R. Kime (Boston: Twayne, 1981), 158–59.

38. Fakahani, "Irving's *The Alhambra*," 49.

39. Williams, *Life of Washington Irving*, 1:364.

40. James Clifford, *The Predicament of Culture. Twentieth-Century Ethnography, Literature, and Art* (Cambridge: Harvard University Press, 1988), 21–54.

41. James Clifford, "On Ethnographic Allegory," in *Writing Culture: The Poetics and Politics of Ethnography*, eds. James Clifford and George E. Marcus (Los Angeles and Berkeley: University of California Press, 1986), 112–13.

42. Washington Irving, *The Alhambra. Author's Revised Edition* (New York: Putnam's, 1887), vii–viii.

43. Prescott's favorable review of *Chronicle of the Conquest of Granada* was published in *North American Review XXVIII* (January 1829): 103–34.

44. "Irving, Chateaubriand, and the Historical Romance of Granada," in *The*

Old and New World Romanticism of Washington Irving, ed. Stanley Brodwin (Westport, Conn.: Greenwood Press, 1986), 93.

45. Michael Davitt Bell, *The Development of American Romance* (Chicago: University of Chicago Press, 1980), 18.

46. Williams, *Life of Washington Irving*, 1:367.

47. The rhetoric of pleasure that, as we have seen, pervades Irving's letters from the Alhambra also makes itself manifest in his descriptions of characters and episodes connected to the ruins of the palace. The connections between this rhetoric and the ethnographic stance in the book are not a mere coincidence, for, as Christopher Herbert has pointed out, nineteenth-century anthropological ideas of culture stemmed as a reaction against "a fixation on the dangerous power and potentially boundless scope of human desire." Herbert, *Culture and Anomie*, 28.

48. Rubin-Dorsky, *Adrift in the Old World*, 238.

49. Mary W. Bowden, *Washington Irving* (Boston: Twayne, 1981), 120–26, 141.

50. Richard V. McLamore, who has advocated for the seriousness of Irving's chronicle, argues that he wrote an indictment on the nature of conquest and usurpation rather than a mere romantic book. *The Alhambra*, too, gains a new meaning in the light of this revisionist approach. See his essay "Postcolonial Columbus: Washington Irving and *The Conquest of Granada*," *Nineteenth-Century Literature* 48 (June 1993): 26–43.

51. Bowden, *Washington Irving*, 143.

52. [Alexander H. Everett], "Irving's *Alhambra*," *North American Review* XXXV (October 1832): 276.

53. Washington Irving, *The Sketch Book*, ed. Haskell Springer (Boston: Twayne, 1978), 246.

54. For a survey of Alhambraism in Western literature see Gerhart Hoffmeister's "Exoticism: Granada's Alhambra in European Romanticism," in *European Romanticism. Literary Cross-Currents, Modes, and Models*, ed. Gerhart Hoffmeister (Detroit: Wayne State University Press, 1990), 113–26. See also M. A. Buchanan's "Alhambraism," *Hispanic Review* III (October 1935): 269–74.

55. On the favorable comments and reactions to Irving's appointment in Spain, see Williams, *Life of Washington Irving*, 2:6–7.

56. Bowers, *The Spanish Adventures of Washington Irving*, 136.

57. Williams, *The Spanish Background of American Literature*, 2:37.

58. Mary Alice Weatherspoon, "The Political Activities of Philip Freneau and Washington Irving," Ph.D. diss. (University of Texas at Austin, 1968), 209.

CHAPTER 6. FIRESIDE TRAVEL WRITING: HENRY WADSWORTH LONGFELLOW'S SENTIMENTAL PILGRIMAGE ACROSS SPAIN

1. Dana Gioia, "Longfellow in the Aftermath of Modernism," in *The Columbia History of American Poetry*, ed. Jay Parini (New York: Columbia University Press, 1993), 64–96.

2. Newton Arvin, *Longfellow: His Life and Work* (Boston: Little, Brown, 1962), 41.

3. Stanley T. Williams, *The Spanish Background of American Literature*, 2 vols. (New Haven: Yale University Press, 1955), 2:161.

4. James Buzard, *The Beaten Track: European Tourism, Literature, and the Ways to "Culture"* (New York: Oxford University Press, 1993), 114.

5. Quoted in Lawrance Thompson, *Young Longfellow (1807–1843)* (1938; rpt. New York: Octagon, 1969), 108.

6. Iris L. Whitman, *Longfellow and Spain* (New York: Instituto de las Españas, 1927), 70–73.

7. Thompson, *Young Longfellow*, 367.

8. Whitman, *Longfellow and Spain*, 185.

9. William Stowe, *Going Abroad: European Travel in Nineteenth-Century American Culture* (Princeton, N.J.: Princeton University Press, 1994), 18–21.

10. On 8 March 1827 Irving wrote to Pierre Munro Irving the following: "Mr. Longfellow arrived save and cheerily the day before yesterday, having met with no robbers" (LII, 223).

11. Cited in Whitman, *Longfellow and Spain*, 40.

12. Thompson, *Young Longfellow*, 366.

13. In an interesting letter that Longfellow wrote to Washington Irving (Cádiz, 24 September 1827) to let him know he had arrived safe and sound—he also gave him some information about local hotels both in Seville and Cádiz—he provides an account of traveling by *galera*, a conveyance he deplored (LL, 1:243).

14. Charles Batten, *Pleasurable Instruction: Form and Convention in Eighteenth-Century Travel Literature* (Berkeley and Los Angeles: University of California Press, 1978), 74.

15. Quoted in Samuel Longfellow, *The Life of Henry Wadsworth Longfellow*, 3 vols. (1891; rpt. New York: Greenwood Press, 1969), 1:132.

16. Ibid., 1:134.

17. Longfellow's first book published on Spain was *Novelas Españolas* (1830), where he hispanized tales by Irving. He also wrote some essays on Spanish Literature: "Spanish Devotional and Moral Poetry," *North American Review* XXXIV (April 1832): 277–315, and "Spanish Language and Literature," *North American Review* XXXVI (April 1833): 316–44.

18. On the principal editions of the book see Whitman, *Longfellow and Spain*, 171–72.

19. George Rice Carpenter, *Henry Wadsworth Longfellow* (1891; Boston: Small, Maynard, and Company, 1909), 37.

20. Arvin, *Longfellow: His Life and Work*, 44. *Outre-Mer* was reviewed in the following periodicals: [John Neal], *New England Galaxy* (6 June 1835); [William O.B Peabody], *North American Review* XXXIX (October 1834): 459–67; *American Monthly Magazine* V (May 1835): 247–48; *Knickerbocker* 4 (July 1834): 72–75; [Lewis Gaylord Clark], *Knickerbocker* V (May 1835): 454–56; *American Monthly Review* IV (August 1833): 157–60. Also, according to Andrew Hilen, a favorable review of *Outre-Mer* and a notice of Longfellow's translation of Manrique's *Coplas* appeared in *Providence Literary Journal* (20 October 1833). Longfellow thought his friend George W. Greene had written them.

21. Longfellow did not seem satisfied with some of Peabody's comments, for he made the following remark to George W. Greene: "The Rev[ie]w of Outre-Mer was written by Peabody. I think it rather in the *cucumber* style—quite cool. No matter" (LL, 1:456).

22. "Outre-Mer," *American Monthly Magazine* 5 (May 1835): 247–48.

23. [Lewis Gaylord Clark], "Outre-Mer," *Knickerbocker* 5 (May 1835): 454–56.

24. Edward Wagenknecht, *Henry Wadsworth Longfellow. His Poetry and Prose* (New York: Ungar, 1986), 39.

25. Terry Caesar, *Forgiving the Boundaries: Home as Abroad in American Travel Writing* (Athens: University of Georgia Press, 1995), 30.

26. Williams, *The Spanish Background of American Literature*, 2:172.

27. Quoted in Longfellow, *The Life of Henry Wadsworth Longfellow*, 1:129.

28. According to Everett, the essay on Italian language and dialects Longfellow submitted to the *North American Review* was found to be "dull and LEARNED." Longfellow's anti-intellectual, lowbrow stance was, at any rate, a momentary maneuver, as Pauly observes, for Longfellow did certainly believe in didacticism and the intellectual apprehension of reality. Thomas H. Pauly, "Outre-Mer and Longfellow's Quest for a Career," *New England Quarterly* 50 (1977): 39–40.

29. Gillian Beer, *The Romance* (London: Methuen, 1970), 5.

30. Raymond Williams, *The Country and the City* (New York: Oxford University Press, 1973), 37.

31. Thompson, *Young Longfellow*, 109.

32. "Be careful not to take any part in opposition to the religion or politics of the countries in which you reside," Stephen Longfellow warned to his son before departing for the Old World. Quoted in Cecil B. Williams, *Henry Wadsworth Longfellow* (New York: Twayne, 1964), 46.

33. Quoted in Longfellow, *The Life of Henry Wadsworth Longfellow*, 1:125–26.

34. Pauly, "Outre-Mer and Longfellow's Quest for a Career," 43–44.

35. Williams, *Henry Wadsworth Longfellow*, 110.

36. George William Curtis, "Longfellow," *Atlantic Monthly* XII (December 1863): 769. Thomas Pauly also calls attention to the difference between Irving's "dreamy outcast" and Longfellow's "pilgrim" in "Outre-Mer and Longfellow's Quest for a Career," 41.

37. "Castles in Spain," in the Cambridge edition of *The Complete Poetical Works of Henry Wadsworth Longfellow*, ed. Horace E. Scudder (Boston: Houghton, 1893), 335.

CHAPTER 7. THE AMERICAN COUPLE ABROAD: GENDER AND CLASS EMPOWERMENT IN THE SPANISH TRAVEL WRITINGS OF CALEB AND CAROLINE CUSHING

1. William Stowe, in *Going Abroad: European Travel in Nineteenth-Century American Culture* (Princeton, N.J.: Princeton University Press, 1994), 56–59, cites these two genres—the letter and the sketchbook—among the available models of travel chronicle in nineteenth-century America. Whereas the typical "Letter from Europe" usually had an eager newspaper audience and permitted a preparation for the writer's later career in letters, the sketchbook modeled after Irving mixed personas—tourist, dreamer, moralist—and genres.

2. Stowe, *Going Abroad*, 45.

3. Leo Hamalian, *Ladies on the Loose* (New York: Dodd, Mead, 1981), x; Nina Baym, *American Women Writers and the Work of History, 1790–1860* (New Brunswick, N.J.: Rutgers University Press, 1995), 132.

4. The Anglo-American canon has often considered women travel writers marginal. Sara Mills's excellent study *Discourses of Difference An Analysis of Women's Travel Writing and Colonialism* (London and New York: Routledge, 1991) shows how, because of gender, they have been slighted in the British literary tradition. In American scholarship, Mary Suzanne Schriber's anthology *Telling*

Travels (DeKalb: Northern Illinois University Press, 1995) and her most recent *Writing Home: American Women Abroad, 1830–1920* (Charlottesville: University Press of Virginia, 1997) have helped nineteenth-century women travel writers to regain some space in American literary history. Even so, in Schriber's last book Caroline Cushing only appears briefly mentioned when it comes to deciding who was the first American woman to have published a travel book on abroad. According to Schriber, Abby Morrell's *Narrative of a Voyage to the Ethiopic and South Atlantic Ocean, Indian Ocean, Chinese Sea, North and South Pacific Ocean, in the Years 1829, 1830, 1831* (1833) should receive that honor because Cushing's letters were printed posthumously, thus leaving authorial intention unclear. See the endnote in Schriber, *Writing Home*, 211.

5. It can certainly be said that before Caroline Cushing's letters there existed a tradition of women's writing on Spain. In *Travellers in Spain* (London: Cassell, 1990), David Mitchell mentions some of those antecedents. Lady Fanshawe, wife of the British ambassador Sir Richard Fanshawe, kept a diary in the 1670s that was published in 1839. In 1691 Madame d'Aulnoy published her popular *Travels into Spain*, translated into several languages, which turned out to be a literary hoax. Finally, Lady Elizabeth Holland, who traveled with her husband and two sons, also kept a Spanish journal between 1802 and 1805. In the United States, one finds a brief, early instance of Spanish travel writing produced by a woman in the essay "Journal of a Tour from Cadiz to Madrid," published in the *Port-Folio* XX (November 1825): 365–74. The editors of this journal prefaced the essay "as the production of a lady of sixteen."

6. The standard biography on Caleb Cushing (1800–1879) is Claude M. Fuess, *The Life of Caleb Cushing*, 2 vols. (Hamden, Conn.: Archon Books, 1965), originally published in New York by Harcourt Brace in 1923. The other biographical sources I have looked up are: Evert A. and George Duyckinck, *Cyclopedia of American Literature*, 2 vols. (New York: Charles Scribner, 1855), 2:291; James Spear Loring, *The Hundred Boston Orators Appointed*. 2nd ed. (Boston: J.P. Jewett, 1853), 513–24; Sister Michael Catherine Hodgson, *Caleb Cushing* (Washington, D.C.: Catholic University of America Press, 1955); William J. Comley, *Comley's History of Massachusetts* (Boston: Comley Brothers, 1879). Many of Cushing's papers are kept at the Oliver Wendell Holmes Library of the Phillips Academy, at Andover, Massachusetts. I have been unable to locate primary sources on Caroline Cushing, so that whatever information is available on her is always cited in reference to her husband.

7. Comley, *Comley's History of Massachusetts*, 268–69.

8. As Caroline Cushing herself demonstrates by way of an anecdote in letter XXIII, foreign women travelers were a *rara avis* in early nineteenth-century Spain. She explains that she and her husband spent the night at an old venta in Alhama where the old couple of innkeepers "felt and expressed a great deal of curiosity at the unwonted sight of a foreign lady travelling among them; while at the same time they paid me every attention which I could desire, and were anxious to anticipate my wishes in every thing" (LD, 2:292).

9. Schriber, *Writing Home*, 52.

10. In the dedicatory page of her epistolary narrative, dating from January 1831, Caroline Cushing explicitly mentions who the main addressee of her letters is: "To you, my dear father, were the sheets of this Journal originally addressed, when the wide expanse of Ocean separated us, and to you I commit them once more, now that I am again happily restored to our beloved country; consigning them to the same indulgent affection and parental kindness, which have contributed so largely to the happiness of my life" (LD, 1:vii).

11. Hodgson, *Caleb Cushing*, 17.

12. Fuess, *The Life of Caleb Cushing*, 1:104–5.

13. Mary L. Pratt, "Fieldwork in Common Places," in *Writing Culture: The Poetics and Politics of Ethnography*, eds. James Clifford and George E. Marcus (Berkeley: University of California Press, 1986), 40–41.

14. Fuess, *The Life of Caleb Cushing*, 1:110.

15. As one can easily notice, Caroline Cushing's exclamation on seeing Granada reproduces the conventional rhetoric of belatedness verbalized by other travelers: "How vain would be any attempt to describe the emotions I experienced, when instantaneously as it were, and without preparation, the whole of this enchanting prospect burst upon my sight. All the romance thrown around it by a Florian, a Chateaubriand, or an Irving, transcends not the reality; and glowingly as the scene had been depicted by my imagination, no sketch of fancy could surpass the beautiful original" (LD, 2:294).

16. Thomas Pauly, "The Literary Sketch in Nineteenth-Century America," *Texas Studies in Language and Literature* XVII (1975): 490.

17. Lawrence Buell, *Literary Transcendentalism* (Ithaca: Cornell University Press, 1973), 192–94. However, among the literary models of travel writing that these critics gave as examples to follow, Buell cites sentimental travel books like Mme. de Stael's *De l'Allemagne*, Goethe's *Italianische Reise*, Sterne's *Sentimental Journey*, poems by Byron and Wordsworth, topographical poetry, and picturesque prose. Terry Caesar also locates in New England thought the source of the general scepticism about travel in American writing. Yet, instead of finding the source of this scepticism in the Common Sense background of New England, he sees it precisely as a result of the New England transcendental bias. Terry Caesar, *Forgiving the Boundaries: Home as Abroad in American Travel Writing* (Athens: University of Georgia Press, 1995), 46–47. This transcendental bias against travel is nowhere more visible than in Emerson's essay "Self-Reliance," which decries what he terms "the idol" of travel, and contains some aphorisms against it (e.g., "Traveling is a fool's paradise" and "The soul is no traveler") that became quite popular thereafter. See Ralph W. Emerson, *Essays and Lectures*, ed. Joel Porte (New York: Library of America, 1983), 277–78.

18. Fuess, *The Life of Caleb Cushing*, 1:114. However, as the reviewer in the *New-England Magazine* saw it, the publication of several books on Spain within a short period ought to be regarded as a positive event: "The very subject of Mr. Cushing's book is a recommendation to it, and particularly so, at this time and in our country, when our attention has been lately so strongly awakened with regard to Spain by Irving's 'Alhambra' and Lieutenant Slidell's very interesting 'Year in Spain'." See "Reminiscences of Spain," *New-England Magazine* IV (May 1833): 427.

19. Alexander H. Everett, "Cushing's Reminiscences of Spain," *North American Review* 37 (July 1833): 85.

20. "Reminiscences of Spain," *American Monthly Review* 3 (June 1833): 468.

21. "Reminiscences of Spain," *American Monthly Magazine* I (June 1833): 225.

22. Ibid., 226–27.

23. Fuess, *The Life of Caleb Cushing*, 1:114.

24. Stanley J. Williams, *The Spanish Background of American Literature*, 2 vols. (New Haven: Yale University Press, 1955), 1:63.

25. Mills, *Discourses of Difference*, 94–97. According to Terry Caesar, however, the opposite is also true, so that "a woman's text gains its authority not only by

renouncing the whole notion of 'higher unity' but also by giving itself over to inward energies based on memory, stray domesticities, and wayward imaginings." Caesar, *Forgiving the Boundaries*, 56.

26. Schriber, *Telling Travels*, xxxiii.

27. Elizabeth C. Goldsmith, "Authority, Authenticity, and the Publication of Letters by Women" in *Writing the Female Voice*, ed. Elizabeth C. Goldsmith (Boston: Northeastern University Press, 1989), 46–47.

28. Mary Suzanne Schriber, "Julia Ward Howe and the Travel Book," *New England Quarterly* 62 (1989): 268

29. Mills, *Discourses of Difference*, 108–22.

30. Alexander H. Everett, "Cushing's Reminiscences of Spain," *North American Review* 37 (July 1833): 104.

31. James S. Loring, *The Hundred Boston Orators*, 2nd ed. (Boston: J. P. Jewett, 1853), 515; Williams, *The Spanish Background of American Literature*, 1:60, 63; Fuess, *The Life of Caleb Cushing*, 1:100–101.

32. Male travelers often regarded foreign women as examples of difference because of their gender and race (or nationality). Yet, their idea of "other" woman became as much a textualization as their idea of foreign sites was, so that if it did not match their ideal of the "American Woman" the male traveler grew disappointed. Schriber, *Writing Home*, 80.

33. Nancy Cott, *The Bonds of Womanhood* (New Haven: Yale University Press, 1977), 19–22.

34. Mary Ryan, *Women in Public* (Baltimore: Johns Hopkins University Press, 1990), 58–94.

35. Mary Kelley, *Private Woman, Public Stage* (New York: Oxford University Press, 1984), ix–xii.

36. L. K. Worley, "Through Others' Eyes: Narratives of German Women Travelling in Nineteenth Century America," *Yearbook of German-American Studies* 21 (1986): 40.

37. Schriber, *Writing Home*, 39–40.

38. Leonardo Buonomo, *Backward Glances* (Madison, N.J.: Fairleigh Dickinson University Press, 1996), 29.

39. Karen Lawrence, *Penelope Voyages* (Ithaca: Cornell University Press, 1994), 20.

40. Mills, *Discourses of Difference*, 76–78.

41. Schriber, *Telling Travels*, xxii.

42. Cott, *The Bonds of Womanhood*, 63–100.

43. Percy G. Adams, *Travel Literature and the Evolution of the Novel* (Lexington: University Press of Kentucky, 1983), 213–23; Schriber, *Writing Home*, 75–76. Cushing also relates that the afternoon of the same day she experienced the dangerous crossing of another mountain pass, where a yoke of oxen had to assist the mules to draw up the carriage. The scene is represented like an apocalyptic, quasi-Dantesque scenario: "The road wound up the side of the steep . . . with only the same small stones between us and the yawning gulphs below. My brain turned giddy as I cast my eyes downwards, the scene being rendered doubly appalling by the dimness and darkness of lingering twilight" (LD, 2:17)

44. James Buzard, *The Beaten Track: European Tourism, Literature, and the Ways to "Culture"* (New York: Oxford University Press, 1993), 149–50.

45. Schriber, *Telling Travels*, xxix.

46. Bonnie Frederick and Virginia Hyde, "Introduction," in *Women and the Journey. The Female Travel Experience*, eds. Bonnie Frederick and Susan McLeod (Pullman: Washington State University Press, 1993), xxii.

47. Schriber, *Writing Home*, 89.

48. Baym, *American Women Writers and the Work of History*, 5–7.

49. Mary Suzanne Schriber lists some of these rhetorical strategies in *Writing Home*, 75.

50. Indeed, as Bonnie Frederick and Virginia Hyde have affirmed, "a wealthy woman's journey is more similar to a wealthy man's journey than to a poor woman's journey." See their "Introduction" to *Women and the Journey*, xix.

51. Through her view of issues abroad Cushing circulated the discourse of American exceptionalism, directly impinging, whenever necessary, upon issues at home. Any occasion in her narrative was opportune enough to praise the rising supremacy of the United States. In Letter XXII, for example, she relates their meeting with several Americans in Málaga and Gibraltar, and asks herself "Where is the city in Europe, in which an American may not always find those, whom he can proudly and cordially acknowledge as the sons of that great and favored Republic, which gave himself birth?" (LD, 2:282–83). However, if she had to be critical with the United States, she did not hesitate to be so. In Letter IX, after witnessing a bullfight and some fireworks, she affirms that "neither upon the present occasion nor any former one, was there the slightest appearance of disorder or riot among the people. . . . Could such a thing take place in America, how different would be the result! How many hundreds of persons we should see extended upon the earth, in a state of the most brutal intoxication; or else engaged in bickerings and disputes. . . . I never witnessed one single instance of intoxication, riot, or quarrelling of any description. This certainly speaks well for the good habits and decorous character of the people" (LD, 2:116–17).

52. Baym, *American Women Writers and the Work of History*, 134–40.

53. The moral reflections triggered by the contemplation of ruins had a paragon in history writing. Nina Baym notes that through textbooks like those of Emma Willard, available to many children, Americans could compare the land of millennial hopes with the rise and fall of civilizations. Nina Baym, "Women and the Republic: Emma Willard's Rhetoric of History," in her *Feminism and American Literary History* (New Brunswick: Rutgers University Press, 1992), 121–36.

CONCLUSION

1. *The Invention of Tradition*, eds. Eric Hobsbawm and Terence Ranger (Cambridge: Cambridge University Press, 1992), 1–14.

2. Terry Caesar, *Forgiving the Boundaries: Home as Abroad in American Travel Writing* (Athens: University of Georgia Press, 1995), 8.

3. James Buzard, *The Beaten Track: European Tourism, Literature, and the Way to "Culture"* (New York: Oxford University Press, 1993), 130–31; William Stowe, *Going Abroad: European Travel in Nineteenth-Century American Travel* (Princeton, N.J.: Princeton University Press, 1994), 126.

4. Ann Douglass, *The Feminization of American Culture* (London: Macmillan, 1996). See in particular the Preface reprinted from the 1988 Anchor edition, xi–xiv, and the chapter entitled "The Legacy of American Victorianism," 3–13.

5. George W. Cullum, *Spain: the Orient and the Occident* (New York: A. Sherwood & Co., 1889), 33.

6. Charles Francis Sessions, *In Western Levant* (New York: Welch, Fracker Company, 1890), 74–75.

7. John Franklin Swift, *Going to Jericho* (San Francisco and New York: A. Roman, 1868), 97.

8. James A. Michener, *Iberia. Spanish Travels and Reflections* (1968; New York: Fawcett, 1969), 11.

Bibliography

Adams, Charles Francis, ed. *Familiar Letters of John Adams and His Wife Abigail Adams, during the Revolution*. Boston: Houghton, 1876.

Adams, Herbert B. *The Life and Writings of Jared Sparks*. 2 vols. Boston: Houghton, 1893.

Adams, John. *Diary and Autobiography of John Adams*. Edited by L. H. Butterfield. 4 vols. Cambridge, Mass.: The Belknap Press of Harvard University Press, 1961.

Adams, John Quincy. *Diary of John Quincy Adams*. Edited by Robert J. Taylor and Marc Friedlaender. 2 vols. Cambridge, Mass.: The Belknap Press of Harvard University Press, 1981.

Adams, Percy. *Travellers and Travel Liars*. Berkeley and Los Angeles: University of California Press, 1962.

———. *Travel Literature and the Evolution of the Novel*. Lexington: The University Press of Kentucky, 1983.

Aderman, Ralph M., ed. *Critical Essays on Washington Irving*. Boston: G.K. Hall, 1990.

Adler, Judith. "Origins of Sightseeing." *Annals of Tourism Research* 16 (1989): 7–29.

"The Alhambra." *New England Magazine* III (July 1832): 81–82.

"The Alhambra: A Series of Tales and Sketches of the Moors and Spaniards." *American Monthly Review* II (September 1832): 177–89. In Aderman, 96–103.

"The Alhambra." *Monthly Review*, New Series, 2 (June 1832): 221–47.

Allaback, Steven and Alexander Medlicott Jr, eds. *A Guide to the Microfilm Edition of the European Journals of George and Anna Ticknor*. Hanover, N.H.: Dartmouth College Library, 1978.

Allen, Harriet Trowbridge. *Travels in Europe and the East: During the Years 1858–59 and 1863–64*. New Haven, Conn.: Tuttle, Moorehouse & Taylor, 1879.

Allibone, Samuel Austin. *A Critical Dictionary of English Literature and British and American Authors*. 3 vols. 1858–71. Philadelphia: Lippincott, 1891.

"American Travellers." *Monthly Anthology, and Boston Review* III (December 1806): 628–29.

Andrews, Malcolm. *The Search for the Picturesque: Landscape Aesthetics and Tourism in Britain, 1760–1800*. Aldershot: Scholar's Press, 1989.

Artola, Miguel. *La burguesía revolucionaria*. 1978. Madrid: Alianza Editorial, 1992.

Arvin, Newton. *Longfellow: His Life and Work*. Boston: Little, Brown, 1962.

Aymes, Jean Rene, ed. *L'Espagne romantique: temoignages de voyageurs français*. Paris: A.M. Metailie, 1983.

Bank, Stanley, ed. *American Romanticism: A Shape for Fiction*. New York: Putnam's, 1969.

Barlow, Joel. *The Works of Joel Barlow*. 2 vols. Edited by William K. Bottorff and Arthur L. Ford. Gainesville, Fla.: Scholar's Facsimiles & Reprints, 1970.

Batten, Charles. *Pleasurable Instruction. Form and Convention in Eighteenth-Century Travel Literature*. Berkeley and Los Angeles: University of California Press, 1978.

Baym, Nina, et al., eds. *The Norton Anthology of American Literature*, 3rd ed. 2 vols. New York: Norton, 1989.

Baym, Nina. *American Women Writers and the Work of History, 1790–1860*. New Brunswick, N.J.: Rutgers University Press, 1995.

———. *Feminism and American Literary History*. New Brunswick, N.J.: Rutgers University Press, 1992.

Beer, Gillian. *The Romance*. London: Methuen, 1970.

Behdad, Ali. *Belated Travelers: Orientalism in the Age of Colonial Dissolution*. Durham, N.C.: Duke University Press, 1994.

Bell, Michael Davitt. *The Development of American Romance*. Chicago: University of Chicago Press, 1980.

Bercovitch, Sacvan, ed. *The Cambridge History of American Literature. Vol. 1, 1590–1820*. New York: Cambridge University Press, 1994.

Bernstein, Harry. "Las primeras relaciones intelectuales entre New England y el mundo hispánico (1700–1815)." *Revista Hispánica Moderna* V (1939): 1–17.

———. *Origins of Inter-American Interest, 1700–1812*. Philadelphia: University of Pennsylvania Press, 1945.

Bhabha, Homi. "The Other Question." *Screen* 24 (December 1983): 18–36.

Bode, Carl. *The Anatomy of American Popular Fiction 1840–1861*. Berkeley and Los Angeles: University of California Press, 1959.

Boon, James. *Other Tribes, Other Scribes: Symbolic Anthropology in the Comparative Study of Cultures, Histories, Religions, and Texts*. New York: Cambridge University Press, 1982.

Bordman, Gerald, ed. *Oxford Companion to American Theatre*. New York: Oxford University Press, 1992.

Bowden, Mary Wheatherspoon. *Washington Irving*. Boston: Twayne, 1981.

Bowers, Claude G. *The Spanish Adventures of Washington Irving*. Boston: Houghton, 1940.

Brown, Charles Brockden. *Wieland and Memoirs of Carwin*. Edited by Sydney J. Krause and S.W. Reid. Kent, Ohio: Kent State University Press, 1988.

Brodhead, Richard H. "Sparing the Rod: Discipline and Fiction in Antebellum America." In Fisher, 141–70.

Brodwin, Stanley, ed. *The Old and New World Romanticism of Washington Irving*. Westport, Conn.: Greenwood Press, 1986.

Brooks, Van Wyck. *The World of Washington Irving*. New York: Dutton, 1944.

Brown, Stuart Gerry, ed. *The Autobiography of James Monroe*. Syracuse, N.Y.: Syracuse University Press, 1959.

Bryant, William Cullen. *Letters of a Traveller*. 2nd series. New York: Appleton, 1859.

Buchanan, M. A. "Alhambraism." *Hispanic Review* III (October 1935): 269–74.

Buckley, James M. *Travels in Three Continents*. New York: Hunt and Eaton, 1895.

Buell, Lawrence. *Literary Transcendentalism*. Ithaca: Cornell University Press, 1973.

Buonomo, Leonardo. *Backward Glances. Exploring Italy, Reinterpreting America (1831–1866)*. Madison, N.J.: Fairleigh Dickinson University Press, 1996.

Bushman, Claudia L. *America Discovers Columbus: How an Italian Explorer Became an American Hero*. Hanover, N.H.: University Press of New England, 1992.

Buzard, James. *The Beaten Track. European Tourism, Literature, and the Ways to "Culture."* New York: Oxford University Press, 1993.

Caesar, Terry. *Forgiving the Boundaries: Home as Abroad in American Travel Writing*. Athens: University of Georgia Press, 1995.

Calvo Serraller, Francisco. *La imagen romántica de España. Arte y arquitectura del siglo XIX*. Madrid: Alianza Editorial, 1995.

Carpenter, George Rice. *Henry Wadsworth Longfellow*. 1891. Boston: Small, Maynard, and Company, 1909.

Carr, Raymond. *Spain 1808–1939*. 2nd ed. 1966. Oxford: Oxford University Press, 1982.

A Catalogue of the Books Belonging to the Library Company of Philadelphia. 2 vols. Philadelphia: C. Sherman, 1835.

Charvat, William. *Literary Publishing in America: 1790–1850*. Philadelphia: University of Pennsylvania Press, 1959.

———. *The Origins of American Critical Thought 1810–1835*. 1936; rpt. New York: Barnes, 1961.

———. *The Profession of Authorship in America, 1800–1870*. Edited by Matthew J. Bruccoli. 1968. New York: Columbia University Press, 1992.

[Clark, Lewis Gaylord.] "Outre-Mer." *Knickerbocker* V (May 1835): 454–56.

Clifford, James. *The Predicament of Culture*. Cambridge, Mass.: Harvard University Press, 1988.

——— and George E. Marcus, eds. *Writing Culture: The Poetics and Politics of Ethnography*. Berkeley and Los Angeles: University of California Press, 1986.

Coe, Samuel Gwynn. "William Carmichael." In *Dictionary of American Biography*, 2:497–98.

Coggeshall, George. *Thirty-six Voyages to Various Parts of the World, Made between the Years 1779 and 1843*. 3rd. ed. 1851. New York: Putnam, 1858.

[Collinson, Peter.] "Account of the Sheep and Sheep-Walks of Spain." *New York Magazine* I, No. 8 (August 1790): 454–57.

———. "Account of the Sheep and Sheep-Walks of Spain." *New York Magazine* I, No. 9 (September 1790): 518–19.

———. "Account of the Sheep and Sheep-Walks of Spain." *New York Magazine* I, No. 10 (October 1790): 567–71.

Colón, María Luisa. *Impresos en español publicados en Filadelfia durante los años 1800 a 1835*. M.A. Thesis, Catholic University of America, Washington D.C., 1951.

Comley, William J. *Comley's History of Massachusetts*. Boston: Comley Brothers, 1879.

Cott, Nancy F. *The Bonds of Womanhood. "Woman's Sphere" in New England, 1780–1835*. New Haven: Yale University Press, 1977.

Crapanzano, Vincent. "Hermes' Dilemma: the Masking of Subversion in Ethnographic Description." In Clifford and Marcus, 51–53.

Crowninshield, Francis B. *The Story of George Crowninshield's Yacht Cleopatra's Barge on A Voyage of Pleasure to the Western Islands and the Mediterranean 1816–1817*. Boston: privately printed, 1913.

Cullum, George W. *Spain: the Orient and the Occident*. New York: A. Sherwood & Co., 1889.

Curtis, George William. "Longfellow." *Atlantic Monthly* XII (December 1863): 769–75.

Cushing, Caleb. *Reminiscences of Spain, the Country, its People, History and Monuments*. 2 vols. Boston: Carter, Hendee & Company, 1833.

[Cushing, Caroline Elizabeth (Wilde).] *Letters, Descriptive of Public Monuments, Scenery, and Manners in France and Spain*. 2 vols. Newburyport, Mass.: E.W. Allen, 1832.

Cutts, Mary Pepperrell Sparhawk. *Life and Times of Hon. William Jarvis*. New York: Hurd & Houghton, 1869.

del Burgo, Jaime. *La aventura histórica de los viajeros extranjeros del siglo XIX y la España desconocida de Cenac-Moncaut*. Pamplona: Editorial Gómez, 1963.

de Figueroa y Melgar, Alfonso. *Viajeros románticos por España*. Madrid: E.P. Sagrado Corazón, 1971.

Dictionary of American Biography. Edited by Dumas Malone et al. 11 vols. 1936. New York: Scribner, 1964.

Digges, Thomas Atwood. *Adventures of Alonzo*. 1775. Upper Saddle River, N.J.: Literature House/Gregg Press, 1970.

"Don Quixote." *Literary Magazine, and American Register* VIII (1 November, 1807): 174.

Douglass, Ann. *The Feminization of American Culture*. 1977. London: Macmillan, 1996.

Douglass, Frederick. *Autobiographies*. Edited by Houston Baker, Jr. New York: Library of America, 1994.

Dulles, Foster Rhea. *Americans Abroad. Two Centuries of European Travel*. Ann Arbor: University of Michigan Press, 1964.

Dupont, Victor Marie. *Journey to France and Spain. 1801*. Edited by Charles W. David. Ithaca: Cornell University Press, 1961.

Duyckinck, Evert A. and George L. Duyckinck. *Cyclopedia of American Literature*. 2 vols. New York: Scribner, 1855.

Emerson, Ralph Waldo. *Essays and Lectures*. Edited by Joel Porte. New York: Library of America, 1983.

Everett, Alexander Hill. *Prose Pieces and Correspondence*. Edited by Elizabeth Evans. St. Paul, Minn.: The John Colet Press, 1975.

[———.] "The Peninsula." *Annual Register* V (October 1829–1830): 414.

[———.] "Irving's *Alhambra*." *North American Review* XXXV (October 1832): 265–82.

[———.] "Cushing's *Reminiscences of Spain*." *North American Review* XXXVII (July 1833): 84–117.

Fakahani, Suzan Jamil. "Irving's *The Alhambra*: Background, Sources, and Motifs." Ph.D. diss. Florida State University, 1988.

Farnham, Carrie E. *American Travellers in Spain: the Spanish Inns, 1776–1867.* New York: Columbia University Press, 1921.

[Fay, Theodore S.] "The Alhambra." *New York Mirror* IX (23 June 1832): 401–3. In Aderman, 94–95.

Ferguson, Robert A. "What Is Enlightenment? Some American Answers." In Bercovitch, 368–89.

Fernández Sánchez, José. *Viajeros rusos por la España del siglo XIX.* Madrid: El Museo Universal, 1975.

Fisher, Philip, ed. *The New American Studies.* Berkeley and Los Angeles: University of California Press, 1991.

Ford, Jeremiah D. M. "George Ticknor." In *Dictionary of American Biography*, 9:526–27.

Foucault, Michel. *Discipline and Punish.* Translated by Alan Sheridan. New York: Vintage, 1979.

Franklin, Benjamin. *Representative Selections.* Rev. ed. Introduction, bibliography, and notes by Chester E. Jorgenson and Frank Luther Mott. 1936. New York: Hill & Wang, 1962.

Frederick, Bonnie, and Virginia Hyde. Introduction in *Women and the Journey. The Female Travel Experience.* Edited by Bonnie Frederick and Susan H. McLeod (Pullman: Washington State University Press, 1993), xvii–xxxiii.

Freneau, Philip. *The Poems of Philip Freneau, Poet of the American Revolution.* Edited by Fred Lewis Pattee. 3 vols. 1902–07. New York: Russell & Russell, 1963.

Frey, John. "Irving, Chateaubriand, and the Historical Romance of Granada." In Brodwin, 91–104.

Fuess, Claude M. *The Life of Caleb Cushing.* 2 vols. 1923. Hamden, Conn.: Archon Books, 1965.

Fussell, Paul. *Abroad: British Literary Traveling Between the Wars.* New York: Oxford University Press, 1980.

García Felguera, María de los Santos, ed. *Imagen romántica de España.* 2 vols. Madrid: Ministerio de Cultura. Dirección General de Bellas Artes, 1981.

Geertz, Clifford. *The Interpretation of Cultures.* New York: Basic Books, 1973.

Gifra Adroher, Pere. "Caroline Cushing's Letters from Spain Reconsidered." In Toda, 509–13.

———. "Rough Memories from a Romantic Land: The Politics of Travel in Alexander Slidell Mackenzie's *A Year in Spain*." In Henríquez, 19–42.

Gioia, Dana. "Longfellow in the Aftermath of Modernism." In Parini, 64–96.

"Glimpses of Spain." *American Whig Review*, New Series, V (March 1850): 292–300.

Goldberg, Isaac. *Major Noah: American-Jewish Pioneer.* Philadelphia: The Jewish Publication Society of America, 1938.

Goldsmith, Elizabeth C. "Authority, Authenticity, and the Publication of Letters by Women." In *Writing the Female Voice. Essays on Epistolary Literature.* Edited by Elizabeth C. Goldsmith. Boston: Northeastern University Press, 1989.

Grabar, Oleg. *The Alhambra.* Cambridge, Mass.: Harvard University Press, 1978.

Guerrero, Ana Clara. *Viajeros británicos en la España del siglo XVIII*. Madrid: Aguilar, 1990.

[Haight, Sarah Rogers.] *Over the Ocean, or Glimpses in Many Lands. By a Lady of New York*. New York: Paine & Burgess, 1846.

Hale, Sarah Josepha. *Traits of American Life*. Philadelphia: Carey & Hart, 1835.

Hamalian, Leo, ed. *Ladies on the Loose: Women Travellers of the 18th and 19th Centuries*. New York: Dodd, Mead, 1981.

Hart, James D. *The Popular Book*. Berkeley and Los Angeles: University of California Press, 1963.

Hart, Joseph. *The Romance of Yachting*. 2 vols. New York: Harper, 1848.

Hart, Thomas R. Jr., "George Ticknor's History of Spanish Literature: The New England Background." *PMLA* LXIX (March 1954): 76–88.

Hawthorne, Nathaniel. *The House of the Seven Gables. The Centenary Edition of the Works of Nathaniel Hawthorne*, vol. II. Columbus: Ohio State University Press, 1962.

———. *The Marble Faun: or, The Romance of Monte Beni. The Centenary Edition of the Works of Nathaniel Hawthorne*, vol. IV. Columbus: Ohio State University Press, 1968.

Hayford, Harrison, ed. *The Somers Mutiny Affair: A Book of Primary Source Materials*. Englewood Cliffs, N.J.: Prentice Hall, 1959.

Hedges, William L. *Washington Irving: An American Study, 1802–1832*. Baltimore: Johns Hopkins University Press, 1965.

Heiser, Merrill F. "Cervantes in the United States." *Hispanic Review* XV (1947): 409–35.

Helman, Edith F. "Early Interest in Spanish in New England (1815–1835)." *Hispania* XXIX (1946): 339–51.

Henríquez, Santiago, ed. *Travel Essentials. Collected Essays on Travel Writing*. Las Palmas: Chandlon Inn Press, 1998.

Herbert, Christopher. *Culture and Anomie: Ethnographic Imagination in the Nineteenth Century*. Chicago: University of Chicago Press, 1991.

Herr, Helena Fernandez. *Les origines de l'Espagne romantique: les recits de voyage: 1755–1823*. Paris: Didier, 1974.

Hertzberg, Arthur. *The Jews in America*. New York: Simon and Schuster, 1989.

Hobsbawm, Eric. *Nations and Nationalism Since 1780*. New York: Cambridge University Press, 1991.

——— and Terence Ranger, eds. 1983. *The Invention of Tradition*. New York: Cambridge University Press, 1992.

Hodgson, Michael Catherine, Sister. *Caleb Cushing*. Washington, D.C.: Catholic University of America Press, 1955.

Hoffmann, Leon François. *Romantique Espagne: L'image de l'Espagne en France entre 1800 et 1850*. Paris: P.U.F., 1961.

Hoffmeister, Gerhart. "Exoticism: Granada's Alhambra in European Romanticism." In *European Romanticism: Literary Cross-Currents Modes, and Models*. Edited by Gerhart Hoffmeister. Detroit: Wayne State University Press, 1990.

Humphreys, Francis Landon. *Life and Times of David Humphreys, Soldier, Statesman, Poet*. 2 vols. New York: Putnam's, 1917.

Hunt, Lynn. "Introduction: History, Culture, and Text." In *The New Cultural His-*

tory. Edited by Lynn Hunt. Berkeley and Los Angeles: University of California Press, 1989.

Irving, Pierre M., ed. *The Life and Letters of Washington Irving*. 4 vols. New York: G.P. Putnam, 1862–64.

Irving, Washington. "Alexander Slidell's *A Year in Spain*." *Quarterly Review* 44 (February 1831): 319–42. In Irving, *Miscellaneous Writings* 30–57.

———. *The Alhambra*. Edited by William T. Lenehan and Andrew B. Myers. Boston: Twayne, 1983.

———. *The Alhambra. Author's Revised Edition*. New York: Putnam's, 1887.

———. "The Alhambra and A Chronicle of the Conquest of Granada." *Eclectic Review* 103 (July 1832): 1–8.

———. *Bracebridge Hall*. Edited by Herbert F. Smith. Boston: Twayne, 1977.

———. *Journals and Notebooks: Volume III, 1819–1827*. Edited by Walter A. Reichart. Madison: University of Wisconsin Press, 1970.

———. *Journals and Notebooks: Volume IV, 1826–1829*. Edited by Wayne R. Kime and Andrew B. Myers. Boston: Twayne, 1984.

———. *Letters: Volume II, 1823–1838*. Edited by Ralph M. Aderman et al. Boston: Twayne, 1979.

———. *Miscellaneous Writings I: 1803–1859*. Edited by Wayne R. Kime Boston: Twayne, 1981.

———. *The Sketch Book of Geoffrey Crayon, Gent*. Edited by Haskell Springer. Boston: Twayne, 1978.

———. *Voyages and Discoveries of the Companions of Columbus*. Edited by James W. Tuttleton. Boston: Twayne, 1986.

Jay, John. *The Correspondence and Public Papers of John Jay*. Edited by Henry P. Johnston. 4 vols. New York: Putnam's, 1890–93.

Jefferson, Thomas. *Writings*. Edited by Merrill D. Peterson. New York: Library of America, 1984.

Joslin, Katherine, and Alan Price, eds. *Wretched Exotic: Essays on Edith Wharton in Europe*. New York: Peter Lang, 1993.

"Journal of a Tour from Cadiz to Madrid." *Port-Folio* XX (November 1825): 365–74.

Kelley, Mary. *Private Woman, Public Stage. Literary Domesticity in Nineteenth-Century America*. New York: Oxford University Press, 1984.

Kowalewski, Michael, ed. *Temperamental Journeys. Essays on the Modern Literature of Travel*. Athens, Georgia: University of Georgia Press, 1992.

Lanero, Juan José, and Secundino Villoria, *Literatura en traducción. Versiones españolas de autores americanos del siglo XIX*. León: Secretariado de Publicaciones de la Universidad de León, 1996.

Lawrence, Karen R. *Penelope Voyages. Women and Travel in the British Literary Tradition*. Ithaca: Cornell University Press, 1994.

Lee, Richard Henry. *Life of Arthur Lee, Ll. D.* 2 vols. Boston: Wells & Lilly, 1829.

Leonard, William Ellery. *Byron and Byronism in America*. 1907. New York: Gordian Press, 1963.

LeVert, Octavia (Walton). *Souvenirs of Travel*. 2 vols. New York: Goetzel 1857.

Levin, David. *History as Romantic Art: Bancroft, Prescott, Motley, and Parkman*. New York: AMS Press, 1967.

Lockwood, Allison. *Passionate Pilgrims: The American Traveler in Great Britain, 1800–1914*. Rutherford, N.J.: Fairleigh Dickinson University Press, 1981.

Long, Orie W. *Literary Pioneers. Early American Explorers of European Culture.* 1935. New York: Russell & Russell, 1963.

Longfellow, Henry Wadsworth. *The Complete Poetical Works of Henry Wadsworth Longfellow*. Edited by Horace E. Scudder. Boston: Houghton, 1893.

———. *The Letters of Henry Wadsworth Longfellow*. 2 vols. Edited by Andrew Hilen. Cambridge, Mass.: Belknap Press of Harvard University Press, 1966.

[———]. *Outre-Mer; A Pilgrimage Beyond the Sea*. 2 vols. 1833–34. New York: Harper & Brothers, 1835.

———. "Spanish Devotional and Moral Poetry." *North American Review* XXXIV (April 1832): 277–315.

———. "Spanish Language and Literature." *North American Review* XXXVI (April 1833): 316–44.

Longfellow, Samuel, ed. *The Life of Henry Wadsworth Longfellow*. 3 vols. 1891. New York: Greenwood Press, 1969.

Loring, James Spear. *The Hundred Boston Orators Appointed*. 2nd. ed. Boston: J.P. Jewett, 1853.

Lueck, Beth L. *American Writers and the Picturesque Tour: The Search for National Identity, 1790–1860*. New York: Garland, 1997.

MacCannell, Dean. *The Tourist. A New Theory of the Leisure Class*. 1976. New York: Schocken, 1989.

[Mackenzie, Alexander Slidell.] *The American in England. By the Author of A Year in Spain*. 2 vols. New York: Harper & Brothers, 1835.

[———.] "The Poor Officer—Traveling Sketch." *Rural Repository* XVII (10 October 1840): 64.

[———.] "Scenes in Campillo." *Southern Literary Messenger* II (August 1830): 540–41.

[———.] *Spain Revisited. By the Author of A Year in Spain*. 2 vols. New York: Harper & Brothers, 1836.

[———.] "A Spanish Bull-Fight." *New-England Family Magazine* I (June 1845): 197–204.

[———.] *A Year in Spain, by a Young American*. Boston: Hilliard, Gray, Little & Wilkins, 1829.

[———.] *A Year in Spain, by a Young American*. 3rd. ed. 3 vols. New York: Harper & Brothers, 1836.

Madrazo, Santos. *El sistema de transportes en España, 1750–1850*. 2 vols. Madrid: Colegio de Ingenieros de Canales, Caminos y Puertos, Ediciones Turner, 1984.

Makover, Abraham B. *Mordecai Manuel Noah, His Life and Work from the Jewish View Point*. New York: Bloch, 1917.

Meregalli, Franco. "George Ticknor and Spain." In Sotelo and Cristina, eds., 2:413–26.

McClary, Ben Harris. "Washington Irving's British Edition of Slidell's *A Year in Spain*." *Bulletin of the New York Public Library* 73 (June 1969): 368–74.

———, ed. *Washington Irving and the House of Murray: Geoffrey Crayon Charms the British, 1817–1856*. Knoxville: University of Tennessee Press, 1969.

McFarland, Philip J. *Sea Dangers. The Affair of the Somers*. New York: Schocken, 1985.

———. *Sojourners*. New York: Atheneum, 1979.

McGann, Thomas F., ed. *Portrait of Spain. British and American Accounts of Spain in the Nineteenth and Twentieth Centuries*. New York: Knopf, 1963.

McLamore, Richard V. "Postcolonial Columbus: Washington Irving and *The Conquest of Granada*." *Nineteenth-Century Literature* 48 (June 1993): 26–43.

Michener, James A. *Iberia. Spanish Travels and Reflections*. 1968. New York: Fawcett, 1969.

Mills, Sara. *Discourses of Difference. An Analysis of Women's Travel Writing and Colonialism*. London and New York: Routledge, 1991.

Mitchell, David. *Travellers in Spain. An Illustrated Anthology*. London: Cassell, 1990.

Mott, Frank Luther. *Golden Multitudes: The Story of the Best Sellers in the United States*. New York: Macmillan, 1947.

Mulvey, Christopher. *Anglo-American Landscapes*. New York; Cambridge University Press, 1983.

[Neal, John.] "Outre-Mer." *New England Galaxy* (6 June 1835).

Nichols, Thomas Low. *Forty Years of American Life*. 2 vols. 1864. New York and London: Johnson Reprint, 1969.

Noah, Mordecai Manuel. *An Address Delivered before the General Society of Mechanics and Tradesmen of the City of New York*. New York: A. Mercein, 1822.

———. *The Selected Writings of Mordecai Noah*. Edited by Michael Shuldiner and Daniel J. Kleinfeld. New York: Greenwood Press, 1999.

———. *Travels in England, France, Spain, and the Barbary States in the Years 1813–14 and 15*. New York: Kirk & Mercein, 1819.

"Noah's Travels." *American Monthly Magazine and Critical Review* IV (March 1819): 341–55.

Núñez, Estuardo. *España vista por viajeros hispanoamericanos*. Madrid: Ediciones Cultura Hispánica, Instituto de Cooperación Iberoamericana, 1985.

"Outre-Mer." *American Monthly Magazine* V (May 1835): 247–48

"Outre-Mer." *Knickerbocker* IV (July 1834): 72–75.

"Outre-Mer." *American Monthly Review* IV (August 1833): 157–60.

Paine, Thomas. "The Crisis. No. 1." In Baym et al., eds., 1:624–29.

Pardo, Arcadio. *La visión del arte español en los viajeros franceses del siglo XIX*. Valladolid: Secretariado de Publicaciones de la Universidad de Valladolid, 1985.

Parini, Jay, ed. *The Columbia History of American Poetry*. New York: Columbia University Press, 1993.

Paulin, Charles O. "Alexander Slidell Mackenzie." In *Dictionary of American Biography*, 6:90–91.

Pauly, Thomas H. "The Literary Sketch in Nineteenth-Century America." *Texas Studies in Language and Literature* XVII (1975): 489–503.

———. "Outre-Mer and Longfellow's Quest for a Career." *New England Quarterly* 50 (1977): 30–52.

[Peabody, William Bourn Oliver.] "Outre-Mer, a Pilgrimage beyond the Sea. Nos. I. and II." *North American Review* XXXIX (October 1834): 459–67.

Pepperrell Sparhawk Cutts, Mary. *The Life and Times of Hon. William Jarvis.* New York: Hurd & Houghton, 1869.

[Pettigrew, James J.] *Notes on Spain and the Spaniards, in the Summer of 1859. With a Glance at Sardinia. By a Carolinian.* Charleston, South Carolina: Evans & Cogswell, 1861.

[Philips, Willard.] "A Year in Spain." *North American Review* XXX (January 1830): 237–59.

Porter, Dennis. *Haunted Journeys. Desire and Transgression in European Travel Writing.* Princeton, N.J.: Princeton University Press, 1990.

Pratt, Mary Louise. "Fieldwork in Common Places." In Clifford and Marcus, 27–42.

———. *Imperial Eyes. Travel Writing and Transculturation.* New York and London: Routledge, 1992.

Prescott, William Hickling. "Irving's Conquest of Granada." *North American Review* XXVIII (January 1829): 103–34.

Rees, Margaret A. *French Authors on Spain, 1800–1850: A Checklist.* London: Grant & Cutler, 1977.

"Reminiscences of Spain." *New-England Magazine* IV (May 1833): 427–30.

"Reminiscences of Spain." *American Monthly Review* III (June 1833): 466–73.

"Reminiscences of Spain." *American Monthly Magazine* I (June 1833): 225–27.

Ribbans, Geoffrey W. *Catalunya i València vistes pels viatgers anglesos del segle XVIIIè.* Barcelona: Barcino, 1955.

Romera-Navarro, Miguel. *El hispanismo en Norte-América.* Madrid: Renacimiento, 1917.

Rubin-Dorsky, Jeffrey. *Adrift in the Old World. The Psychological Pilgrimage of Washington Irving.* Chicago: University of Chicago Press, 1988.

Ryan, Barbara. "Alexander Slidell Mackenzie." In James J. Schramer and Donald Ross, eds. 224–30

Ryan, Mary P. *Women in Public: Between Banners and Ballots, 1825–1880.* Baltimore: Johns Hopkins University Press, 1990.

Said, Edward. *Orientalism.* New York: Vintage, 1978.

Sánchez, Alejandro. "Els somniadors del romanticisme." *L'Avenç* 51 (1981): 66–73.

Santoyo, Julio César. *Arthur Lee: historia de una embajada secreta.* Vitoria: Obra Cultural de la Caja de Ahorros Municipal de la Ciudad de Vitoria, 1977.

———. *Viajeros ingleses del siglo XIX.* Vitoria: Obra cultural de la Caja de Ahorros Municipal de la Ciudad de Vitoria, 1978.

Sarna, Jonathan D. *Jacksonian Jew: The Two Worlds of Mordecai Noah.* New York: Holmes & Meier, 1981.

Scenes in Spain. New York: Dearborn, 1837.

[Schoenberger, H. W.] "Mordecai Manuel Noah." In *Dictionary of American Biography,* vol. VII: 534–35.

Schramer, James J. and Donald Ross, eds. *American Travel Writers, 1776–1864. Dictionary of Literary Biography,* vol. 183 Detroit: Gale, 1997.

Scriber, Mary Suzanne. "Edith Wharton and the Dog-Eared Travel Book." In *Wretched Exotic: Essays on Edith Wharton in Europe.* Edited by Katherine Joslin and Alan Price. New York: Peter Lang, 1993. 147–64.

————. "Julia Ward Howe and the Travel Book." *New England Quarterly* 62 (1989): 264–79.

————, ed. *Telling Travels: Selected Writings by Nineteenth-Century American Women Abroad.* DeKalb: Northern Illinois University Press, 1995.

————. *Writing Home: American Women Abroad, 1830–1920.* Charlottesville: University Press of Virginia, 1997.

Serrano, María del Mar. "Viajes y viajeros por la España del siglo XIX." *Geo Crítica* 98 (September 1993): 6–58.

Sessions, Charles Francis. *In Western Levant.* New York: Welch, Fracker Company, 1890.

Simms, William Gilmore. *Views and Reviews in American Literature, History and Fiction.* Edited by C. Hugh Holman. 1845. Cambridge, Mass.: Belknap Press of Harvard University Press, 1962.

Smith, Harold S. *American Travelers Abroad: A Bibliography of Accounts Published Before 1900.* Carbondale: Southern Illinois University Press, 1969.

Sotelo, Adolfo, and Marta Cristina, eds. *Homenaje al profesor Antonio Vilanova.* 2 vols. Barcelona: Dept. de Filología Hispánica, Universitat de Barcelona, 1989.

"The Spaniards; Their Character and Customs." *Southern Literary Messenger* V (August 1839): 519.

"A Spanish Execution." *New York Mirror* XII (30 August, 1834): 66.

Spear Loring, James. *The Hundred Boston Orators Appointed.* 2nd. ed. Boston: J.P. Jewett, 1853.

Spengemann, William. *The Adventurous Muse. The Poetics of American Fiction, 1789–1900.* New Haven: Yale University Press, 1977.

Spiller, Robert E. *The American in England during the First Half Century of Independence.* 1926. Philadelphia: Porcupine Press, 1976.

———— et al, eds. *Literary History of the United States*, rev. ed. New York: Macmillan, 1953.

————., ed. *The American Literary Revolution, 1783–1837.* New York: New York University Press, 1967.

Springer, Haskell. *Washington Irving: A Reference Guide.* Boston: G.K. Hall, 1976.

Stimson, Frederick S. *Orígenes del hispanismo norteamericano.* México: Ediciones De Andrea, 1961.

————. "Spanish Themes in Early American Literature, 1770–1830." Ph.D. diss. University of Michigan, Ann Arbor, 1952.

Stowe, William. "Conventions and Voices in Margaret Fuller's Travel Writing." *American Literature* 63 (June 1991): 242–62.

————. *Going Abroad: European Travel in Nineteenth-Century American Culture.* Princeton, N.J.: Princeton University Press, 1994.

Swift, John Franklin. *Going to Jericho; or, Sketches of Travel in Spain and the East.* San Francisco and New York: A. Roman & Co., 1868.

Thompson, Lawrance. *Young Longfellow (1807–1843).* 1938; rpt. New York: Octagon, 1969.

Thoreau, Henry David. *Walden.* Vol. 1 of *The Writings of Henry David Thoreau.* Edited by J. Lyndon Shanley. Princeton, N.J.: Princeton University Press, 1971.

Thorp, Willard. "Pilgrims' Return." In Spiller et al. 827–42.

Ticknor, George. "Amusements in Spain." *North American Review* XXI (July 1825): 59–78.

———. *George Ticknor's Travels in Spain*. Edited by George Tyler Northup. *University of Toronto Studies* 2 (1913).

———. *History of Spanish Literature*. 3 vols. 1849. rpt. New York: Ungar, 1965.

———. *Life, Letters and Journals of George Ticknor*. Eds. George Hillard, Mrs. Anna Ticknor, and Anna Eliot Ticknor. 2 vols. 1876. Boston and New York: Houghton, 1909.

Toda, Fernando, et al., eds. *Actas del XXI Congreso Internacional de AEDEAN*. Sevilla: Secretariado de Publicaciones de la Universidad de Sevilla, 1999.

Twain, Mark. *Innocents Abroad. Roughing It*. Edited by Guy Cardwell. New York: Library of America, 1984.

Tyack, David B. *George Ticknor and the Boston Brahmins*. Cambridge, Mass.: Harvard University Press, 1967.

van de Water, Frederic Franklyn. *The Captain Called It Mutiny* New York: Washburn, 1954.

Vaugh, Jack A. *Early American Dramatists. From the Beginnings to 1900*. New York: Ungar, 1981.

Vilar, Mar. *La prensa en los orígenes de la enseñanza del español en los Estados Unidos (1823–1833)*. Murcia: Universidad de Murcia, 1996.

Wagenknecht, Edward. *Henry Wadsworth Longfellow. His Poetry and Prose*. New York: Ungar, 1986.

Wallis, Severn Teackle. *Glimpses of Spain; or, Notes of an Unfinished Tour in 1847*. New York: Harper, 1849.

"Washington Irving's Alhambra." *Westminster Review* XVII (July 1832): 132–45.

"Washington Irving's Alhambra." *Spectator* LXIX (9 July 1892): 66–67.

Weatherspoon, Mary Alice. "The Political Activities of Philip Freneau and Washington Irving." Ph.D. diss., University of Texas at Austin, 1968.

Wheeler, Valerie. "Travelers' Tales: Observations on the Travel Book and Ethnography." *Anthropological Quarterly* 59 (1986): 52–63.

White, Hayden. *Metahistory. The Historical Imagination in Nineteenth-Century Europe*. Baltimore: Johns Hopkins University Press, 1973.

Whitman, Iris L. *Longfellow and Spain*. New York: Instituto de las Españas, 1927.

Williams, Cecil B. *Henry Wadsworth Longfellow*. New York: Twayne, 1964.

Williams, Raymond. *Keywords*. New York: Oxford University Press, 1976.

———. *The Country and the City*. New York: Oxford University Press, 1973.

Williams, Stanley T. *The Life of Washington Irving*. 2 vols. New York and London: Oxford University Press, 1935.

———. *The Spanish Background of American Literature*. 2 vols. New Haven: Yale University Press, 1955.

Wines, Enoch Cobb. *Two Years and a Half in the Navy*. Philadelphia: Carey & Leah, 1832.

Wolf, Simon. *Mordecai Manuel Noah, a Biographical Sketch*. Philadelphia: The Levytype Company, 1897.

Worley, L. K. "Through Others' Eyes: Narratives of German Women Travelling in Nineteenth Century America." *Yearbook of German-American Studies* 21 (1986): 39–50.

Wright, Nathalia. *American Novelists in Italy*. Philadelphia: University of Pennsylvania Press, 1965.

"A Year in Spain. By a Young American." *Literary Gazette* No. 736 (26 February 1831): 132–33.

"A Year in Spain." *Southern Literary Messenger* II (August 1836): 593.

"A Year in Spain. By a Young American." *Maine Monthly Magazine* I (September 1836): 143.

"A Year in Spain—By a Young American." *New Yorker* I (6 August 1836): 317.

"A Year in Spain. By a Young American, third edition." *American Monthly Magazine*, New Series, II (August 1836): 204.

"A Year in Spain." *Knickerbocker* VIII (September 1836): 366–68.

"A Year in Spain. By a Young American." *Southern Review* VIII (November 1831): 154–71.

"A Year in Spain." *Fraser's Magazine* III (May 1831): 436–46.

Zardoya, María Concepción. "España en la poesía americana." Ph.D. diss. University of Illinois, Urbana, 1952.

Index